The Silence *of the* Volcano

Creating the Life we Deserve

ALMUDENA KONRAD

Foreword by Tristine Rainer

TheSilenceOfTheVolcano.com

About the Author

ALMUDENA KONRAD earned her Ph.D. in Computer Science from the University of California, Berkeley, and currently teaches at Mills College at Northeastern University. Her journey is anchored in a profound commitment to education, with a primary focus on empowering the younger generation to pursue dreams beyond academia. She is married and a mother, residing in Alamo, California.

To my precious mother,
my guiding force,
who through her actions showed me
the transformative power
of internal anger—the fuel of change.

Contents

Foreword

THERE'S A NEW GENRE of personal memoir in town, called in publishing circles the prescriptive memoir. Unlike earlier literary cries of suffering that began the memoir vogue, i.e., *Angela's Ashes, The Liar's Club, Running with Scissors,* the emphasis has shifted to the wisdom and specific life hacks learned within stories of seemingly insurmountable problems. It is as if the genre has matured out of the inward gaze identified with first person writing and now reaches out to take the reader's hand, a seasoned mentor inviting the student into a private laboratory where transformative discoveries can be observed in immediacy, intimacy, alive, hands on.

Almudena Konrad has the perfect pitch for this new type of memoir. Instead of giving us just the formulaic story of the American immigrant who survives through courage and triumphs through unshakable ambition, she offers a quiet and practical book, neither sentimental nor exaggerated.

I've read hundreds of memoirs and worked with bestselling memoirists to prep their books for publication, but none have helped me in my own life as this book has. Today, when I face discouragement, a depressing problem or overwhelming challenge, I think how Almudena faced and overcame such incidents in her life to achieve happiness. Reading this memoir has infused me with courage and a belief that we each have unbeatable resilience once shown how to use it. This is what her memoir demonstrates and implants in the reader. Empowered happiness, with steps specific to each life situation. A priceless gift.

TRISTINE RAINER
Author of *The New Diary and Your Life as Story*.
(both Penguin/Random)
Director Center for Autobiographic Studies.

Prologue

WHEN I WAS A LITTLE GIRL all I could think about was how scary the world seemed. My father was a normal man, *I thought*. All fathers must be monsters with the scents of tobacco and alcohol, while all mothers must be like angels with soft hands and fragrant aromas. My parents defined my only possible reality. My memories of him remain distant, filled with intense emotions that could not be placed as good or bad without a sense of guilt. My only role was to ensure the world around him was perfect— a towel waiting for him as he got out of the shower, his clothes meticulously prepared in his bedroom, laid out neatly on the bed, cleaned, and impeccably ironed. I often wondered why his breath was so loud, slow, and deep. Did he do it to scare me? His mental state was unstable, and his desire for dominance *intense*. I was too young to understand; I was already suffocating in this world, unaware that an alternative reality existed. It felt as if destiny was set in stone, and I was born to be his servant. I grew up reserved yet observant, sensitive yet aware. Could I ever lead a life filled with love, connection, and purpose? Did my father shatter me?

My story extends beyond my father's limited presence; it revolves around a more profound theme—our innate power to shape our destinies regardless of our beginnings. It carries a burning and essential message: that our past, the circumstances beyond our control, the trials we endure, and even the existence of evil itself cannot prevent us from living a fulfilling life. It is through our courage, fueled by strong emotions such as anger, that we cultivate resilience and fight for the things we want.

As I grew up, I discovered an unexpected source of strength in my profound resentment toward my father—a strength that fueled my determination to fight for the life I truly deserved. Like a silent volcano, I withheld destruction, channeling my anger to triumph over adversity and the conquering of dreams. In the pages of this memoir, I share my childhood struggles, adolescent adventures, experiences as an undocumented immigrant, the meaning and price of accomplishments, and, above all, the transformative power that resides within each of us.

PART ONE

SURVIVE

CHAPTER 1

A Lonely Beginning

"Loneliness comes with life." – Whitney Houston

FROM INSIDE MY MOTHER'S WOMB, I was nurtured to never feel alone. I was coming into an imperfect world and a dysfunctional family with a cruel father but a good mother. From a young age, despite my mom's devotion to me, I felt lonely with a strong sense of wrong and an intense desire for good. I wanted to live and be happy, and without ever questioning my circumstances, I persisted.

The year I was born, 1969, was a year of great innovation and technological advancement. The birth of the Internet. Humans made their history by landing on the moon. The Beatles, the Rolling Stones, and Bob Dylan were in their prime. In the heart of the civil rights movement, I was lucky to be born.

My mom at the time was 23 years old and she had already endured an unbearable 28-month-long marriage. She was the mom of two 19-month-old twin boys–my brothers, Chino and Memel and was living in an apartment in Madrid, away from her family in southern Spain. My father was not present the day I was born, and years later I was told that he showed disappointment in having a daughter and not another son.

I have heard stories of those early years living in Madrid. My father spent most of the time sailing, having affairs with other women, and forgetting about his new family and financial responsibilities. As a result, my mom became lonely, living the life of a single parent, concerned with constant financial struggles. Several times she drove down to her family in the south with her three little ones. But every time that my mom left looking for emotional and financial support, my father, sooner or later, would show up unpredictably, full of rage, and force her back to Madrid.

Eventually, fate guided my father to a new job in the port city of Cadiz, my mom's hometown. While she was happy to be near her family, our circumstances did not improve. Now, my father would spend more time at home during the longer breaks between his trips, constantly exposing us to his temperamental character.

My earliest childhood memory takes me back to our first rental home in Cadiz when I was just five years old. It was a day like no other—my father had returned from one of his trips to Africa, filled with happiness and affection, and with plenty of captivating stories to share. He told a story, just for me. During his travels, even though he was an engineer, he had supposedly learned new hairstyles from women around the world, and he promised to try a new hairstyle on me. I remember feeling affection for him, with the desire to connect with him through my hair. I wanted so much to be loved by my father. That night, he was enthusiastic and quite entertaining, telling my brothers and me about his adventures in Africa. I believed everything he said! I held on to that feeling of care and love, of having a good dad, for as long as I could. My mom in the kitchen did not participate in celebrating his arrival or listening to his stories of other women. She sent me to my room.

A few years later, he decided to finally show me one of the hairstyles that he had learned on his travels. I had anticipated this moment for years, even though I never dared bring it up. He seemed to be in a happy mood that afternoon, eager to give me a stylish new haircut. I recall the rush, the small window of opportunity to perhaps enjoy being with my father. I sat in a chair in the kitchen. I could hear his typically loud breathing suddenly quiet, a cigarette hanging from his mouth. The smell of tobacco together with his usual, strong Old Spice aftershave invaded my senses. I was nervous but excited. He put my long brown hair up in a ponytail and held it with his left hand. With his right hand, he used kitchen scissors to cut the whole thing off, leaving my head looking like an artichoke. I walked to my bedroom quietly, without a word to say nor daring to complain, pretending to be fine, with sadness overtaking my face. I remembered his proud smile. In my bedroom, I cried in silence in fear of being heard. My father thought my pain was funny and did not allow my mom to follow me, "Let her be, she'll get over it." Throughout the evening and into the night I waited for my mom to enter my room to make me feel better. But that never happened. The next day, while my dad was not at the house, my mom did her best to fix my hair, but I looked like a boy—I looked just like my older brothers. And I didn't like that. I loved skirts, dresses, laces, necklaces, bracelets, and my long wavy hair. I played with all kinds of dolls and loved dancing alone. A short-haired girl was not who I wanted to be. My father deceived me. All I could think was that he'd made me ugly on purpose.

Years later my mom told me that my father had forced her to cut her long hair very short only a few years after their marriage. I felt empathy for her and, at the same time, relieved to know that we'd shared the same experience.

I have good memories of attending the first few years of an all-girls Catholic school as a child. I loved the Catholic nuns, and I especially adored Sister Sor Maria Jose. She taught me through her actions to silence my struggles. She was the perfect example of compassion and self-sacrifice. Sor Maria Jose told me that one day God would call me to become a nun so we could collectively join the suffering of Christ. My young, vulnerable mind was eager to follow. My purpose was to be the good and obedient girl so clearly defined not only by my father, but also by the Catholic post-Franco society that we lived in. I quickly learned that pretty much everything a woman did was a sin. Every night, I prayed on my knees. I made personal sacrifices to God many times a day through long prayers or certain food restrictions with the hope that I would avoid eternal life in hell. I begged God to make my mom happy and my father good. I constantly prayed, and with growing fear, observed my heart—a heart with a predisposition for goodness—clashing with moments of hate for my father. I lived in an incessant cycle: feeling guilty about my thoughts and asking God for forgiveness. I mostly recall my mom's suffering and my feelings of helplessness.

At home, I learned to be quiet to avoid conflicts with my father. I stayed observant and obedient, always paying close attention to the treasure of my life: my mom. I spent most of my days by her side, constantly looking for reassurance that I was doing things correctly and finding ways to make her happy. I was not alone but felt lonely battling my struggles. I created an invisible friend, Adelaida, to share my stories with during difficult moments. I would spend hours in my room pretending she was real. Sometimes we played with dolls, but quite often I was mean to her, as we often engaged in arguments that I would always win by calling her names, making her disappear from my thoughts, and threatening to never bring her back into my mind. She was the only thing I could control. I played this game for many years.

CHAPTER 2

Disguised Feelings

"We must accept finite disappointment, but we must never lose infinite hope." – Martin Luther King

MY MOM, THE DAUGHTER of a high-ranking military Catholic man, was secretly an open-minded woman who did not practice or believe in Catholicism. Unlike most young women in the sixties living in the south of Spain, my mom went to college prior to her marriage and received a degree in education. She then attended Bellas Artes—an art school—and spent most of her time painting and reading.

During the sixties, my mom was a progressive teenager with dreams of traveling to England and exploring the world. She once fell in love with a Puerto Rican man, a student of medicine, who had a similar ideology to hers, but her father did not approve of him. I still have one of her most valuable treasures: an aquamarine ring that he gave her as a present when they were both college students. The ring is a nostalgic talisman of forbidden love.

Like other women living in fascist Spain under a patriarchal family structure, my mom was a victim of the inequalities between women and men. Women belonged inside the house. They were first the property of their fathers and then of their husbands, with no freedom to make choices and without laws to protect their rights. At least my grandfather gave his daughters, my mom and her sister, the gift of a college education. He expected both young women to be educated but obedient.

My grandfather approved my mom's marriage to my father, a wealthy, fascist, and Catholic man from Madrid who was temporarily in the port of Cadiz studying at the Naval University. My father's family also had a military background, something that my grandfather valued tremendously. My father set his sights on my mother, who was living in the Pabellon Militar, and after months of short conversations, he asked to meet my grandfather. My father's charm was undeniable, along with his educated and well-spoken Castilian accent, he left a strong impression on my grandfather instantly.

My young mom left her family in southern Spain with great enthusiasm to embark on a life of adventure. But, as she described it to me, her 28-year prison sentence started the night of her wedding. For years I have refused to ask, why that night?

Despite the misery in her marriage, I saw some of my mom's light spark in her when she would play castanets with me or teach me flamenco moves. My arms would shoot up in the air, and my facial expressions would turn as serious and as confident as a flamenco dancer. While dancing, I would glance at my mom, searching for her soft smile as she watched me, momentarily forgetting about the worries of her world.

My mom had a love for reptiles and tremendous compassion for all animals. I was terrified of most creatures, but she put effort into reducing my fears. I paid close attention to how softly she would speak to mice, spiders, lizards, mantises, and all living creatures—regardless of how scary some of them looked to me.

Since I was a child, I admired my mom for her strength in enduring the difficulties of our lives. But as her daughter, I was most impressed by her academic abilities, especially her passion for literature, philosophy, and history—subjects I struggled with tremendously. School was not easy for me. The challenge of communicating through writing and speaking, coupled with my fear of making mistakes, made my school years stressful. My mom used to tell me that she wasn't a math or science person, but I can't recall a time when she couldn't answer my endless school questions, regardless of the subject. She would often sit with me and my siblings to work on school projects, and she would even write some of our essays. I remember one day when I asked her to explain the meaning of *Purita Campos*, words I had come across in children's books. She looked at me with a curious but serious expression and said, "Almudena, *Purita Campos* is the name of the artist next to the book's drawings." I knew I had asked a question that might seem obvious, but she took the time to explain, and I will never forget that day.

My mom and I took care of the house responsibilities together. I recall being quite young, insisting on cooking at a kitchen stove higher than my height and having to use a stepping stool so I could be next to her. She often looked sad but was always present for her children, finding ways to provide us with the bare necessities, and making sure that we had Christmas presents every year, regardless of her financial struggles. She found ways to make special moments.

Sometimes, I asked my mom to draw profiles of women's faces, and she always did without saying much. When she was drawing, she would sit quietly next to me, engaged completely with the pencil and the paper, perfecting her drawing without interruption or distractions. Those short moments were sacred and felt endlessly peaceful. As a sensitive daughter, I grew up studying her facial expressions, recognizing her suffering, and figuring out ways to make her proud. I didn't see her smiling much, but when she did, I felt all was right in the world.

She loved me and still does, but she would never say it. She didn't have to. I don't recall a kiss or a hug. Her moments of affection were words of protection— "go to your room," meant go, stay quiet and away from trouble. I knew how she felt. She was not happy and feared for the safety of her children. Her actions spoke louder than her words. As a child, I never wanted to be away from her, not even for a split second. I remember waiting by the door whenever she had to use the bathroom. I would often ask my mom if I was going to be as beautiful as she was. I wanted to be just like her.

For most of my childhood, I did not love my father, but there were still times I worshipped some of his skills. I admired his engineering abilities. He could fix a variety of mechanical problems, spoke several languages, and was a great chess player. But that was the extent of his intelligence as I remember him.

He traveled all over the world for work during my early childhood years. He loved the United States. Many times, he would cook for us an American breakfast consisting of scrambled eggs and bread with plenty of butter. I didn't enjoy it very much. In the morning, all I ever wanted as a child growing up in Spain was a cup of chocolate milk and a piece of freshly baked bread soaked in olive oil. But on these random mornings, this was too much to ask. He would force us to eat his American breakfast, usually on the weekends and during the summer when we had time to experience his craziness, becoming victims of his eccentricities. If we ate slowly, he would pick Chino to demonstrate his authority. He would forcefully press Chino's face inside his plate, scaring us and pressuring us to finish eating as we watched Chino with food dripping from his face and glasses.

My brothers perhaps had it more difficult than me. My dad did not hit me until I was a teenager, but my brothers were victims of his violence since they were very young boys. My father yelling, "Chino, take off your glasses," still brings deep pain. Chino was a happy boy but very mischievous—the perfect target for my father's unstable mood. As soon as my father called for Chino, he would run to him, removing his glasses as fast as he could so my dad could easily slap his face. My father would hit once, twice, and even more, depending on his mood. He never hit softly, and never without rage. I would close my eyes but feel the pain. Chino would put his glasses back on and run off to play. He would often whisper under his breath, "You hit me, but I'll continue." I never saw him crying; he was always playing, always absorbed in our children's world. Once my dad hit him so much and so hard that he went to school with bruises all over his face and a painful ear. Memel years later told me that he cried that night. I didn't see my brothers crying or complaining, feeling only my own pain and a lack of understanding for the violence we all had to endure. What did Chino do to deserve such treatment? I wished that he would learn to be a quiet, obedient boy, but he never did. His determination to be playful was his strength. How could I ever not love my brothers? The bond through suffering is indestructible.

With every incident in which I felt we were wronged, my heart would tear. I saw him as less and less of a father and more of a figure leaving indelible marks and creating dark thoughts. Internal voices were growing out of despair—voices that reclaimed justice. My internal world was burning, unable to confront my day-to-day living.

The small windows of time when my father was happy and in a good mood were flashes of hope, but these moments didn't last very long. Without warning, my father would backtrack in a matter of seconds from extreme enthusiasm about something ridiculous to severe anger for unknown reasons. My brothers and I would whisper as quietly as we could, making sure he couldn't hear us or see our lips moving, "Papa is in a bad mood." My father's anger was dangerous: reactive, uncontrolled, and unpredictable. With his anger, he kept the family frightened and his needs met.

My father had many traits that easily camouflage abusive behavior. He was charming, handsome, highly manipulative, and corrupt. He was fearless, overconfident, and amusing. He could make anyone trust his phony exterior. As my brother Memel once said, our father alternated between being our rock star and an ogre. Outside of our family home, he had the gift of the gab and was able to portray leadership qualities. Behind closed doors, he was cruel. He told me stories of when he was 13 years old, living in a boarding school in France, and having enough money to hire prostitutes. I don't know if these stories are true—like so many stories he told about his travels and affairs with women around the world—but the fact that he bragged about such a life in front of his wife and children was disturbing.

I was never able to make sense of my father's behavior, even though it seemed amusing to many people. Some even laughed at the things he would say always inappropriate, offensive, degrading, and disrespectful remarks toward women. I learned that whatever felt wrong at home was meant to be kept a secret. I so badly wanted to yell to the world that my father was not okay; that we were not okay; that our smiles were only pretend; that he wasn't funny or entertaining to us, his family; and that I hated him. I used to daydream of his death, wondering if his heavy smoking and drinking would soon free us from him. My fear of him was real, but my imagination was free and fearless. My daily smiles and kisses were a requirement for just being his daughter—they were not something I would have intentionally chosen to do. I wish I could erase the memory of those kisses, the feeling of his face, the smell of his aftershave. My mom, however, never adhered to any demands compelling appreciation, and she paid the consequences for expressing her misery. There was fear all over our faces, barely concealed under our forced grins.

We all found our unique shields. Chino was the funniest and cutest, Memel academically the strongest and closest to perfection, and I was the quiet, hardworking, sensitive, and easily breakable daughter. My mom, brothers, and I never discussed our fears or feelings. My father's temper and the way we lived was our only reality. Expressing unfavorable opinions of him or negative emotions meant misery for us all. Complaining about our situation, taboo. I silenced my anger, thoughts, and sadness with a building rage. Living with suppressed and disguised feelings was the norm.

CHAPTER 3

Becoming Who I Hate

"Girls are the future mothers of our society, and it is important that we focus on their well-being." – Miriam Makeba

THE BEST MEMORIES from my childhood were the births of my two younger siblings. I remember them as presents from my mom to me. I recall holding Ana the day she was born in the hospital. I was only seven. I cradled her, sitting on the only chair across my mom's hospital bed, and stared at her the same way that I held my dolls. "*Gracias, Mama,*" I mumbled a few times. I felt intense happiness. I will never forget the memory of holding my first baby.

A year later, Carmen was born, and with the same affection and love, I held her tight against my chest, pressed to my heart forever.

I became protective of Ana and Carmen the moment I saw them outside of my mother's womb. They gave me purpose. My mom let me bathe them and feed them. I spent the rest of my childhood as a responsible *mini mom.* I don't think I ever understood that they were not my babies or possessions. With the mind of a child, I cared for them in the same way I cared for my most precious dolls.

One of my earliest, most vivid memories is of my mom, pregnant with Carmen, stepping out of the house and leaving me in charge of baby Ana under the supervision of a maid from the neighborhood, who often used to come to the house asking for work. This young maid decided to take Ana from my arms to give her a bath. The quiet me turned into a little monster, screaming at her. I cried, possessed by some demon, until my mom came home. I remember this episode as a terribly upsetting one because I lost control of my most precious, self-assumed responsibility— my little one. As soon as Mom came home, I immediately stopped crying and pulled myself together. She quickly understood the situation. She knew how difficult it had been for me. Without asking for an explanation, she told the maid never to touch the baby again, and that Ana was under my care and not hers. I felt empowered. My mom didn't need to question her; she trusted me. In my eyes, no one could do the job as well as I did. I didn't understand that I was only a child myself. I was seven years old with a strong sense of responsibility. But like my father, for the first time ever, I also expressed out-of-control rage.

My mom, four siblings, and I spent most of our childhood moving to new homes and cities because of my father's inability to keep jobs, homes, or friends. He worked a few years for Sea-Land, a US company based in southern Spain in the port of Algeciras, the city where we lived and where my younger siblings were born. During this time, he often traveled to Oakland, California to solve engineering problems. Sometimes, engineers from the United States would come and stay at our house. I perceived these American men as quite tall with nice personalities.

Their voices were gentle, and they seemed to speak slowly. I didn't understand a word of what they said, but I liked the sound of their voices. Sometimes my siblings and I would make fun of them, but they seemed to have a sense of humor and plenty of patience when dealing with little rascals. They were interested in initiating conversations with us and not so much in drinking with my father. I believed they were religious men with a higher sense of purpose beyond solving complex engineering problems. I remember one engineer in particular, Nick. Even though I was young, I found him handsome and dreamt of him taking my mother, with all of us, away from my father. My twin brothers connected with Ron, another engineer who frequently stayed with us. As a result of their friendship with him, both of my brothers ended up going to Oakland as young teenagers after my father pushed them out of the house.

While my father was working for Sea-Land, he gave us the experience of living under a facade of financial success. In reality, we were still struggling financially. My father controlled all income—even my mom's teaching salary—and spent every nickel on parties, friends, and prostitutes, and at one point in my childhood, even on a few nice homes.

I remember one of our homes, *Villa Coca*, well: a large, old Mediterranean-style villa with access to acres of property. The bedrooms had intercoms to communicate with the kitchen, and all the rooms were spacious with big windows and sliding doors. Outside, we had a white Andalusian horse, a monkey in a cage that my dad had brought from Africa on one of his trips, another little monkey inside the house, and plenty of wild snakes that would hiss in the spring. There was a story in town: the previous owner of the house collected snakes, and after a poisonous one bit him, he set them all free. These stories terrified me.

I will always remember our larger monkey. His face was bitter, and he was always in a rage. He showed aggression toward us, which I responded to by insulting him and sticking my tongue out in his face. Reflecting on it now, it saddens me to realize how little understanding I had of his situation. My mom, an animal lover and defender, suffered quietly.

One day, while I was holding baby Carmen, walking in my backyard completely distracted, he got a hold of my hair from his cage and pulled it hard several times, shaking me angrily. Carmen stayed in my arms. I pulled away from him and screamed as loud as I could, running inside to my mom in the kitchen. I understood that this was his revenge. I knew that I deserved it for all of the times I had made fun of him. After his death, my guilt stayed with me forever. I am sorry, Charlie.

Later on, we moved to another gorgeous, much newer villa, *El Escorpion*. The large backyard, more manicured than the wild one of *Villa Coca*, had a pool and a statue of a naked woman holding a jar of water on top of her right shoulder. I loved her—the image of a beautiful but sad woman who resembled my own mother. My father's friends constantly came to the house to have parties in our backyard. Once, he invited a large group of hippies to live in the backyard for a few months. They played guitar and taught me to sing a few songs. They were good people who smoked plenty. I became used to the smell of Moroccan hash. Every night, my mom would send me to bed early with little Ana and Carmen, who were now toddlers, even though I wanted to stay outside with the hippies. I would go to my room, get in bed holding Carmen tight while listening to the sound of the guitar strings through my window. Ana was quite independent from an early age and always slept in her own bed, next to ours.

Later at night, my dad would often come in, grab my hand, and take me to another room in the large house so that I could say good night to his young lover, a teenager attending high school in our town. She was living with us, and no one dared question the situation. My father made his young lover the queen of the house. I hated her as much as I hated my father in those days. I stood in the dark room, watching my father lying by her and kissing her goodnight. Then my father would ask me to kiss her goodnight too. Young me could not make sense of the situation. I still don't think I do. Sometimes, I can hear her voice and laughter ringing in my ears, irritating the living shit out of me.

My father and his young lover would make fun of me in the car while they drove me to school. She enjoyed calling me *mosquita muerta* (dead fly). And my father, somehow, made fun of this. She laughed at me; she humiliated me. Her giggle, more than anything, infuriated me. It was painful to sit there and listen to her the entire ride. I stayed quiet, keeping my hatred for them deep inside, tallying every moment I was shamed, strongly believing that at some point I would get my revenge and waiting for the day I could make both suffer.

My worst moment at *El Escorpion* was the morning I woke up to find my mom, without a voice or facial expression, leaving our home with my younger siblings, Ana and Carmen. Maybe she told me of her plans, but all I remember is her silence that morning. Terrified about what would happen to her, I cried the entire day. My father didn't let my twin brothers or me go with her. I walked from room to room, trying to find a way out. All the rooms seemed large and empty. I could endure difficulties if she were with me, but not without her. Before I acted out on any crazy escape plan, she came back, late in the night.

I don't know what happened the day before she left. I refused to ask for fear that she would have to relive some terrible event, maybe causing her to leave again. Or maybe I didn't want to hear. I know that my father had hurt her. She would never leave my brothers and me otherwise, even though she had already lived through unbearable moments. Years later, she told me that she left home to look for help from family members, but in fear of my father, no one did. They were all terrified of his violence, and the government had no laws to protect women after Franco's regime. In Spain, the first law to protect women against domestic violence was passed in 1997 (decades later), after the case of Ana Orantes, a woman, a beautiful brave soul, who after decades of abuse was burned alive by her husband after making a public announcement on television asking for protection for her and her children. Women living under conditions similar to my mother's were terrified—completely on their own with no support from the government or society. If my mother had made the decision to separate from my father, she would have had to give up her children to an insane man, and we would have grown up without a mother. And this would quite possibly have changed my life story in ways I could not imagine. There were no women's shelters during those days in Spain, or family members crazy enough to take my mom and her five kids against my father's will. All I cared about that day was that my mom came back. And everything seemed bearable again.

To keep our lives interesting, my father brought a homeless man to our home and gave him the title of chef. He lived in the garage. I visited him often and watched him cook in a small, tiny kitchen area that he had built himself. He was nice, skinny, and foul-smelling. His morning buttery toast cooked on the stove is still my favorite breakfast which, now and then, I make for my sons. Our homeless chef had a special way of making me happy. The taste of that toast still reminds me of his goodness. One day, my father showed up in the garage to find both of us having a conversation, and in front of him for no reason at all, he called me dumb. I cried and left quickly because I was embarrassed and thought that the homeless chef would believe him and think I was dumb. No other insult could ever hurt me as much as being called dumb. I ran to the kitchen inside the house, feeling furious, and while my mom was cooking, I sat by the counter to do my homework without being able to focus on anything but the word "dumb." A few minutes later, my father showed up with his best drinking buddy—a neighbor who would frequently visit my father. I was still angry. They both approached me, and my father told his friend that I cried when he called me dumb. My father's friend laughed loudly and drunkenly. I honestly did not dislike this man, but his laughter felt like salt on my very open wound. I turned around, dug my pencil into his shoulder, and left the lead inside his skin. They were too drunk to care. I stared at my mom as she stared at me, waiting for my father's reaction. They walked away and left the house.

Many memories of those years live vividly in my mind, perhaps not so much the details but the emotions attached to them. I recall my brothers climbing at times onto the roof of our house. Once my father found them, and though I don't remember the punishment, I know it must have been cruel because I recall the sadness that I felt for both of them as I fell asleep that night.

I have countless memories of my brothers standing together side by side, backs straight, arms held tightly to their bodies, enduring my father's slaps non-stop until one of them would give in and accept the blame, often for something ridiculous. Memel mostly took the blame, even in situations where he wasn't at fault. They were good brothers, and even though we had our fights, they were good to me. Memel was cool. He loved imitating Elvis Presley, and, oh boy, did he do it well. He also had the perfect, handsome, sharp look of Elvis. Chino was the funniest brother I could have asked for. With his creativity, he invented games to make us believe that we were living different lives. My favorite one was when we played the cat and the girl, where he pretended to be a lost cat, and I played the character of a girl who had to conquer his trust to become my pet.

A little while after the rooftop incident, my dad arranged for my twin brothers, Ana, who was only about three years old and quite mischievous, and me to attend a Catholic summer boarding school named Campano, thanks to connections with his drinking buddies. The morning he told us of his decision, he was in a bad mood, saying that he was sending us away because my brothers had gone to the roof and that we didn't deserve to live with our mom. He made it sound like it was our fault that our mom was not a happy wife. Ana only lasted three days because she would not eat until our mom came back to pick her up. My twin brothers and I stayed for the summer in different units—my brothers with the boys and the priest, and me with the girls and the nuns. On my first night, girls came to my bed, and as I was lying there, they covered me in toothpaste. They told me that they would come back to mess with me again when I was asleep. I was too young, too shy, and too scared to do anything. From that night on, I went to bed every night with tears and fear, missing my mom, and praying to God that the girls would not come back. They never did, but my worry about them didn't cease. In the morning, the girls would shower together naked, all of them laughing and having a good time—all except me. My only contact with the water was on days when we had pool activities. This made things worse because they started to call me *sucia* (dirty). I hated pool days. Besides having to get up in the pre-dawn hours to jump in a pool full of cold water, I struggled to control my breathing during swimming or scuba diving practice.

The girls in my unit seemed to be connected, and I was the only outcast. I felt like the ugly duckling—too dirty, and too small to be around the cool girls. I avoided talking to any of them because I was intimidated. My only conversations were with the nuns, and only to speak about God or religion. One of the nuns, Sister Sor Eugenia, enforced discipline in the dorm, making some of the girls cry by yelling and assigning extra work like cleaning and praying. She was tough as nails, but she never bothered me.

I thought I was alone, but maybe Sister Sor Eugenia had an eye on me. I told her once that one day I hoped to become a nun.

When my mom picked me up after the summer, I was very dark, too skinny, extremely dirty, and borderline depressed. But I gave her a smile and said, "Sorry, Mama, I have not taken a shower the entire time." My brothers made fun of me as siblings do and we all laughed, putting the terrible experience behind us.

Our lives in *El Escorpion* were coming to an end. I was about 10 years old when my father took his gambling addiction to an extreme during one of his drinking binges and lost our house on a bet. Even though I loved the house, I was happy to leave *El Escorpion* and all of its memories behind.

My father had a falling out with his young lover since she decided to leave him for another man. She was now back living in Cadiz with her parents. And for that reason, we all quickly packed, leaving our friends and school behind, and followed her there, my father hoping to win her back.

The drive was not pleasant. My father, as always, sped with the four of us—Memel, Chino, Ana, and me—squeezed into the back of the car without seatbelts. My mom held Carmen in the front seat. As I had done many times before, I put my body on the floor of the car next to my brothers and rested my face on the edge of the seat. I closed my eyes, scared of the speed. Suddenly nauseous, I placed my hands over my mouth and gagged, inhaling the vomit as it collected on my palms. I don't remember the rest. My mom describes this ride as one of the worst moments of her life; she feared we would lose our lives. During conversations about our childhood with my mom, I always notice how easy it is for us to go back to those memories and talk about them as if they were normal, though our hearts still hurt, and anger still rises. My mom always ends her stories with the word *cabron* (fucker).

Once we arrived in Cadiz, I was happy to be back because my best friend, Mili, lived there, and our families were close. As soon as I saw her, I shared all my stories, and she told me hers. She was my best and only friend. We were so different but so close. She was tall, with a much whiter complexion and shiny, soft, voluminous black hair. She laughed loudly; I laughed much less. She was extroverted and had a greater sense of humor. We often fought other girls around her neighborhood. She was strong and provocative, but I showed up with more anger. She called me *bichito* (little bug). I used to tell her that she was longer (as in taller) than a day without bread. She often held my hand when we had sleepovers because I was scared of the dark. At times, we pulled each other's hair in the middle of the night, fighting for more bed space, but we always ended up laughing and hugging.

I attended middle school at a different Catholic school than Mili. It was a short walking distance from our new apartment in Cadiz. My father was having angry episodes more frequently. Maybe things were not going so well for him since his young lover had left him, or maybe I was just older with a better perception of reality. I became an expert at reading my mom's facial expressions so that I could act quickly to avoid further trouble with my father. I also learned my father's patterns. From morning to early afternoon, I would stay away from him as much as possible, doing household chores. Then I would look for the right opportunity to offer him some wine. Once he started to drink, I knew we would get a few hours of peace. Buzzed, my father would be in a good mood and make us feel like a family. He could be very funny and entertaining but highly unpredictable. Hours later, as he continued drinking, we hid from him. Most of the time I would go to my room or take a walk outside, always caring for Ana and Carmen.

One afternoon, I sat at a park outside our house with young Carmen next to me. We were killing time by watching a group of young men playing soccer when the ball accidentally flew toward my head. It hit me so hard that I dropped to the ground and lost a few seconds of consciousness. I woke up to my father punching the young man in the face. He must have seen the incident from the balcony. I saw blood and felt my tears falling. I did not feel pain for myself but for the young man. He might have been a teenager, I am not sure, but I was scared for his life. My father hit him hard, and I cried nonstop. My father took me to the emergency room because I wouldn't stop crying. I kept crying until I finally fell asleep that night, praying to God for the well-being of the young man. After the incident, I walked to school for the rest of the year with the fear that the soccer boys would recognize me and take revenge. They never did.

School was not peaceful for me either. A bigger and stronger girl from my middle school enjoyed calling me names and making fun of me as soon as she saw me at school. I was now 12 years old, still reserved and small, with a school uniform too big for my body and legs too skinny to hold my leotard in place. One of those school mornings, as I sat in the first row of the classroom, the bully approached me. Before she could insult me, I felt a burst of uncontrollable rage. I got up and pulled her hair as hard as I could until I brought her to the floor. And then I slapped her. When the nun opened the door, she found me on top of her, gripping her hair so tightly that the nun had a difficult time separating us.

The nun called my mom. My mom defended me in the meeting. Her questions and arguments were too fast for me to follow, but her determination to make a good case for me was loud and clear. Even though my mom didn't know the story, she told me right away that it wasn't my fault. She always had blind trust in me. Nevertheless, the nuns and my mom agreed that I would stay after school to bring all the garbage down the stairs from the upstairs classrooms. Still feeling angry, I threw the garbage all over a private room the nuns used for their own prayer. They called my mom again, and I don't know what she told them this time, but somehow, she protected me, and I stayed at the school for the rest of the year. My bully never bothered me again.

I appreciated the strong education in science I received from the Catholic school and the nuns. The physics, chemistry, and math that I learned during those years helped me for the rest of my academic life. I can still recite the entire periodic table while thinking of a nun standing in front of the classroom. But I didn't agree with their fear-based teaching strategies, and even less with their extreme Catholic practices. Church every single morning before class, constant confessions, and in-classroom praying with discussions that no longer aligned with my beliefs. I started to question the validity of the only religion I knew, Catholicism. That was my last year in Catholic school.

Resentment continued building rapidly inside me. I often

pulled Mili's long beautiful hair when we had disagreements, especially when we had sleepovers, and she would invade my space or take my blanket. That year, I punched my older brother Memel in the nose because he mocked me after my dad had called me pretty in a sarcastic manner. I had never punched anyone before, and I could not understand where this urge came from. Memel didn't seek revenge, but I spent hours crying in the bathroom thinking he would. I know I made him upset, and I felt really bad. I never apologized to him. We grew up using few words, and "sorry" was not one of them. I don't recall anyone ever apologizing for anything that happened inside those walls.

I was working hard to be good, to be like my mom, but the more I tried, the more I found myself resembling my father. The times that I showed aggressive behavior made me think that my hatred for him was manifesting itself and turning me into an angry person, too. All my prayers and sacrifices, my good intentions and behavior, made no difference. God had betrayed me!

CHAPTER 4

Unworthy of Love

*"Everybody needs a safe place, and it should
be their home." – Debbie Rowe*

BY THE TIME I WAS 13, we moved to *Chiclana*, a town on the
coast of Cadiz where I spent my teenage years. I call *Chiclana* my
hometown.

I could no longer keep track of the houses, cities, and towns
that we'd lived in. Changing schools was particularly stressful for
me. Our lives were awfully restless and unpredictable as we
constantly followed my father's unsteady wishes. By the time we
got to *Chiclana*, my mom was unable to find a teaching position
for several years, and my father was not interested in working
much. My mom was having a hard time finding ways to feed us,
buy us clothing, and pay the rent. There was a little store at the
corner of our first rental where my father would ask me to do
grocery shopping and tell the owner that my parents would come
on a later day to pay. That is how we bought food until the end
of each month, when my mom somehow scraped together the
funds to pay the bill, often with the help of both of my grandmas.
Every time I entered the store, the owner with his loud voice

would embarrass me in front of other customers reminding me that we had a large debt to pay. Somehow, he still let me buy some food even if it wasn't all the items on the list.

In that same year, when we relocated to *Chiclana*, I went back to a public non-Catholic school. Unfortunately, the new school also had rotten kids who took pleasure in constantly teasing me during class breaks and along my lengthy walks to school. They never touched me—it was just insult after insult, most of them referring to my body and the fact that I still had not grown any breasts as my classmates had. One morning, I had the brilliant idea to wear my mom's black bra on my flat chest underneath a white T-shirt. I am proud today of that risky idea, but unfortunately, it only brought more negative attention. I didn't make any friends at school, so my walks and the entire year felt pretty challenging. I could not wait to turn into a woman and fill into a bigger body. I was tired of being teased, of being quiet, and of not having the courage to speak up in any way. To the bullies in the new school, I never responded or reacted. I ignored their comments and swallowed my anger. Stepping into a co-ed learning environment for the first time was a new experience for me. But I soon discovered that some of the boys were just as repulsive as the bully girls. Beyond the school walls, there were moments when I found myself involved in uncontrollable physical fights, but this only happened when Mili joined me in my neighborhood or during weekends spent in hers.

That year, my father was always at home without a permanent job and with plenty of time to bring turmoil into our lives. During the times when I was not at school, he ensured that my mom and

I never sat to take breaks from doing chores around the house. It was so tiring that when my father would step out of the house, usually to go for a drink, I would take the opportunity to sit on a chair near the window, resting but keeping an eye on making sure that I could see him coming back. Then, I would quickly go back to my household chores.

In my thirteenth summer, my father arranged for me to travel alone by train to Madrid to visit his mom. My father's violent tendency toward his three brothers and his own mom distanced us from our family in Madrid. I only remembered my paternal grandma from the one time she visited us in the south, recalling how my father had burned all her black conservative dresses and made her cry. Without any explanation or justification, he imposed punishment upon his own mother for purchasing toys for Ana and Carmen.

Before I left for my trip to my family in Madrid, my mom made sure to tell me that my father's brothers—a dentist, a gynecologist, and a physicist—were good men and that my paternal grandfather had been a well-known brain surgeon, loved and respected by the people in his life, who died from an infection at the age of 33 during the civil war in Spain. The four boys, including my father and his brothers, were raised in a privileged household where they each had their own live-in nanny. My father's nanny told my mom a story about him as a two-year-old boy: My father was sick with a high fever at the same time that his own father was dying, and no one paid attention to him. After battling his illness and high fever for too many days, my father was never the same. My mom reassured me that my father's family in Madrid was good and that my father's behavior was not genetic.

I felt a little bit better about visiting, but I was still shy and not so excited to go visit a big family of strangers. As soon as I arrived, I noticed that my strong southern Andalusian accent was drawing attention. Members of the family kept saying that my southern accent was funny, making me uncomfortable and less willing to say much. At first, I stayed with one of my uncles and his family. On my first night there, my aunt and cousin put away my hand-me-down clothes and old tennis shoes on top of a closet. Why do I still remember this? My possessions had been put away without my permission. But as always, I did not speak or show disappointment. I just complied and forced a smile. In their minds, they were doing something nice for me. The next day, they took me to a high-end store called *El Corte Ingles*, famous in Madrid, to purchase a few girly and vibrant pink, fuchsia outfits. The gleam of my patent leather shoes made a statement in itself. Although those clothes didn't truly reflect my personality, I had no access to the jeans, tennis shoes, and T-shirts that I had brought along. Eventually, I departed and sought comfort from my paternal grandma.

At grandma's house in Madrid, the maid, dressed in a traditional uniform with elegant white gloves, would bring me breakfast in bed on a silver tray—coffee with toast, full of butter and strawberry marmalade. She seemed happy. In poverty-stricken Spain after the Civil War and World War II, people from the countryside were lucky to get jobs in the city. My grandma's maid worked seven days a week, day and night, with only a few hours of a break on Sundays to attend church. I liked her. I liked her so much that I spent my afternoons in her room next to the kitchen listening to *radionovelas* on a tiny radio with a little antenna. She would spend hours ironing the family clothes; she even ironed the bed sheets and dish towels. I observed how happy she seemed to be when she was working. At home, I also did lots of ironing, but I was not happy. It brought flashbacks of my father destroying my hard work, taking his perfectly ironed shirts, wrinkling them with his hands, squeezing them into little fabric meatballs, and asking me to repeat the job. As an adult, I refused to iron for decades. Only in my 50s did I make peace with the ironing board.

At Grandma's in Madrid, lunch and dinners were fancy. The maid would set the table with a traditional, elegant tablecloth and silverware. Grandma had a little bell she would shake to call the maid for assistance while dining.

During my visit, there was a family party. There were a lot of family members I had no recollection of ever meeting before. People would constantly come and ask: "Are you Jose Hilario's daughter?" Family members and friends were intrigued. It seemed like my father was a popular man in that large crowd. I wondered if these people loved my father or if they knew how scary he was. They *all* knew him in some unique way. It was the most elegant party I had ever attended. Silver platters full of the most exquisite hors d'oeuvres were being served. I went crazy with my first caviar experience. I might not have been a talker, but I was definitely an eater. I wore my shiny new shoes and felt like Cinderella in the ballroom, but instead of a prince approaching me, it was my godfather, who told me that he was happy to see me again for the first time since my birth. He gave me the equivalent of 50 dollars, which was a lot of money for any adolescent in the early '80s. That night I went back to stay with my uncle and aunt. I gave the money to my aunt even though she didn't ask for it. Somehow, I felt it was wrong to keep it. The next day, she took me back to *El Corte Ingles* and bought me more *a la mode* outfits—it was painful watching my aunt spend my money on clothing that I didn't care about and knew I wasn't ever going to wear once I got back to southern Spain. It was even harder to watch her try so hard to get a word or sincere smile out of me. But I said nothing, instead I ruined my shopping experience—my fault for not being able to speak my mind.

I paid attention to my cousin. She was my age, quite pretty, and very comfortable dressing like a princess in expensive and colorful dresses. She definitely had style and felt so comfortable running around the house looking girly, speaking her mind, and showing her emotions. She loved her dad and I remember her crying once because her dad said something silly that I can't recall. Her dad held her in his arms like a 13-year-old baby, and wiped her tears, calling the tears *lágrimas de cocodrilo* (tears of a crocodile). They were very affectionate with each other. My uncle was sweet and such a joker. He had the same Castilian accent as my father did. His expressions were similar, and they even looked alike. It was freaky! I felt inside a movie watching a different version of my father and myself.

It was hard to believe that my father was from the same family, made from the same gene pool. *He was nothing like any of them!*

After my summer in Madrid, I went back to my dysfunctional home in the south, happy to be with my mom and siblings and my sleeping buddy, Carmen. My mom was my safe place. I'd missed her every day. When I got back, I recalled her gentle smile. She gave me two kisses that day. That night, I saw her at the kitchen table counting the money we needed to buy food for the coming days. *I wish I kept those 50 dollars*, I thought. My father could not keep a job for long, and when he worked, he spent most of his income on himself and his friends. I was upset about the inequality and the unfairness of the world. My mom deserved a good life. I learned to never say no when my friends offered me food. I loved strawberries, yogurts, bananas, and shrimp, but we could never afford these at home.

When I turned 14, we had to move to an even cheaper rental. Our new rental, *Villa Lichi*, was between the town and the beach, at the end of a dirt street from the main road that connected the two. In the beginning on the street, there was a nice house where a family with five teenage boys lived. We kids all became friends. At the end of the street, there were four old homes. One for the landlord, Maria, and three other cheap rentals.

Our first summer in *Vila Lichi* was an adjustment. I quickly became traumatized by the black large ugly-looking cockroaches inhabiting our rental home. At night, they would visit my bedroom, passing freely through the walls. While I was in the shower, these disgusting creatures would come out of the drain. I was terrified of them. My fear of them was beyond rational. I would scream in panic and pray in my own way to some type of divine power, so they would disappear from my life. My father made it worse by bringing and forcing these disgusting creatures near me so I could make peace with them. These moments would bring me to an inconsolable powerless cry.

Maria, our landlord, would occasionally bring us cooked meals, generously sharing what little she had. I remember her short, black, greasy hair, and the lingering scent of alcohol that surrounded her. She would often allow me to use her phone for brief one-minute calls to my friends. She was good to us. Meanwhile, my father, the resourceful engineer, would surreptitiously tap into her phoneline from the rooftop to make his own calls. There were instances when Maria would unexpectedly appear at our doorstep, and my father would answer the door in the nude, leading to laughter and shared drinks between them.

I was always angry at my father for not providing the family environment that we deserved. Because he didn't care to work, I lived all my teenage years in misery. To make things worse, that summer my father decided to send my 15-year-old brother, Chino, away to Oakland, California with Ron, our friend engineer from Sea-Land who had often visited our home over the years and was visiting again that summer. Chino was the one who could bring a smile to my face with his radiant energy and positivity. He was young and brave. The most mischievous of all of us. I missed him a lot. He spent years in Oakland, attending high school in a low-income neighborhood. Through letters, he told me stories of how different the environment was in Oakland. The classrooms were inside trailers, and the students divided themselves by race. Blacks, Mexicans, and Asians mostly stayed away from one another, something that he had never experienced in Spain since we grew up in a society with almost no ethnic diversity. Chino quickly adapted and joined the Black students. If we thought we had it rough in Spain, his new life quickly gave him a different perspective on the meaning of survival. Without knowing a word of English, he quickly had to adapt to a new culture where most teenagers grew up in tougher economic and social conditions. On his first day of school, dressing like a European boy with tight jeans, Chino got in trouble. He punched another male student who had slapped his butt, perhaps making the wrong assumptions about his sexuality. With a laugh, Chino once said to me: "That was my last day wearing my tight European jeans in high school in America. Baggy pants became my new thing."

During this challenging summer, I also got chickenpox. My father took this opportunity to remind us that his children were lucky because he happened to be the best doctor in the world. It was funny until it wasn't. He once pulled out his own bad tooth with pliers, never went to a doctor, and injected his own penicillin whenever he felt sick. To cure my infectious varicella disease, he sent me to the roof of the house in a bikini so that the sun could burn my blisters, and forced me to drink cognac because, according to him, alcohol was the most effective remedy of all. The family was too scared to intervene against his unconventional parenting style. After a couple of sips, I fell asleep lying on the roof. I woke up feeling excessively hot and burned, and experiencing the most severe headache of my life. As my illness progressed, I silently endured the consequences of his illusive healing methods.

My father made that year a living hell. Sometimes, he would bring the hose inside the kitchen to clean the ceiling, windows, and walls, and after having fun with the water, I had to spend the rest of the day with a mop soaking it up and drying the cabinets, walls, and floor. He was delusional and committed to making the perfect servant out of me. In the afternoons, he would lay rows of wine glasses on the kitchen counter, and with an empty bottle of wine, I practiced pouring water into the glasses like a sommelier. He would come back after his nap to see if I was still practicing, and then he would ask me to show him what I had learned by serving him a glass of wine like an expert so that I could become someone he was proud of when his friends came over for a drink. In front of his friends, he would tell me that I was classless like my mother, and that he was going to make a lady out of me. He bragged to his friends and to us, about his wealthy upbringing and his Castilian Spanish accent, but he could never see his own boorish behavior.

My mom continued looking for teaching and other job opportunities. She worked most of my childhood as an elementary school teacher to provide some type of financial stability. But as we moved to new towns, she had to restart the process of searching for new jobs over and over again. Although she never complained, I felt her struggles, and they became my obsession. That summer, I watched my mom, with superhuman determination, working as a flamenco instructor during the day while studying at night. She was preparing to take four exams so that she could earn a competitive position in public schools as a special education teacher. My *abuelita*, her own mom, had paid the fees of the program and bought the books, even though my mom could not attend the classes in person at the academia. She studied on her own, drinking Coca-Cola at night and strong coffees during the day. Later, when it came time to take the four exams over a period of four months, my father took an engineering job in a Kurdish base in northern Iran. Meanwhile, my grandma paid for my mom's trips to Malaga, a city in southern Spain, where the exams were proctored. During her trips, I stayed with my younger siblings, hoping and praying that she would get this chance. Out of more than 200 testers for only four teaching positions, my mom passed them all with the highest scores. She was the only one from the province of Cadiz to pass all four exams. The only one that didn't attend the academia. My mom achieved the impossible and showed me through her efforts that there was no limit to the power of will.

My father came back sooner than expected because Iranian jets had bombed the Kurdish base where he was working. He returned unscathed and re-immersed himself in our lives, now bragging about how he'd survived a bomb attack in Iran. He felt indestructible. As soon as he heard what my mom had accomplished while he was gone, he said to her, "Whatever you earn, I will spend on prostitutes." Those were his only words.

Soon after, my mother's job required her to relocate. She moved with my younger siblings to a nearby town for her new teaching position. Meanwhile, my brother Memel and I remained with our father in *Chiclana*. With my mother's absence, I found myself catering to my father's incessant demands, as he seemed incapable of managing a simple task without the presence of a helper. From preparing his morning coffee to lighting his cigarettes, his requests were endless. Even something as simple as stepping out of the shower required a woman by his side, whether it be my mother or myself, ready with a towel in hand.

❀ ❀ ❀

Right after turning 14 years old, I made a new friend whose parents used to rent a nearby home during the summers. A French boy, probably a year older. In the afternoons after cooking and cleaning the kitchen, he would take me to the beach with his windsurfing board. His parents would drive us. Holding on to the end of the board, he would sail far from the shore, and in the deep ocean he would sit next to me and say, *"Je t'aime a la folie."* I was quiet but enjoyed hearing his words. I never told anyone. I was not sure what the sentence meant after *je t'aime,* but his words stayed with me forever.

On one of those summer afternoons, I walked with one of the neighborhood teenage boys, about two years older than me, down to the only store nearby, which was about 20 minutes away. During our walk, I enjoyed listening to him. I don't remember his words, just the feeling of joy. When I got home from our short walking trip, my dad was furious and in an awful, ugly mood. His face was distorted with rage. He called me *puta* (whore) several times, together with other sexual insults in his unique tone of violence, a voice that without ever being loud could scare the bravest of the brave. At least that was my perception. He said that he never wanted to see me around any of the neighbors' boys again. He gave me the mop and told me to keep myself busy in the kitchen. The last thing he said to me that day was, "The mop can give you as much pleasure as any boy." That afternoon, he hurt me more than he ever had before. I felt hatred, unworthy of love, and *very, very pissed off.*

Days later, my dad put a ridiculous-looking helmet on my head and made me walk *Villa Lichi* Street facing the house of the teenage boys, carrying large heavy garbage bags in my hands, just so he could ridicule me in front of my new friends. I walked fast through the entire *Villa Lichi* Street looking down, then made a turn to the main road until I found the garbage bins. I came back walking with the stupid helmet still on, frozen by the fear of my father, frozen, unable to disobey his authority. My father was at the end of the street, shirtless in shorts with a big belly and his flip-flops, with a cigarette in his mouth, proud of his ways. I can still hear in my memory the teenage boys' voices outside their houses. My thinking was that my dad wanted them to think that I was dumb, and maybe then, they would stop interacting with me, but if I looked down, if I didn't look at them, they would never know that it was me underneath the helmet. The boys never made fun of me; they respected me, and in a way, they felt my pain. One of the youngest in the family once brought me a bucket of wild yellow daisies while I was hanging the laundry outside the house. Yellow daisies became my favorite flowers. His kindness was everlasting.

These events marked the end of my summer. The end of my goodness. The end of holding back.

CHAPTER 5

The End of Obedience

*"I believe that if you'll just stand up and go,
life will open up for you."* – *Tina Turner*

THERE IS NOTHING MORE DARING than a hurt and broken teenager. Nothing is more powerful than a strong desire for revenge.

At the age of 15, vulnerability no longer defined me. Years of bearing the pain of being a sensitive and observant child, witnessing my mother's suffering, and enduring degradation and insults had instilled in me a fearlessness that surpassed my own comprehension. My father had shattered me to a point where I no longer cared about the consequences, as my life, I thought, couldn't possibly become any worse. Embracing my rebellious spirit, I embarked on my own personal revolution. I renounced my faith in the Catholic Church, and rejected the notions of God, marriage, and family. No longer meek, but rather spirited and outspoken, I became a social force during my high school years, unafraid to challenge and provoke my father for the first time ever. Fueled by anger, I found myself in reckless and perilous situations, fearlessly defying the life I had been forced to live under my father's tyranny. The once shy and compliant girl rapidly transformed into a defiant and furious teenager, resolute in her determination to fight against his oppressive presence.

In those days, I didn't think highly of most men, with the exception of a few of my friends and brothers, whom I had adored, loved, and idolized since I was little. My brothers have always been good men. I grew up wanting to be like them: strong and big. But I was the opposite: feminine and small with a delicate physical constitution. I longed for the attributes that my brothers had. I enjoyed driving fast motorcycles, dancing in nightclubs, smoking cigarettes, pretending to be tough, lying topless in the sun, swimming in the deep ocean, and laughing at men if I had the chance. My newfound image of masculinity felt empowering, somehow imposing a sense of strength and control. I had not yet met a woman in power, in control of her destiny, and in a position of authority; any woman trying to cross that line was deemed an outcast. But, oh, did I want to be her.

I found strength in Black female singers; they became my idols. There was a time when I acted like a mini-Spanish Tina Turner. I would walk like her, wear similar miniskirts, and often sing and dance to her song *Two People* in front of my friends. I now wonder how a woman from such a different culture, more than 5,000 miles away, made me feel so empowered. I identified with her in all but my looks and culture. Tina Turner had been a victim of brutal abuse, but it didn't stop her from becoming a powerful woman, influential and beautiful. I also idolized Whitney Houston and Diana Ross. My bedroom walls were covered with pictures of them. My friends would ask me to impersonate Tina and sing *Smooth Operator* like Sade. I really didn't have a voice for singing. But I had the disposition to entertain my friends; they had my heart. The only thing that I looked forward to in those days was going out on the weekends. I discovered a new world. Sometimes, my father didn't fuss or was too drunk to care; other times, I just left while he slept. Eventually, he couldn't control me, and intimidation didn't work anymore.

During the day, my father would ask me to roll and light up his Moroccan hash cigarettes—a concentrated form of marijuana. Often, I would take a few puffs before I passed them on to him, leaving me lightheaded and disoriented, and helping me in a way deal with my anger. Hash, I ended up not liking it so much. But I enjoyed lighting up his nicotine cigarettes. Eventually, I liked them so much that I started to steal them from him. They seemed to calm my nerves. By the age of 15, I was completely addicted to Marlboro cigarettes, an addiction that lasted seven years. Nowadays, I sometimes hold my writing pens like cigarettes to feel that calming effect.

At night, Carmen would hide little love notes under my pillow with stolen cigarettes that she secretly grabbed from my father's stash. She knew how to show love for me. Carmen and I would fall asleep holding each other every single night. She held me so tight that at times she hardly let me breathe. Getting in bed sometimes meant that I would have to wrestle with little Carmen after feeling hairy creatures brush against me under our blankets. I was not against sleeping with dogs as much as I was afraid of fleas and ticks, but feeling Carmen's arms around me brought some peace to my agitated world.

Difficult encounters with my father continued for another three years, until the day I turned 18. On a typical weekend morning, as I walked to the front of the house to hang the laundry, my dad made a comment about how my breasts were growing and looking good while at the same time reaching out his arm to touch me. My first reaction had been in the past to gently block him while moving to the side and ignoring his intentions. But by now, I had seen plenty of boxing in the house between my father and my brother. Memel, at the time, was a black belt in Karate and a sharp boxer, but with a gentle heart. My dad was vicious and always ready for a fight. That day, without much thinking, I turned around and did a back-knuckle punch to his nose, right on target. It was perfect. I was proud of my strength, and for just a moment, I was another version of myself: strong, fearless, and commanding respect.

Unfortunately, my father didn't share in my pride. He was about to hit me when I quickly began crying and yelling non-stop while displaying my now-injured fist. I don't recall anyone else in my family demonstrating their emotions in this way, and I did so sparingly. But behaving crazily bailed me out of further trouble this time. My father, without a word, took me to the emergency room. I kept crying, pretending to be in excruciating pain, scared that he would hit me at any moment, until I saw the doctor, knowing that at that point my father would turn on his charm and forget about the incident to protect his own side of the story. The doctor shot me a look of disappointment after my father told him that I had hit him because I was a rebellious teenager who did not do things right. My dad's favorite thing to say to my mom, my siblings, and me: *You don't do anything right.* The doctor expressed sympathy for him. I have never been so glad to get physically hurt—my dislocated finger perhaps saved further injury to my face.

Every fight with my father, every sexual comment made, and every intention to grab my breast brought me closer to feeling lost and isolated in my tormenting reality. I cried at night when no one could see me, my tears fueled by frustration. My mom was working in another city, so I was spending lots of time at home with just my father and Memel while Chino was still living in the US.

My mom and maternal grandma were my beacons of hope during those days. When I was a little girl, my *abuelita* called me *muñequita de cristal* (crystal doll). She knew I was sensitive and that I cried easily. I recall the day when I was in the kitchen, a young girl, about 6 years old, watching my *abuelita* cook, feeling a sense of peace when I suddenly heard my father's voice: "*Munini,* come here right now." I dashed outside like a soldier responding to her sergeant. He was holding a green chameleon by its tail and asked me to hold it. Terrified, I ran back to the kitchen, seeking my *abuelita's* protection, but my father cornered me between the sink and the kitchen table. I dropped to the floor, holding my knees, screaming with terror. He placed the chameleon on top of my head for a split second. I covered my eyes while crying uncontrollably. In the background, I could hear my *abuelita's* upset but firm voice: "Jose Hilario, she is just a girl, please." My father, left with the chameleon, whispering, "She will learn not to be so weak." I rushed to my *abuelita* and held her tightly, still crying in agony. With a gentle voice, she assured me the chameleon was my friend and that he had been just as scared of my father as I was.

My *abuelita* nurtured my broken spirit during my childhood, and even more so during my challenging teenage years, trying to piece the fractured parts back together. She gave me much love and always inspired me to work toward something, to not allow anyone to burn my spirit, and to rise from the ashes as strong women do. She thought I was good, and that I was going to achieve a happy life. She helped me in any way she could; she would even hide my cigarettes from my grandfather and other family members because she knew that I needed them. She would listen to my non-stop home stories, and with a gentle expression, she made me feel like there was hope. I used to tell her that I hated men, that I would never get married, and that I would never love a man. "Not all men are like your father. There are great men in this world," she would say with conviction. I never understood her positivity, but she understood my pain. No matter what the situation was, my *abuelita* always put a smile on my face.

On Tuesdays, I would ride my Vespa from my high school to her house for lunch. She would always cook my favorite pasta with delicious homemade tomato sauce. Afterward, I would go to her fridge, dip my fingers into the *Nocilla* (Spanish Nutella), and suck on sweet, condensed milk. This became routine. After lunch, we would sit outside in the sun by her rose garden and knit while I listened to heavy metal music. AC/DC and Scorpions were my favorites, even though I did not know any English. I am not sure that my grandma enjoyed how loud it played on my cassette player, but she never complained about my music. As long as I was happy, she smiled. During this time, she would ask me to comb her hair, put moisturizer on her legs, and do her nails. I still remember her telling me, "You are the only one who knows how to do my nails. I like them fine and long, so I can look younger." The desire to look younger was a foreign concept to me. She was in her early sixties and had a light complexion, shiny and curly black hair accented with some gray, soft hands, and a tender smile; she was already beautiful.

Before I headed back to high school for the afternoon session, my routine was to go to her bathroom and spray her perfume all over me. My friends knew I was coming back from Grandma's house. I could not afford perfume, and the scent was distinctively hers. In the evening, I would return to her house, where she would prepare a whole *tortilla de patatas* (potato omelet) and reserved the most delicious parts of the *puchero* (Spanish stew), just for me. She once took me shopping. We walked for about half an hour to the nearest store to buy basic clothing like jeans and t-shirts, but instead, she bought me a large pink jacket—fluffy and bold. She knew that it was not very practical, but she still bought it for me because I liked it. I felt special!

At dinner time, I paid attention to my grandpa, sitting on the couch and watching the news on TV, mostly fussing about politics as the anchors talked to him through the screen. My *abuelita* would serve my grandpa dinner on a tray. He barely noticed her. I only saw my grandma really upset once, gently raising her voice because my grandpa didn't like his dinner that night. I could not make sense of how he took for granted her dedication to him. Her dinners were perfectly put together and had the most delicious homemade taste.

My grandpa was a particular and methodical man. He had fought in the Spanish Civil War on the side of General Francisco Franco, who had a leadership style similar to Hitler's. Since the war, my grandfather followed Franco's conservative beliefs and was unable to see different perspectives. He was a good grandpa but quiet and rigid, well-respected because he was generous and treated people well. The people in town would call him *El Capitan.* I saw his goodness as a child when he sat next to me to teach me how to color without going outside the lines.

My grandma didn't agree with my grandfather's political and Catholic beliefs, and she hid her opinions, spiritual beliefs, and the books that she read—most of them beyond her generation— from her husband. She strongly believed that young people had the power to change their circumstances and the world for the better. I didn't think that she had dreams or desired a different life. It seemed that she accepted her life as if her life's purpose had already been decided: to better the lives of her children and grandchildren. We all took for granted her kind dedication to details. She didn't hold degrees, pursue personal fulfillment, or achieve external recognition, but her contribution to this world is alive today through all the people she touched. She once said to me with wise compassion, "Your father doesn't want to be a bad man. He is sick, and no one can help him." It took me years to understand the meaning of her words.

My grandma somehow convinced my father to let me stay with her during the weekdays since she lived near my high school. This perfect arrangement did not last long. One night, my father came to my grandma's peaceful home. I was in my pajamas, ready to lie down in the cozy bed made by my grandma when I heard my father walk in. He was in a bad mood. He scared all of us without raising his voice. He asked me to get in the car and told my grandparents that I would never come back, and that my place was at home, cleaning, cooking, and helping my mother with the chores. *Fucking jerk.* The sadness on my grandma's face still pains me to this day. My grandfather was a strong man, but he, like the rest of the men in my family, didn't dare challenge my father. *Why?* I asked myself. *Why can't anyone stop this man from behaving like a lunatic?*

This moment has lived in my dreams for years. In *Abuelita's* house, I hide behind the door of my bedroom. I can hear the roar of a hungry lion walking slowly around the house. I sense him. I know he is there to hurt me. The door between us will not protect me. At *Abuelita's*, I am supposed to feel safe. But I don't. I know the lion will find me.

Living under my father's roof became unbearable. Every day, I greeted him with a hello, a kiss, and a smile. It was what he expected. But one morning, I had had enough. I was still 15 years old, but the incident in *Abuelita's* house had brought me to a new level of misery. As I was walking toward the bathroom, he came into the hallway between my bedroom and the bathroom, blocking my path and asking for a smile, a scowl overtaking his own face. "You have no reason not to," he said. I hated his voice of authority, so I responded with my own: "No." He slapped me hard before asking me again. "You can keep hitting me, but I am not going to smile," I responded. This was the first time in my life I showed no fear of him. There were no tears, no yelling. He slapped my face one more time, grabbed me, and shook me hard.

When he didn't get a reaction from me, he filled a large bucket of water mixed with bleach and told me to clean the walls outside the house until they were spotless. I spent the day outside without food or water, skin boiling in the heat, scrubbing the hot walls with bleach and no gloves, hatred building inside me, mentally preparing for a way out of his life, or his out of mine. I could either run away or find a way to end his life.

That night, I ventured to a field near my house, filled with the poisonous herb known as *cicuta*, which is well-known in Spain. Gathering it, I returned to my kitchen with a conscious determination fueled by hatred. While my father was drinking with his friends in the living room, I prepared an appetizer of anchovies, substituting the parsley with *cicuta*. I presented it to him, but he immediately recognized the danger. "You think you can kill me, but not even the bombs in Iran could succeed. This will only give me a stomachache," he scoffed. I pleaded and wept, urging him to demonstrate his strength. Though intoxicated, he wasn't foolish enough to consume the *cicuta*. He laughed at me, requesting more wine. As I served the wine to him and his friends, my tears fell, frustrated by my failed attempt to end his life.

My father took every opportunity to degrade me, embarrass me, and make me feel filthier than dirt. His words were shameful— they tortured my mind for years. My femininity was entertainment to his corrupted mind.

In front of friends, with a dark smile, he used to call me

beautiful, followed by inappropriate sexual comments about my breasts and my skinny body. I was still a virgin, but he made sure that I knew I was sexy and appealing to men. He often provided advice on how a woman should satisfy a man. "A man needs to be able to say thank you after sex. Do men say thank you to you?" he would ask, planting the seeds to make me believe that a woman's value was determined by her sexual performance.

My high school girlfriends and I became friends with the cool guys in town. They were older, in their late 20s, had nice cars, and owned villas at the beach and bars in town. We trusted their smiles, words, and images of caring. Ignorant of their intentions, we unwittingly played their game. One evening, my friends and I rode our Vespas to a party in a house at the beach. I only remember bits and pieces of the night, with very few vivid details remaining etched in my memory. I was dancing with my friends to the continuous playing of David Bowie in the background when one of my high school girlfriends' boyfriend held my hand and led me to a bedroom. Without hesitation, I followed him. I recall experiencing a sense of security as we stepped into the room. I was not attracted to him, but neither was I afraid. I was head over heels in love with Rob Lowe, and this guy, holding my hand, was the complete opposite. While I found him ugly and unattractive, I didn't voice concern or ask any questions—I simply followed him blindly. In the bedroom, he kissed me and touched my body in a way that I had not been touched before. He was kind and quiet. Without understanding my role in this game, clueless of the consequences, I found myself under his body having sex, feeling his kisses, his passion, and his intense desire to control my entire being. I was lacking my own emotions as I could hardly breathe under his sweaty chest. I didn't know what I was supposed to do or feel or say. I didn't know I had a choice.

For years I have wondered if I was being obedient, unable to confront the situation, or if I was actually being rebellious and a risk taker. I still don't know what I was thinking. Because of ignorance or curiosity, I crossed the line. There was no going back, and it was my fault—*ALL my fucking fault.* To me, that night meant perhaps the possibility of something new. To him, it meant nothing. Perhaps I was just one more young woman to add to his list. I lost my virginity that night and never shared the experience with anyone until this writing. For one, he was my girlfriend's boyfriend, but even worse, I felt ashamed. I went along with him. I didn't stop him. I didn't enjoy any part of the experience— absolutely nothing. I didn't understand why I felt this way. I imagine that, if I had been a young man, perhaps I would have a different story to tell. Maybe I would have been on top in possession of him. I hated this double standard. I recall my high school male friends bragging about their sexual encounters. But I did not feel the same about mine. I didn't want to feel wrong about my sexuality, but I did. One part of me felt taken advantage of, used for his personal satisfaction, but another part of me felt that it had been my fault for going along with the experience. I wanted to forget. The entire incident created deep internal anxiety and uncontrollable thinking.

I now understand, that when we are young women, we are unaware of our own vulnerabilities and strengths. We can become victims of our own sexuality. Only positive role models can teach us at this early age that our worth and successes do not come through our sexual bodies but through our remarkable abilities to persevere and thrive. While as women we should take pride in our bodies and enjoy our sexuality, it is important to learn that our bodies are ours and ours alone. Our sexual power is our ability to consciously and confidentially engage in sexual activities that align with our values. These powers need to be developed early in our lives so we can avoid long-lasting unwanted ramifications— unintended pregnancies, abortions, sex with the wrong people or emotional pain. Looking back, at the age of 15, I had no understanding of my own sexual agency.

A few months after my first sexual encounter, I met a guy from Belgium in one of the *chiringuitos* (beachfront bars). I had just turned 16 and he was a couple of years older than me. He had a cool look, with a punk-inspired hair style and a wardrobe consisting of only black baggy pants and tight white muscle tees. He was cute and in no rush to push me outside my comfort zone. In no time, we become crazy about each other. We spent our summer together hanging at the beach and a nearby campground where he was staying with friends. In my stories, he was my first real lover, as I try to erase from my mind the confusing David Bowie night. On one of the nights with my new lover, I came home late and rushed into my mom's bedroom. The room was dark, and my father was not at the house. I confessed to my mom that I had had sex with a cool Belgian boy. She remained calm but

I don't remember her words. I felt relieved to be able to share with my mom that I was not a virgin, as I had never told her about my first experience. Soon after, my mom took me to a gynecologist and had an honest conversation with me about sex and pregnancies. With my cool boyfriend, I felt alive and experienced the excitement of young love. After a few months, he and his friends returned to their country, and I never saw them again. I was now back to just me and my teenage struggles.

In an attempt to escape my tormented teenage mind, I recklessly pursued dangerous situations. On one occasion, as my father and I were driving late at night after visiting my mother and younger siblings, the car broke down several kilometers away from the nearest town and even farther from our home. We parked on the side of the road, and my father fell asleep in the car. I got out and started walking on the right side of an isolated, dark two-lane road. I saw a car approaching, driving toward me. I quickly lifted my hand and showed the sign of a hitchhiker. The car stopped immediately. We were a good distance away from my father's car. There were two men inside, and without hesitation, I opened the door and got in. I remember a short conversation. I stayed mostly quiet as the men gave me a sermon about the dangers of walking alone on the road at nighttime, especially for a young woman. I told them that my car had broken down, but I didn't mention that I'd left my father behind. My desire to run from him outweighed any fear I had of strangers. They were good men with only one intention: driving me to my destination, the dancing club in *Chiclana*, where I knew I could find friends. The owner of the club, who knew both of my parents, offered to give me a ride to get my father. My only thought entering the car that night was getting away from my father. Running away. The only reason I came back for him was out of fear of what would happen when he found a way back home.

I imagine what could have happened to me the night I went hitchhiking. I thank the Universe for keeping me alive and physically unharmed. Somehow, I survived my teenage years. But many young women with the same desire to run away find themselves in worse situations. Over the years I keep hearing stories of runaway teenage girls found dead, bringing me back to the fearless years when I walked with a broken soul.

At home, my frustrations grew by the day. My father hardly allowed me to do my homework and used to tell me that I was as stupid as a washing machine. I still managed to go to *Abuelita's* on Tuesdays for lunch. She and my mom seemed so perfect. I used to wonder why my mom didn't leave us and how she found the strength to stay with us, her children, every day despite her unhappiness. Her presence was larger than life. My mom and my grandma were my strength. Their words kept me from crossing the line between hope and despair. But my journal at *Abuelita's* house became full of hateful sentences. I could only see darkness. I had to get out.

On my 17th birthday, Chino returned from California, bringing a ray of light into my life with his infectious optimism, captivating American tales, and his mastery of breakdance. His dance became popular among our high school friends. Chino was the cool kid, and I so much yearned to be a part of that hip American lifestyle. He was quite Americanized but still with a strong connection to his roots. Together, Chino and I enrolled in a public computer science academy, commuting daily, immersing ourselves in the world of computer programming. Without much thought, I followed in his footsteps simply because he was fun to be around.

In the early summer, both my father and Chino fell seriously ill. Memel was fulfilling the mandatory military service required of all young men during that time in Spain. My father and Chino both battled high fevers for several days, and I took on the role of caregiver. I diligently monitored my father's temperature and administered painkillers throughout the night. He would lock his door and only allow me in when I knocked, for I had threatened him with the possibility of taking this opportunity to end his life. The idea of a life without him was a distant dream that I had never imagined could become a reality. I spent my nights lying beside Chino, hoping for his recovery, and secretly wishing that the illness would permanently cripple my father's health. After a week, both recovered, and life carried on, yet my hate toward my father continued to intensify with each passing day.

As I was getting close to my 18th birthday, my mom told me, "Almudena, this is not your life; this is mine. You will soon be free with an entirely new life ahead of you." But my present was my only reality. Growing up with my father made me feel weak, stupid, shameful, and empty. I couldn't imagine a future for me, let alone foreseeing a world in which I was happy. I knew I had to do something. I spent my days and months planning my escape from a house where no one had a voice but my father. I was 17 when I told my father that on my 18th birthday, I would leave the house forever. He marked the calendar and challenged me with a you-don't-have-what-it-takes kind of arrogant smile. I needed to prove him wrong, show my courage, and—eventually—my value.

PART TWO

CONQUER

CHAPTER 6

The Courage to Take the First Step

"The secret of happiness is freedom, and the secret to freedom is courage." – Thucydides

THE NIGHT BEFORE MY 18ᵀᴴ BIRTHDAY was a long one. In my mind, I ran through the many ways I could find the courage to leave my family the next day. Holding my little sister, Carmen, next to me, I stayed awake as long as I could. Having experienced my father's aggressive tendencies for too long, I imagined that maybe that could have been the last night of my life. But my feelings of hatred had grown stronger than my fear of him.

In the morning, without much thinking or planning, I left home. Tears fell intensely as I watched my younger sisters cry, staring as I walked away from the beat-up house. Sounds of them pleading and begging me not to leave still haunt me. The image of Carmen and Ana on the doorstep of our rental home has caused me to wake up in despair many times, even more than three decades later. Over the years, nightmares of big ocean waves swallowing my sisters as they beg for my help have brought back memories of this painful separation.

As I walked away from my house, part of me felt dead, hearing their still-young voices calling for me while my mom was inside the house with not only a broken heart but a terrifying marriage. I kept walking, telling myself that I would reunite with them along the way. It took every ounce of my being not to stop myself from turning around and running back to them, to our damaged life. I wanted to protect them and be there for them. I wish I could go back to those girls, to that mom, and to that teenager, to give them hugs and tell them that they were going to be just fine. But that moment has passed.

With my clothes packed in plastic bags, I walked for hours in the heat of southern Spain to Mili's older brother's farmhouse. The walk was long with mostly isolated dirt roads, quite far from town. I was hot. I kept walking with a mix of hope and tormented thoughts. When I arrived at their house, Mili's brother and his partner, Rosa, never questioned my arrival or lack of plans. They knew my father well and that was enough explanation for showing up upset and in tears. They provided food and shelter and a quiet, peaceful environment. I had no plans—no sense of direction. Mili stayed with me the entire summer. We enjoyed days at the beach and nights at the *chiringuitos.*

At the end of the summer, I made a phone call to Maria, my mom's neighbor and landlord of my family's home. She immediately told me that my father had left for *Barcelona* for a job and that she would go and bring my mom so I could talk to her. My mother was happy to hear my voice. She said to me, "Almudena, your father wants you to go to *Barcelona.* He wants you back in our lives, and he is willing to make peace and make things better. You don't have to live with us again, but you can visit us anytime if you are on good terms with your father." I agreed because I wanted to be able to visit my mom and siblings at the house. I traveled for several hours to *Barcelona* by train, taking Ana with me, hoping that she would make my encounter with my father less uncomfortable. She was 11 years old and nearly understood my fear for my father. She had suffered enough herself to be able to share this experience with me.

The encounter in *Barcelona* was casual, and my father and I did not reflect much on our rough history. He kissed me, hugged me, and told me that he loved me. I kept as quiet as possible and remained vigilant of the situation. My father could be an overwhelmingly affectionate man. His hugs, cologne, and soft big lips were suffocating and something I never enjoyed. On the first day in *Barcelona*, he took us to the circus, ending the night eating *percebes* (goose barnacles) at an expensive seafood restaurant near the ocean, showing off his upbringing through elegant table manners and well-spoken abilities. I had experienced that pretentious behavior too many times and always felt it was fake and sick. Ana and I went back to the south after only a couple of days of living in a fucked-up reality, a world that only my father lived in. The only enjoyable part of the trip was the time I spent alone on the train with Ana, but at least now I was on good terms with my father and could visit home freely.

On my return, after months of disorientation and confusion, still living with my friends in their farmhouse, I made the decision to continue my studies in computer science in *Granada*, a city located approximately five hours east of my hometown by train. With *abuelita's* help, I bought a train ticket and set out on a new adventure with money my mom had saved for me, safely tucked in my pocket. I sat on the train for hours, giving me plenty of time to think. The sounds of the train made me sleepy and relaxed, which, when paired with the views from the window, provoked a deep reflection on my situation. I was 18 and free. For the first time, I was holding my own hand, owning my destiny. I knew that the next steps were going to be critical. *Granada* was a fresh start, distant enough, and filled with opportunities.

Granada is a multicultural college town. There is a mix of Arabian and Castilian architecture and endless student nightlife. The city is frosty in the winter, located in the foothills of the *Sierra Nevada* mountains an hour north of the Mediterranean Sea. A perfect place to study, work, and socialize. *La Alhambra*, its magnificent and breathtaking royal Moorish palace, captivated my attention with its sad, drastic history: In 1492, the Castilian king and queen expelled the Arabs from *Andalucía*, forcing Muslims to convert to Christianity. Other myths about the romantic affair between the last Muslim Sultan of Granada, Boabdil, and his Catholic Spanish lover also define the palace. Stories of love, power, and conquest have always captured my attention.

I associate history with my mom. Her stories of European history, despite my lack of interest in history and my ability to forget the details, have taken up a great amount of space in my brain and heart. What has truly stuck with me, even as the memories fade, is the hidden message behind her stories: even great women, including powerful queens and empresses, have suffered throughout history, and many of their lives ended horrifically regardless of their effort, strength, contributions, and intelligence. I had to wake up to the reality of women's place in the world, and from my own experiences, I learned to be extremely careful with the men in my life. *La Alhambra* would bring me back to my mom's stories growing up and remind me of the misfortune of women. Her stories gave me the strength to persevere and fight for a different destiny.

As soon as I arrived in *Granada*, I quickly found a babysitting job and an apartment to share with four college girls. This was not hard to do since all the cafes and stores had lots of listings for rentals and jobs for students. It was truly a dream to live in this majestic city full of opportunities for young students, including many international students, all of whom were young and driven. In a matter of weeks, I enrolled in a technical school to continue my studies in *Informatica* (computer science). The building where I lived was full of students and social life. There I met Juan, the first man to ever show me the meaning of true love. With him, I felt trust and great kindness. He was spiritual and strong academically, a student of biology, and a painter. For three years, we spent every night together, reading poetry, and listening to Joan Manuel Serrat—*Penelope* was our favorite song. I was not always the nicest girlfriend, and my temper would rise out of nowhere, but he would respond to my outbursts by leaving little notes under the door of my apartment, asking me to come back to him. His notes always ended with: "You know our *contraseña* (password)," which was a specific knocking rhythm right outside his bedroom wall. Once with him, his kisses and hugs reminded me that I was lovable beyond my beauty.

With Juan, I realized how little I knew about the world, about men, about love. My perception of reality had been very limited.

I was consumed by emotions I did not want to feel, with thoughts that had mostly blossomed in my corrupted home. I started a new episode of my life, and pictured a new me, running away from victimization by hiding my real story—ignorant of the fact that I had trauma and that I was not OK. Instead of sharing the truth about my past, I pushed it deep into my soul, keeping it as much as I could to myself. I changed my life story. I became a new person, concealed beneath a wild and fearless spirit, radiating with young vitality and sparkle. My upbringing did not define how I wanted to feel about myself; it gave me the courage to rebel, to not comply, and to not give power to the messages from my childhood.

Soon after my arrival in *Granada*, I brought Carmen along. She was only 10 years old, living with me and other college girls navigating life in a big city. Each morning Carmen got up on her own, had breakfast, and took a bus, crowded and full of adults, to go to school. At the end of her school days, as soon as she came home, I became obsessed with feeding her healthy tasteless meals like vegetable purees and other plain soups. To compensate for the torturous meals, on the weekends we both ate plenty of chocolate croissants at the cafe right below our apartment. My girlfriends and Juan often looked after her. Together we did our best. I didn't know how to be a mom even though I thought I was doing a great job. It wasn't until I had children of my own that I understood how brave Carmen was at that young age, keeping up with the life of college students.

Carmen became part of many of my adventures. She still is my life companion. Younger than me but full of wisdom and wit—a strong beautiful girl full of life and funny jokes.

The saddest day of my life happened a year after living in *Granada*. I was sitting at the cafe with Carmen and decided to make a phone call to my friend Mili, concerned because my family was not answering my calls. She fell silent for a while, and I sensed that something was wrong. My *abuelita* had passed away unexpectedly due to a stroke. No suffering in my life had ever prepared me for this moment. As I was on the phone with Carmen next to me, I slowly felt the phone drop from my hands. Then, I yelled and cried aloud as my world collapsed in a way it never had before. For the first time, there was no hope, no turning back, no opportunity to rebel and fight.

The next day, after an endless night of crying without sleep, I took my usual long, freezing walk to work. Each step of the way felt heavier, the morning darker, and the temperature much colder. I arrived early at my babysitting job. Little Maite was excited to see me and ready to play before I took her to school. I explained to her dad the reason I was crying. He appreciated that I showed up since he had to go to work. That day, I felt dead inside, guilty because I had chosen to walk away from my entire family, because I had not made it a priority to visit my grandma much in the past year—one of my deepest regrets. But this pain gave me the strength to go to work that morning and to attend all my classes because she always believed I was destined for something greater. I couldn't let her down now, especially since I felt that she might be watching me from somewhere in the vast Universe.

I cried over her loss for years, and I still cry at times. I have her picture, her sweater, her special earrings, and many great memories. My *abuelita* is and always will be with me.

CHAPTER 7

Disappointments and Failures

"When one door of happiness closes, another opens, but often we look so long at the closed door that we do not see the one which has been opened for us." –Helen Keller

AT THE AGE OF 21, after three years of living in *Granada*, I returned to my hometown to live with my parents with a Technical Degree in Computer Science from *Aynadamar* Polytechnic Institute. Juan and I never formally ended our relationship, but moving back to my hometown created a sense that it wasn't meant to continue, especially as neither of us had a phone and our towns were several hours apart. For the next year, though, I still thought about him, thinking that he would show up at any time. I once asked a fortuneteller to read to me my future—something common in south Spain. I asked her if Juan would come back to me. "You will travel far—*mi niña* (my girl), and this boyfriend of yours will not be with you." These were the only words I remember from her. I thought it was bogus, and I continued my life somehow trusting that Juan would not let go of me.

Luckily for me, the year I returned home, my father was mostly traveling on ships around the North Atlantic along the coast of

West Africa and did not spend much time at home. Chino had left again to live in California, entrusting his job as a software engineer to me. Thank you, brother! It was my first opportunity to make a difference for myself. I enjoyed coding in COBOL, the main computer programming language that I learned. At the time, computers had no Graphical User Interface (GUI), and all the interaction with my IBM computer was at the command line using an early version of the operating system Unix. For me, this was fun! Magic! My mom was one of the earlier adopters of IBM computers in the late '80s, and with her humble teacher salary, she managed to buy one for the house. She taught herself to code in the early programming language BASIC and even used some of her computer programs to teach her special-ed children at the school where she worked.

I have said for most of my life that my tendency to be analytical comes from my father. I also inherited his thin body type, olive skin, and big lips. On the contrary, my mom has dark blonde hair with fair skin and an hourglass body figure—a Spanish version of Brigitte Bardot. For so long, I have hated that I look like my father. But the older I get, the more I identify myself with my mom, not so much in my appearance but in our shared thirst for knowledge and passion for reading. I've accepted that my physical resemblance to my father is nothing more than a genetic mishap.

There are many things that I cannot remember about the year right after obtaining my computer science degree. However, I recall well the technologies I had learned. At the age of 20, I was able to code in several programming languages: COBOL, BASIC, FORTRAN, PASCAL, C, and Assembly. I was living in my hometown, engaged in my new job, where I spent most of my days meeting customers who owned businesses, including wineries, and troubleshooting bugs in their code. I also created accountant programs for local businesses.

I loved my life for a short while. During my lunch breaks, I would drive to the beach in my topless bikini to take a nap, laying in the sun with baby oil all over my already tanned body. I found a balance between work demands and the pleasures of life.

At the end of the day, as most Spaniards do, I would meet with friends for a quick *tapa* (Spanish appetizer) and a drink. My days were full of work, relaxation, and social interactions. I was happy!

After one month of working, I gave my mom my first paycheck, proud that I was able to help with monthly expenses for the first time in my life. Even though my father was working away from home, he was a spender and did not bother sending money to my mom. We relied solely on my mom's teaching income. I kept working and was highly motivated to keep helping my mom.

In the early '90s in the south of Spain, it was not common to be a young woman working in the software industry. And as much as I loved my coding job, it terminated after I had an argument with my boss over not getting paid for my second month of work and for his constant sexual advances on me. At the time, this behavior—well known now as sexual harassment—was considered normal, and to speak against it was frowned upon, so I sadly left my job and got paid for only my first month of work.

The beach and my social life kept me busy and content for a while. The beach in my hometown is a secret paradise on the coast of the Atlantic Ocean, with miles of soft, light-colored sand, clear water, gentle waves, and *chiringuitos*. Nighttime on weekends and summers are endless, with family and friends gathered by the ocean. My favorite memories are on that beach, watching the sunset with loved ones next to me while listening to Spanish music coming from the bars. The sound of the waves, the music, and people laughing and talking, together with the smell of the ocean, and the feeling of sand and salt on my body, still bring me pure joy. That feeling of freedom never goes away. I can close my eyes and be there in a second, all my senses coming to life as if I were living the moment again. The image is vivid and powerful, attached to the people in my past that I have loved. I have spent countless hours walking that shoreline on my own, feeling the immense power of the ocean that has always brought peace to my soul. That ocean was not just a part of my life; it was my life.

On a hot day after spending hours at the beach with my friend Carmela, we drove to her house, had dinner together, took a shower, and went back in her yellow car to the *chiringuitos*. Carmela was older than me, blonde with tanned beach skin, and a loud, confident personality. She had a house at a beach with a pool, and even though I never saw her working, she seemed to be in a good financial situation. Hanging out with her was fun. As soon as we arrived at the beach, a group of young women greeted us with giddy excitement, sharing news of two handsome German motorcyclists who had just pulled up on two impressive bikes. My hometown, with its stunning ocean views and lively nightlife scene, was a popular destination for young tourists from Northern Europe. The community was tight-knit, and any news spread like wildfire. Thus, it didn't take long for word of the attractive

Germans to reach the ears of most young women in town.

Carmela and I walked purposefully toward the *chiringuito* to check the enigmatic Germans. As we stepped inside, my eyes locked onto a stunning blond man whose beauty surpassed even the glowing descriptions I had heard. I felt his eyes on me, awakening all my senses and every fiber of my being. I kept my eyes on his for a split second with unintentional intensity. Carmela and I sat at the bar, and I ordered my favorite drink, a *Gin Lemon*. My skin was bronzed and radiant, accentuated by my favorite blue miniskirt and a tiny blue top adorned with numerous African leather bracelets. My lips were painted a bold red, while my eyes were outlined with a thick application of black eyeliner and mascara. My hair fell down my back in wild beach curls and my soul was on fire.

A friend of Carmela's came over to talk to us—he obviously liked her and made the comment that my makeup was going to age me fast. Then he looked at Carmela and told her that her skin would stay young forever. *What a loser*, I thought. *What a way to hit on my friend, by picking on me.* As I was getting annoyed by his comments, the gorgeous blond German suddenly approached and sat right next to me with a beer in his hand and a loud confidence. He quickly conquered my gaze and full attention. He spoke just a few words of Spanish. I spoke no German or English—the languages he spoke. When that happens, your body is your only language. Sitting next to him, without thinking twice, I held his hand and said, "Let's go to see my friends." I felt attracted to him without any doubts. I felt trust, maybe blinded by an oxytocin rush.

I thought his name was Mongo—probably the wrong spelling and pronunciation. But that is what I decided to call him. Mongo and I rode on his motorcycle to my friends' *chiringuito* in a different beach area. I knew Mili was there waiting for me, and I wanted so much to introduce him to her. Mongo lost track of his friend that night and I lost track of Carmela.

We found Mili, and she quickly gave me her blessing and a wink. I knew I'd scored!

Mongo and I stayed together for the rest of the summer. Days were spent at the beach and nights sleeping in the dunes with campfires and a ridiculously small tent. We swam at night naked in the ocean. Every day, we would drive to my house to see my mom, Ana, and Carmen. Ana—14 years old—in a way fell in love with Mongo. At times, she would join us at the beach watching Mongo licking ice cream off my body.

At the end of August, Mongo had to head back to Germany. On the morning of his leaving, he dropped me off at my house. We kissed each other goodbye, showing indifference toward the love we shared. But as he left, I was consumed by a strong mix of passion and sadness. In his absence, the world felt bleak and empty. I was terrified by my feelings. I didn't cry and tried my best to hide my pain.

I spent the day trying to distract myself, cooking, cleaning, and hanging out with Ana and Carmen. In the evening, I lay in my bed unable to process or understand my emotions. Like most summer nights in Spain, it was hot, but I was too upset to leave my overheated bedroom. I found myself looking at the ceiling of my bedroom unable to shake the deep ache in my heart. That's when I heard Ana's voice outside my bedroom, shouting excitedly, "*Munini*, the German is back. He is outside with his motorcycle."

Without a second thought, I bolted out of my room, ignoring the fact that I was barefoot in just a T-shirt. I did not believe it. As I ran outside the house, I thought for a moment that this would be one of Ana's jokes. To my surprise, Ana had told the truth: Mongo had returned. I hugged him and kissed him with no words. I felt the world shift back into place, my heart overflowing with joy and relief.

Mongo and I spent one more night at the beach sleeping in the dunes. The morning arrived faster than expected, and again he left—this time forever. With his broken Spanish, I thought he asked me to go with him. I ignored the possibility that perhaps he wanted more than just a summer with me. I knew so little of him. In my mind, he was just a lover that I had to let go. He came back the next year at about the same time, to find that I was gone. Gone to a place where no motorcycle could reach.

After my separation from Mongo, I went back to hanging out with Mili, Carmela, and other friends, but with a quiet broken heart. I told my girlfriends that I didn't care about Mongo, that he had just been on a hot summer adventure.

I started to search, without much luck, for other coding job opportunities. When I couldn't find one, an acquaintance who owned a real estate agency offered me an interview for a receptionist position. Recalling the interview is something I would prefer to avoid as it represents one of the most humiliating moments of my life. Upon arrival, the interviewer handed me a script and asked me to take a seat at the reception desk and answer incoming phone calls. It seemed like a straightforward task that anyone capable of speaking could handle with ease. To my surprise, however, I found myself struggling to even answer the simplest office phone calls correctly.

My communication skills were lacking, and my self-confidence was nonexistent. During the phone calls, I failed to sound professional. My mind would go blank, causing me to remain silent when I should have spoken, and then quickly hang up before the calls were over. I felt nervous and damned. I could hear my father's mocking jokes about my slow thinking, which only added to my feeling of inadequacy. I couldn't even pass a basic phone-answering interview. It was disheartening to realize that such a seemingly simple task was out of my grasp. I left the interview feeling like a failure. Unaware of my potential, I focused on hating my weakness: my inability to speak with confidence and conviction. I questioned my intelligence, torturing myself with doubts about my future.

Despite my setback, I continued to search for other opportunities. In the fall, I decided to study for the entrance exams to work as an engineer at Telefonica, the main telephone company in Spain. The exams consisted of a set of standardized tests with a specific curriculum designed for people with computer science and engineering degrees. To avoid another failure, this time, I planned my course of action. With the help of my mom, I enrolled in an academy in a nearby town, and with impeccable discipline and motivation, I attended daily classes over winter followed by studying in the evenings. I overprepared, studied like never before, and gained the confidence for the first time that I was going to get a dream job position. I felt it! One of those positions belonged to me. I felt over-prepared on the day of the exams, and because they were all written questions, I was optimistic.

I recall the excitement of taking the bus to check the list of successful applicants who had gotten the position, remembering how my mother a few years earlier in a much more difficult situation had passed three sets of special education exams for her much more competitive teaching position. I imagined how I was going to tell my mom, make her proud, and help her financially. Upon arriving in a large room full of people and scanning the listing on the walls, I couldn't find my name. I spent hours searching, asking people, and not making sense of the fact that I could not find my name. The confusion was overwhelming. With tears, I left the place. I strongly felt that I deserved one of those positions and couldn't comprehend why I had failed. Despite my intense disappointment, I didn't want to draw attention to my immense failure. I bottled up my anger and moved on. But no matter how much I tried to pretend to be okay in front of my mom, she sensed my pain, intensifying its effect on me.

Days on the beach following nights with friends seemed, one more time, to quiet my mind temporarily. The nights were so long that they often trickled into the morning, where a breakfast of chocolate and churros waited for us.

It was now the beginning of spring, the time when the ocean would speak to me with daily invitations to enjoy its beauty and power. On one of those spring mornings, I went to the beach, as usual by myself, for a quick swim and my regular walk. I was feeling the anger of my failures and the disappointments in my life. Mongo was gone forever, Juan never came back for me, and most of my friends—including Mili—except for Carmela, were in committed relationships. There must be something wrong with me, I thought, when I could not hold on to a relationship or find a job. I ran to the water for a swim, with the only intention of shaking the anger out of me. I knew the ocean had the power to change my emotions. But the waves that day seemed as upset as I was. For the first time in years when swimming in that ocean, I could not find my way out of the water. Each time I tried to surface for air, a larger and more powerful wave pushed me back into a struggle for survival. I exerted all my energy to resist the forceful undertow, but eventually my body gave in. I felt a sense of relief, maybe the need to let go, since my life seemed pointless. It was in that instant that I felt someone bringing me back to shore. A friend of mine, Juan Manuel Bejerano, was also that day walking on his own on the same beach and saw me struggling. I don't recall anyone around me before I ran to the water, but somehow, he was nearby. He rescued me from the water. The people of my town call him *El Loco*—The Crazy One. He was crazy enough to fight the waves and save my life. We have both relived the story of that day later in our lives without being able to make sense of how he brought me out of the water in a state of unconsciousness. After the event, I went back to my house with my Vespa and my disturbing thoughts. I didn't say anything to my mom; she had enough to worry about already. I knew she was concerned about me since I could no longer pretend to have any sense of happiness. I wanted so much for her to be happy—but how could I help her? Instead, I was hurting her with my constant failures.

I thought that night: *How could the waves betray me? They first tried to kill me but then they let me go free to the same torturous life.* Nothing made sense. What was the Universe trying to tell me? A few days later, I rode my Vespa to the very end of the beach, an area still quiet and underdeveloped with only a few homes around. I parked by the dunes, walked near the shore, and lay topless in the sun. I was waiting for my friend Chantal. She and I would meet at the end of the beach to sunbathe nude during this quiet time of the year. I adored her French charm and allure, but above all, I admired her strong sense of independence and confidence.

As I drifted in my thoughts, I suddenly noticed a young man, fully clothed in jeans and a T-shirt, peering at me from behind a dune. I quickly covered myself and headed toward my Vespa. He pursued me, pushed me onto a sandy dune, and groped my breast. It felt as if I were outside of my body. I stood motionless, refusing to look at him. Once again, I felt defeated; in the same way I'd given up inside the waves just a few weeks earlier, I lacked the strength to fight. Luckily, he vanished quickly, leaving no physical harm but robbing me of my sense of freedom. No more solo beach adventures. No more long walks or sunbathing topless. I have never dared to walk alone on a peaceful beach again. I miss that feeling dearly.

These were defining moments. The Universe was sending me signs that perhaps I had to look beyond to find opportunities to find my own sense of freedom; and that the comfort of my friends was not going to make my dreams a reality. Even my ocean was communicating to me that I had to let go of everything I loved. I didn't belong in my town if I wanted to conquer more than perhaps being someone's wife and, if lucky, a job in one of the *chiringuitos* or grocery stores.

One weekend night, I was sound asleep at home when Fernando, a past flame from when I was only 16, suddenly appeared at my house and woke me up. He invited me to go to the beach and have a drink at a *chiringuito*. While there, he confessed his love for me and expressed his desire to have a serious relationship. Our previous attempt at dating five years prior had not gone well and only lasted a few weeks. This time around, I was older and feeling drained from constant failure. I was happy to see him again, even if it was just for a good time with no expectations.

Fernando possessed many qualities that I found attractive in a man. He was seven years older than me, handsome with a toned physique, passionate, romantic, and lots of fun. He also had a good heart, was financially well-off, had been through a divorce, and was already a father. I enjoyed being with him, at the beach, at his house, and visiting his beautiful Spa Club. We quickly became a couple and spent all our time together. He brought some special moments into my life, but I still kept walking toward internal darkness, with growing thoughts of fear and limitations. I built a strong desire to move forward in a different direction so I could achieve my only goal, to be financially independent, but my many failures made it seem unattainable. Traveling down this road of unfortunate events led me to think hard about leaving my town again.

My love for the ocean, my friends, Fernando, and my family could not help with my constant disappointments that year and my growing internal frustrations. I could not reconcile the environment that I loved so much with the only goal I had. I was willing to leave everything behind to start a new beginning, to find my own dreams, new hopes, and opportunities. My father would soon be back. I didn't want to live with him again and his abhorrent self upon his return from his travels. I had to get out fast.

I called Chino, who was living in California near Silicon Valley, working as a software engineer, and recently married. He was now 23. In his letters, he told me about the work that he was doing there and the many opportunities available for people with coding skills. I had never been outside Spain, and the idea of leaving as far as I could from the only place I had ever called home felt thrilling and promising. I recall listening to the song "*Cadillac Solitario*" (Lonely Cadillac), a big hit in Spain in the '90s. I would often joke with friends about traveling to California to see my brother and to someday drive a big old Cadillac. Inexperienced, young, and naive, limited to my hometown's bubble, I believed that in California I would have a chance to meet celebrities like Whitney Houston and Tina Turner. Traveling to California became my dream.

CHAPTER 8

A Dollar in My Pocket

"You can't just sit there and wait for people to give you that golden dream. You've got to get out there and make it happen for yourself."
– Diana Ross

ON MAY 1ST, 1991, when I was nearly 22, I left Spain. I left everything and everyone I ever loved and the only language I spoke. I spent the night before my trip with Fernando at the *chiringuitos*. We had only been dating for a few months but were strongly connected. At the end of the night, we sat in his car listening to Gypsy Kings and talking about our future together. He insisted that I didn't need to go and that he would always provide for me. Maybe he was sincere, maybe not. I would never know. I promised him that I would come back. My last promise ever, since I was just about to quickly learn not to make promises about the future ever again. I was sad that night. I knew I was leaving a lot behind, and that the price for new adventures and the possibility of new opportunities was going to be filled with struggles and sacrifices.

At the time of my departure, my father had come back from his trip. We were communicating with caution, keeping our distance, and staying out of each other's way. I don't remember who paid for my ticket—my mom, my father, or Fernando—or who gave me the only dollar that I carried in my wallet for luck. Today, I keep that wallet with the same dollar bill tucked away in my closet.

I don't know how thoroughly I planned my trip, but I left Spain with no money; instead, I packed a pair of new shoes and a sewing kit that my mom had purchased for me. I appreciated my new shoes so much that I never wore them; they are still unused in my closet, saved with the one-dollar bill. They remind me of the morning before the day I left Spain, my mom and me walking in downtown *Chiclana*, looking for inexpensive but pretty leather shoes. I recall my father's words: "Don't worry about a thing; in the US, everything is easy." I knew it was hard for my mom to let me go again, but with the sewing kit and my new shoes, I was off to a good start.

My first stop outside of my country was at Heathrow Airport in London. With the help of an older lady and my nearly forgotten high school English, I made it to the hotel. She must have seen confusion on my face because she made the effort to walk with me to the bus that would take me directly to the hotel. Only a few hours had passed since I'd left my home and country, and I was already desperate to speak and hear my own language. I felt overwhelmed; international traveling so far had been a lot more difficult than expected and still, I was pretty far from my destination. In the hotel room, I couldn't figure out how to use the knobs of the shower since the design was completely different from what I was used to back in Spain, so I went straight to bed and lay there with my eyes open, not thinking much, until the time to go back to the airport in the early morning finally came.

I made it to the plane with the help of the people around me with not a word in English other than *very thank you*. On the flight to San Francisco, I slept the entire time, about 12 hours. I woke up as we were landing in the lap of a friendly gentleman seated beside me. He had lots of curly black hair and a trusting smile. He spoke some English. I remained silent.

At the San Francisco airport, I was picked up by Lina, Chino's wife. I recall that she cried when she first saw me. I felt quite alert and enthusiastic to see her. Communicating with just a few words, she took me to eat at a drive-through. My first American experience was watching Lina order food through a little speaking box, something I had never seen before. We then drove down the longest bridge in California, the San Mateo-Hayward bridge, to her apartment in Hayward, where my brother was waiting for us. The length of the San Mateo-Hayward Bridge and the size of the freeways were beyond my imagination. I kept wondering why the streets were so empty. I saw freeways, big cars, bridges, and buildings, but hardly anybody was out on the streets. I was in a different world. As soon as we arrived at the apartment, Chino's smile, his unique dimples, and his funny personality instantly made me feel closer to home.

I stayed with Chino and Lina for a few months on a tourist visa, discussing the possibilities of pursuing an education in the US. They took me to a few famous places, such as Los Angeles, Disneyland, and San Francisco, and we drove along the beautiful wild Pacific Coast. Because my mind was constantly preoccupied with my future, trying to figure out my next steps, I could not fully appreciate these unique places.

During the first few months, I enjoyed mostly observing the diverse array of races, ethnicities, and cultures coexisting within the same country. My first conversation with an Asian person was when I met Lina, and prior to that, my exposure to other races had been limited to gypsies or African men selling goods on the streets of Spain. The Mexican people particularly captivated me; their manner of communication and expressions were quite different and interesting to me. Meeting Chino's Mexican and Black friends, I was able to expand my understanding of diverse cultures. Through Lina, an immigrant from the Philippines, I learned about her own culture, met many members of her family, and gained knowledge about the complex history between Spain and the Philippines, of which I had previously been completely unaware. My high school history classes either failed to cover that period or I had slept through the brutal and violent conquest of the Philippines by the Spanish in 1565.

It wasn't until I arrived in California that I was confronted with the reality of the role of the Spanish in destroying and exploiting indigenous civilizations, especially in the Americas. The streets in California had Spanish names, and signs of Spanish missionaries were scattered throughout the state. Regrettably, I had been blind to this sad part of history; in my school education, I had been taught to view my people, the Spaniards, as heroes in history. Supposedly, my ancestors had brought *good* religion and *prosperous* culture to the Americas. I experienced mixed emotions, as these cultures welcomed and embraced me without any resentment, treating me as if I were one of their own. I felt lucky, but I could not understand the admiration so many people showed for a country that had been so cruel to its people. There was no doubt in my mind that Californians, regardless of culture or race, loved Spain.

As I tried to make sense of this new world, being with Chino next to me felt safe; he was the only person who could make me feel at home, but I knew it was a short-term situation. I spent my days learning English while Chino and Lina went to work. I would watch the same movies over and over, taking notes, and studying on my own to prepare for the Test of English as a Foreign Language (TOFEL) exam, required by most academic institutions in the US. Chino and Lina still remind me today about how obsessed I was with watching the same movie, *Presumed Innocent*, over and over to pick up on English words and sentences. *It's gotta be so good,* became my favorite thing to say. I had underestimated the difficulty of learning a second language and I was now starting to realize that speaking English was going to be a struggle and a much slower process than I had anticipated.

Taking a turn for the worse, just a few months after my arrival, I was involved in a car accident. Chino was driving when another driver, a young man, drove through the exit of the freeway in the wrong direction, resulting in a head-on collision. I don't recall the accident, but I do remember waking up inside the ambulance with blood all over my face, hair, and hands from an opening in my scalp, telling the paramedics in Spanish that I was choking on something, but no one understood. I felt blood in my mouth and pieces of broken teeth. The accident left me devastated without front teeth and—again in my life—with the kind of short hair I so much dislike in myself. At the hospital, the nurses were forced to cut a lot of my hair to stitch up my skull. When I looked at myself in the mirror, all I could see was my missing hair. I felt exposed, without a shield, without a place to hide my sensitive low-confidence self. I identified myself with Samson, the character in the Bible, who loses his strength as a warrior after his lover, Delilah, cuts his hair while he is sleeping—my long hair always had that kind of meaning and power to me. I was also left with many thousands of dollars of medical bills to pay off. I was deep in debt from the start.

Something positive came out of the car accident. I stopped the heavy smoking addiction that I had started at the age of 15, which had seriously been damaging my vocal cords and who knows what other organs in my body. I knew that smoking was a nasty habit—it was hurting me and I needed to find the strength to quit. Without understanding my seven-year addiction, I was able to quit cold turkey right after the doctor at the hospital, who had just finished putting several stitches in my head, told me, with a nurse translating next to him: "Absolutely zero smoking for at least a few weeks. You should consider quitting, young woman. Smoking is not good for you." I took his advice seriously. No man had ever spoken to me so directly, looking into my eyes with such confidence and a caring yet firm disposition. His words replayed in my head like a broken record. Besides, in California, smoking was not as cool as it was in Spain. As a matter of fact, I was surprised that it was not cool at all, and even prohibited at *all* establishments.

Right after the car accident, without a plan, I made a phone call to Fernando and another to my family back in Spain to let them know that I was not coming back. I was already missing my mom and siblings, especially as I started to recognize the challenges ahead of me. Compared to my situation in Spain, my goal of achieving financial independence now seemed like a much more unrealistic dream. I had no work permit or understanding of the language. I felt lonelier than ever with barriers at every turn. In Spain, I thought I was insignificant, but in the United States, I really was nobody. But for some reason, I was blindly determined to stay. I knew that I was in a difficult situation, but I had a strong desire to succeed even if I had to move in random directions looking for opportunities. My *abuelita's* wishes for my future were still part of me. Her, the desire to help my mom and sisters, and a lot of hope became my only sources of strength; all previous religious beliefs had left me. Growing up with concepts such as heaven and its limited access to only certain chosen people, or the fact that one could commit crime after crime and still be forgiven after a confession with a priest, together with unrealistic expectations such as a woman needs to stay married no matter what her situation is or bear the child of a rapist, made it easy for to simply walk away from the Catholic Church and the God I'd spoken to for so long. In my childhood, endless, exhausting prayers resulted in nothing but aching knees and a tired heart, realizing that to face adversity I was the only one having to make those hard choices and that only I would become completely responsible for the consequences. Only I could forgive myself. No God could be made accountable for my choices, good or bad. No God was ever listening to me. My *faith* now more than ever came from within, with prayers to the spirit of my *abuelita* and to an unknown Universe with infinite divine powers, all beyond my individual understanding.

I had decided that I wanted to work as much as I could, doing jobs that would not ask for a work permit or proof of residency, to save money to go to college to study electrical engineering. Back in Spain, I had enjoyed the engineering curriculum for the Telefonica exams, and I was now trying to read a book that I found on the shelf of Barnes and Noble, *Digital Signal Transmission.* I could hardly understand any of the content in the book, but it became my obsession to learn about Digital Communications.

Friends and family would ask me how I was going to pay for an education in the Bay Area (California), where the cost of living or college education was one of the highest in the world. No one tried to discourage me, but they wanted me to see a clear picture of my reality. I was on a six-month tourist visa with no money, no financial support, and the pressure to find my own living arrangement. I still remember my trusting optimism. In reality, *I had no plan.* But I didn't have a choice either; going back was not an option in my stubborn mind—I would have felt like another failure—and dreaming big was much more exciting than returning home.

Chino and Lina found me a babysitting job with one of their friends, a single mom, also from the Philippines, who had two boys. The older son, about five years old, smiled a lot at me, probably wondering why I could not speak English or cook mac and cheese. I was making pennies, but I had no other options. I got my driver's license and a bank account, and my brother gave me an old but still-working Isuzu. I loved that car. With my ridiculous income, I was able to start paying off my medical bills. I sent monthly checks for only $10 to the hospital.

It was time for me to find a different living situation. Chino and Lina lived in a one-room apartment, and I had been using their living room for months sleeping on their couch. A friend from Bolivia gave me the name and phone number of a family who needed a live-in nanny. Lina made the first call, and the next day I drove to my first interview to work as a live-in nanny with the Gilio family. They had two children: a baby girl, Gina, and a toddler boy, Joey. Arlene (aka Mama Gilio) was fantastic! Right away she made me feel like I was part of the family. She liked me, I liked her, and the next day I was moving in as her nanny. The day I arrived at her home, she bought me an outfit—a red satin blouse with black pants that were exactly my size—and had placed it in the center of a full-size bed covered with new bed sheets and a fluffy blue comforter. There was an elegant decorative hat hanging on the wall above the bed. That hat is still in my bedroom today, many years later.

Arlene and I hardly understood each other's language, but we smiled and laughed a lot. She provided room and board in exchange for my help with the kids. I felt safe and loved in their home. I made money cleaning homes and doing extra babysitting jobs over the weekends.

The Gilio family had a blue Cadillac that I often enjoyed driving, a manifestation of the jokes I had made back in Spain about driving a Cadillac in California. It was super cool to drive their humongous American car. I spent a few months with the Gilio family learning English without attending school and doing lots of reading. Mostly I read physics books on quantum mechanics and lots of self-help books.

Arlene introduced me to several books written by John Bradshaw. I slowly read a few of them with the help of a dictionary, such as *The Family*, *Creating Love*, and *Homecoming*. Even though I understood probably only a third of what I read, for the first time ever, I learned about the concepts of the inner child and family dysfunctionality. I never knew that our behavior, our thoughts, our accomplishments, and even our own perception of reality could be influenced by how we were loved as children. These books were life changing. I found relief as I started to understand the concept of the inner child. It was the beginning of healing my own quiet girl, a process that continues and will probably go on forever as I continue reflecting and rediscovering myself. The messages we receive about ourselves when we are children hold great power and can be dangerous, as they can influence our entire lives, guiding our path and making our choices. I had an epiphany at this moment in my life. The realization that science had an explanation for my difficult childhood and solutions for recovery—taking small steps in learning to love myself and stopping the negative self-talk—gave me hope that I could have a special life. It was possible that I could accomplish more than I'd ever dreamt! From those days on, I became a devoted explorer of the science of the mind.

Arlene and I became best friends. She treated me like a younger sister, never introducing me as her nanny to her friends. Instead, she pointed out good qualities about me. I later learned that a person's true character is exposed by how they treat those perceived to be living in a lower class. Arlene treated me as her equal. We talked about kids and psychology, went to her gym together, and she even bought me outfits and jewelry. I wanted to be like her, wearing pearls and even using some of her English expressions. She meant so much to me. I don't think she ever realized that she was helping heal my damaged soul. Just being her loving self, she made a great impact on my life.

My writing and reading in English became good enough to start college, but my speaking and listening still had a long way to go. After taking the TOEFL exam, I enrolled in community college. The college provided me with the legal paperwork, basically an I-20 form, accepting me as an international student with a huge new responsibility to pay each semester's high international tuition. But immigration never issued the student visa, which would have given me legal international student status. I didn't know that the I-20 had to be taken to the US immigration office to request a student visa. I was, without my knowledge, an undocumented immigrant working as hard as I could, and getting paid under the table so I could pay my expensive international student college tuition.

I took every cleaning and babysitting job that I could find. I cleaned homes all day on Saturdays and Sundays for three dollars an hour and did babysitting jobs for five dollars an hour. A ridiculous compensation even in the early '90s but still appreciated. *Beggars can't be choosers*, I thought.

Most people did not treat me with the respect I felt I deserved, except for those from marginalized backgrounds or fellow immigrants, something I had a difficult time comprehending. The fact that I was cleaning homes or taking care of kids for money gave people the green light for disrespect. It took me some time to realize that most Americans saw me as an immigrant with no rights and of less human value. I came to understand that my low socioeconomic status wasn't the only reason for this bias. It was also because of my Latina appearance and Spanish accent. This contradicted the way I felt about my culture, the pride I had in being from southern Spain, and the immense respect I had for all my Latin American friends. At times, people's perceptions of me would quickly change once they heard that I was originally from Spain. Their typical response would be: "Oh, you're from *Spain*." Somehow, this seemed to increase my human value in their eyes.

My new Mexican friend Wendy quickly became my partner in crime. She was two years younger than me, also undocumented, and had similar difficulties, but with wit and a much better understanding of how to navigate the system as an undocumented immigrant. To her, the picture was crystal clear and accepted. Basically, if we were to survive in California, we would have to ignore the fact that we were *not welcome* unless we worked harder than anyone else and for less. And even then, we'd still be treated as inferior. California was not looking like the land of opportunity I had envisioned, but rather a highly competitive culture lacking empathy, in need of significant growth and improvement. I always understood that I could not expect job opportunities without a work permit but being treated poorly for my looks and my accent, or their perception of my abilities, made me furious.

Regardless of our difficulties, Wendy and I spent most of our days laughing and sharing our daily challenges. We took many college classes together and helped each other as much as we could. She wanted to study genetics; I wanted to study electrical engineering.

In our chemistry class, Wendy would enter the classroom in the early morning with coffee in her hands, a slow pace, and the greatest smile. She was always late, but she was always happy. The professor did not appreciate her. But I did. Wendy and I had an unspoken understanding of the meaning of being late. Wendy was not late because she was lazy, and she did not smile because she was disrespectful. She was late because she worked harder than any other student I ever met to make a living on her own and still go to college. And she smiled because she appreciated the good things in life. To us, daily life challenges seemed insignificant, while big struggles were just a part of the life we chose. Both of us, filled with determination, woke up every day ready to pursue the future we envision—fearless of hard work.

There was a hidden message from society that somehow as a Spaniard, I had the traditional colonial advantage as a US immigrant; that somehow, I was superior in race and language. This bothered me! It could not have been farther from the truth! On paper, I was a white privileged European woman with no access to any type of financial program, but in the reality of my new Californian life, I was less than a second-class citizen.

Wendy and I felt connected to the same struggles. Most people thought we were sisters. We were of the same height and had similar thin body types, big lips, and big brown eyes, although Wendy's skin complexion was slightly lighter than mine. With her big confidence, she strode through campus like she was the Queen of Spain with me following her, learning from her experiences as we navigated the challenges of living in this country. Like my sister, Carmen, Wendy had the striking combination of dark hair and contrasting skin tones typical of women from southern Spain. Her English was flawless—at least in my opinion—and her personality was explosive. Her boyfriend, a successful American businessman, was older than us, and Wendy was deeply in love with him. She had an open heart, something I could not understand. He was kind, trustworthy, and reserved, but to me, *being madly in love was a sign of trouble.* In a way I wanted her to fall out of love. But she never did! With him, we took our first trip to the snowy mountains of South Lake Tahoe.

I have many stories of what it was like to work as an undocumented Spanish immigrant in the early '90s.

Once a family offered me a job to work in their homes on Saturdays as a cleaner and cook. After spending the day cleaning the entire house, in the early evening, I cooked a delicious dinner, setting up the table for the mom, dad, teenagers, and me. The mom removed my plate and put it on the kitchen counter. I followed her and gently told her that I could not work in her house if I could not eat at the same table. But she insisted that I could not eat with the family. I packed my bag and left, emotional and offended. Worst of all, I did not get paid.

I got a job cleaning another humongous house in San Mateo

Hills on the weekends. The lady of the house lived alone and had a bizarre obsessive personality. On my first day, she told me that she was going to call me Amanda and that I had only a 15-minute break to eat lunch that she would prepare for me. She requested that I not bring food of my own. The entire day she would follow me, observing my cleaning, and giving me detailed instructions. She never spoke about anything else; she just gave me instructions. "Amanda, roll the rug and make sure that you vacuum the carpet underneath," was my least favorite instruction, which never made sense to me. The rugs in the house were large and heavy, and every Sunday the carpet beneath needed to be cleaned. Her behavior and demands were strange. But I never fussed over or questioned her requests. She once insisted on giving me a very old dress. I noticed that she was getting upset at my intention of rejecting the dress. I took it as I felt I had no choice. Months later, after many torturing Sundays, and hearing the irritating way in which she would call me "Amaaaandaaaa ..." I quit. "Return my dress right away," was her only response, screaming at me, furious that I wanted to quit. I did return the old dress, since it was an ugly dress that could only be worn by a frog. I was happier ever after.

But not all was dark and gloomy during my years of financial struggle. I once experienced great generosity working as a babysitter. A family living in San Francisco, who hardly knew me, wrote me a check for a sum of money large enough to cover my entire international student tuition. This surprising gesture allowed me to continue my education for one more semester. With gratitude, I still think of them. Perhaps they have long forgotten their gesture of kindness, but it will forever be in my memory. I continued working for this family during the weekends to pay off my debt. I was happy that I was able to pay my tuition, but I was heading toward financial catastrophe, as I still was trying to pay my hospital debt and adding more as time went by.

I was living a day at a time, constantly in survival mode. Driving a car without insurance, without a work permit or medical care, and pretending to be a financially capable international student in front of the college administration was draining. At times I wondered what I had gotten myself into by leaving my hometown in the south of Spain. I missed my mom tremendously. I called her as much as I could at phone booths, and I often felt sadness right before falling asleep. I was happy to be thousands of miles away from my father, from a place that did not provide the opportunities that I wished for and strongly felt I deserved. But how close was I to making a difference for myself, my mom, and my younger sisters in a place that was so vastly different from my expectations? I felt that my future did not look so promising.

CHAPTER 9

I Live Here

*"I have someone who believes in me,
I can move mountains." – Diana Ross*

EXACTLY ONE YEAR AFTER I ARRIVED in the US, the Gilio family took me on their vacation trip to Maui where we also celebrated my 23rd birthday. Arlene bought me a flowery bikini, a cute little black dress, and a Hawaiian outfit. I was ready to have fun! I enjoyed myself like a pig in a trough those days. My first vacation ever, my first stay at a luxury resort, and my first taste of good living. I hung out at the beach and swam in the open ocean all day long with one-year-old Gina. I ate plenty of delicious food at nice restaurants and enjoyed my daily *Piña Colada*. I was back in the ocean, feeling its power with a newfound hope for my American life.

As soon as I came back, I realized that the last few days had been just an illusion, just a dream—one that, in reality, I could not afford. But the experience introduced me to the possibility of a better life.

At the end of the summer, on August 9th, 1992, I met Mike. That day, I spent it with Chino taking family pictures to send to my mom. At the end of the day, upon my return to Arlene's house—my home at the time—Arlene's nephew, opened the door in a black tight workout outfit. That moment marked the beginning of a long relationship with ups and downs and everything in between. He asked who I was, and I quickly responded in my broken English, "I live here." There was not a drop of romanticism or flirtatious behavior in me in those days. My only goal was financial survival so I could pursue an education in the US. But in that instant, in those steps, my goals and worries slightly took a break, and my mind became primitive as I noticed his muscular body, his well-defined and strong forearms, his white smile and perfectly combed hair, and his deep blue eyes. His look was beyond pleasant to my eyes, with a touch of overconfidence that made him even more interesting. Deep under a layer of superficiality, I felt goodness, flashes of kindness, and a sense of trust. We stared at each other at the doorstep with no more words but a deep sense of curiosity, clearly possessed by each other's presence. We walked to the living room, sat on the couch next to each other, and talked for hours. With our bodies near each other, we forgot about the others in the house, absorbed with each other's words, gestures, and energy. Eventually, Arlene and Joe went to bed with the kids, but I don't recall saying goodnight.

In our conversation, Mike first asked me questions about the book that I was carrying in my hands—Stephen Hawking's *Universe,* a simply written introduction to his early work on theoretical physics, my first reading on quarks, and other groundbreaking theories. I recall being passionate about Stephen Hawking's ideas, and I made an effort to share them with Mike since he seemed curious. I explained to him, using a mix of Spanish and broken English, that I was learning theoretical physics, mostly the world of quantum mechanics, to which he responded with impossible-to-follow questions. I was putting a lot of effort into discussing concepts that, in reality, he had zero interest in learning about in those days. He didn't speak any Spanish and his English was fast and loud with a lot of American humor—the perfect way to get a foreigner lost in conversation. I was good at pretending, nodding, and smiling. It seemed like we were having completely different conversations. We both used plenty of hand gestures and facial expressions, and we put tons of energy into making our points. Clearly, we didn't understand each other, but we continued talking, not wanting the night to end. I wish I could hear our first conversation again today because I know we were completely out of sync, unable to truly follow each other but finding excuses to stay next to each other. I was drawn to him as he was to me in a way that our words didn't need to convey.

At the end of the night, I thought he would pick me up the next day to take me out to dinner and watch a movie. Since I barely understood his fast-spoken English, I wasn't a hundred percent sure of what the plan was.

The next day, he came back at the same time and took me to see the movie *Unforgiven*. On the drive to the theater, he spoke on his car phone with a friend, and he hung up on him as his friend was still talking, which I thought was quite rude. He also made jokes that I didn't find funny and/or could not follow. I thought he was a little bit odd on our first date, but for reasons I can't explain, I already felt strongly attracted to him. Even though the movie was nominated for an Oscar, it was boring to me since, besides having a hard time understanding English, I could not relate to Westerns. As a matter of fact, in Spain, I had never gone to the cinema. I came from a culture where young people didn't go out to movies or fancy restaurants. There was no formality about setting up a date. Instead, relationships would start in our evening social gatherings at the *chiringuitos* at the beach, or at the bars or clubs in town. On my first night out with Mike, I would have rather gone dancing or for a walk in the evening on a beach, but we didn't. My Spanish expectations were not met by American norms when it came to having fun.

After the movie, we went out to dinner at Il Fornaio, still one of my favorite restaurants. During dinner, he talked about how he was a stockbroker and a bodybuilder, topics of conversation as foreign to me as the language that he was using. I summarized our conversation with: *He cares about money and building muscles.* I focused on eating as much as I could, taking advantage of the opportunity to eat good quality food. I finished my plate, plenty of bread with olive oil, and continued eating out of his plate since he seemed more interested in talking than eating. It was now me who looked odd to him. After our dinner, I asked him to go for a walk to help digest all the food I overate. He agreed to my not-so-romantic suggestion and went for a walk with me outside the restaurant, going around and around the block, with him still talking. At the end of the night, he drove me to Arlene's house, and at the door, he surprised me with a passionate kiss, completely unexpected since I was not feeling my best and I didn't think the night had gone so well. That night marked my first and only experience with formal dating in my life.

Apparently, he had never gone on a date with a woman who could eat more than him. And I had never been with anyone that could talk as much as he did. Decades later, he still often tells this story to our friends. Eating out at expensive Italian restaurants, and walking afterward to compensate for my overeating, became our norm. I quickly realized that Mike was a talker and that even though he had a lot of questions, if I kept quiet, he would smile at me holding his words for a second, and then he would keep talking, answering his own questions. That worked perfectly for me.

As poor as I was during those years, I would not eat unless the food was of great quality, either homemade or from the best restaurants, and always with proportions far from tiny. Back in Spain, my friends used to joke and say that no man would ever be able to afford to take me out to eat. But I found a man comfortable with my expensive, obsessive gobbling.

Mike would call me every day on the only phone at Arlene's house, toward the end of the day, and I would always answer with the same sentence and a strong Spanish accent: "What happened?" translated from the Spanish salutation, *Que pasa?* The sentence *What's going on?* made no sense to my stubborn Spanish brain since I was literally translating word for word. I used this greeting for longer than I can remember. Every day, after his workouts, toward the last hours of the night, he came to Arlene's house to see me and say goodnight. Mike and I saw each other pretty much every day after our first date. Breaking my loneliness forever, we embarked on a life adventure that has now lasted over 30 years.

Early in the relationship—despite his self-obsessed personality common amongst young, good-looking men—it seemed like he deeply cared for me. He loved my imperfections and always spoke positively of me. My absent-minded and forgetful behavior together with my difficulty in learning to communicate in English did not seem to bother him or influence his strong opinion that I was a smart woman. No one in my life, not even myself, had ever had that perception of me being bright. And no man had ever paid more attention to my brain than my body. I was perfect in his eyes, but so imperfect in mine. His words of encouragement were music to my ears, as he constantly supported my dreams and goals from day one. He never told me, *I will take care of you*; instead, his words were, *You can do it. You are smart. You are unique.* I liked that. I loved that. He pushed me to be a stronger version of myself and to believe in myself. He was a great support in a world and culture still foreign to me. I had never dreamt of a man like him, relied on one, or even known they existed. His love felt real, his attachment intoxicating, and his confidence reassuring.

Regardless of our early strong connection, my relationship with Mike became far from perfect; he was conceited and arrogant to the world around him. Most of our fights happened after family or friends' gatherings, always related to his inappropriate unfiltered remarks, and his rudeness toward strangers. Going to the movie theater with him was always upsetting; he would frequently cut lines to buy tickets, leaving me feeling embarrassed. During the movies, he would open cans of stinky tuna, completely disregarding the people around us, as he felt the selfish need to maintain his body-builder weight. These incidents were impossible to overlook and always resulted in intense disagreements between us. His strong masculine presence and presumptuous voice felt threatening and irritating to me. I often responded with aggression to his obnoxious behavior toward others and his overconfident responses during our fights.

While my nature was typically humble and soft-spoken toward those around me, I tended to be defiant toward men in my relationships. Unfortunately, Mike was unable to acknowledge how his comments and behavior were often provocative and uncomfortable. As a result, and despite my efforts to control my reactions, I found myself becoming increasingly enraged with him. During our fights, I fired up with *burning* rage. I broke the bedroom door at his apartment several times, damaged the front interior panel of his new convertible Corvette by hitting my shoe against it, slapped his face a few times, and showed him the worst of me during our fights.

Mike consistently responded with surprising calmness and tolerance, even when my temper was at its worst. In fact, the more enraged I became, the more patient and understanding he seemed to be. It worked like magic. In reality, he was a peaceful man with a loud dysfunctional ego—unable to hurt, not even a tiny spider. His heart was big, with a lack of understanding of the workings of social interactions. After our fights, he would wait for my tantrum to stop and then he would try to talk things through, to get close to me, to hug me—at times waiting for hours or even days. For him, it was easy to say sorry. But his words and apologies meant nothing to me.

His vanity and disrespect were traits that clashed with my people-pleaser personality. We both were living at the farthest end of our extremes. But his rudeness was never toward me, just like my desire to please the world was not toward him. The reasons for our fights were insignificant to him, but to me, they were worth going to war over. My aggression toward Mike, and my ability to explode with anger, perhaps came from childhood wounds, from the fear that his masculine rudeness one day could take over our relationship. My high intolerance of men's control was playing a role in subtle ways. I didn't know another way to fight back my fears—other than the expression of anger. Fights between us went on for years.

My brother Memel also came to the US shortly before I met Mike and stayed with Chino and Lina for a while. Memel didn't exactly warm up to Mike as my boyfriend, but despite that, Mike and Memel quickly became good friends. I recall the day Memel showed up at Mike's apartment in the morning, and Mike refused to open the door because, besides feeling lazy about getting out of bed, he was unaware of Memel's visit. This to me, again, seemed like a sign of rudeness when, in reality, it was a cultural difference. I wasn't at home with Mike that morning, but when he told me with such arrogance, I didn't say a word. Instead, I immediately picked up a couple of shoes, threw them at him, packed my stuff, and left him. Mike followed me to my brother's house and begged me to come back with him. I noticed that day his fear of losing me. I could not understand such deep emotion. He was in a kind of pain I could not relate to, but it felt real. He showed no pride, only love and fear. For the first time in our relationship, I could see and feel his pain. I went back with him still upset but grateful to see that he followed me, and that he didn't give up on me or hold any grudge. That was our dance. I needed him, and I loved him with a heart not trained for love. My anger weighed heavier than the way I deeply cared for him. Regardless of my feelings or emotions, I had been quick to walk away from my relationships in the past, perhaps because I didn't believe that long-term love was possible—or perhaps because I put myself first for self-preservation. But for Mike, losing someone whom he loved was painful and not an option. I wonder, if he ever let me go, would I have let go of him?

For a long time, I tried to convince myself that my relationship with him would be temporary. My mom kept the many letters that I wrote to her during these early years of my relationship with Mike. The letters describe him as a handsome but arrogant man whom I would soon remove from my life. Secretly, I hated the fact that I loved him, though I tried to hide it and never dared to share it with anyone. It made me angry to recognize not even the tip of this feeling. To me, love was a sign of weakness, a trap, a free invitation to a miserable future, so I stayed as detached as possible, keeping my real emotions deep inside. When Mike said, "I love you," I would reply with "Of course." It never bothered him because he was convinced that I loved him. He was, and still is, made of thick skin. "You love me," he would say, happy to have me in his arms.

I've always held a strong belief that our partners should treat us the way we deserve from the very beginning. They should love us despite our faults, sympathize with our mistakes, and, most importantly, show respect to those we hold dear. I fought passionately for those ideas.

In retrospect, I wonder if I expected too much from Mike

while holding back in return. My occasional bursts of aggressive behavior toward him felt unexplainable and uncontrollable to me. I didn't like it, but I didn't know another way to control his toxic arrogance. Now I like to think that perhaps my anger was a form of self-protection—*my only weapon.*

I often reflect on how women are hardly ever encouraged to express strong negative emotions like anger; instead, we are raised to be loving, caring, friendly and people-pleasers. A man who blindly falls in love with a woman can be perceived as weak. But a woman is supposed to drink the punch, become delusional, possibly destroy her future in the hands of a man, and still be perfectly accepted by social norms. Falling in love can be a dangerous drug. It makes us crazy. It blinds us from logic. It leaves us defenseless. It hinders our thinking. While I did fall in love with Mike, I never allowed myself to be blind to this love, but instead prioritized protecting myself, my values, and my goals.

Mike didn't have a conventional upbringing either. His parents divorced when he was three years old, and immediately after, Mike was left in foster care. During the divorce trial, neither his mom nor dad fought for Mike or any of his siblings. Even though he was young, he still remembers his tears as he waited at the entrance of the house of the foster family for his mom. Mike tells me stories of how he would ride a bike as a young boy after school and how no one cared where he was, what he did or what he ate. He still believes, whether true or not, that one of those foster families fed him dog food every night. He mostly grew up in foster care and worked since he was a young teenager. He never stopped searching for a reason to understand and accept his parents' choices. I now understand his rudeness toward the world as a young man.

For many years, Mike and I did not share our childhood stories. The signs of damage were all over us, but we held onto false images of our lives with pride and displayed only our individual strengths, showing each other a partial version of ourselves. Me with my image of cold-heartedness, and Mike with his image of grandiosity, continued our relationship.

Family and friends believed that Mike would never commit to me or any other woman who did not have certain standards of materialistic beauty and professional success. Most of them discouraged our relationship. Some of my close friends and family members even made the effort to introduce me to supposedly better men. Mike was not a well-liked guy. A friend of the Gilio family once insisted that I meet a successful young French man. He was sophisticated and had lots of knowledge about wine, but I was thinking about Mike during the entire afternoon with the French guy. Besides, the whole uppity act was a complete turn-off for me. Mike's own sibling once advised me to be conscious and said that Mike would never marry me, that he was free-spirited and that he would not commit to me. I was not interested in marriage or any sort of serious commitment, so this didn't dissuade me. We needed each other in our own flawed ways.

A few months after I started dating Mike, my ex-boyfriend Juan from *Granada* showed up at Arlene's house with a large painting of the *La Alhambra* Palace that he'd painted for me. He didn't speak English and was not much of a traveler, but there he was, standing in front of me in California, even though we had not talked since the day I left *Granada*. He told me how he had found my grandpa in *Chiclana* and got my US address from him. As soon as Arlene came home, Juan and I went out. I was surprised but happy to see him again, to learn that he had not forgotten about me. He was perhaps the most perfect man one could spend a lifetime with, but that day, for reasons I still cannot comprehend, I told him that I was living a new life and had no intention of going back. He was surprised by my financial situation in the US and my determination to stay regardless of the many challenges I was facing. My decision that night made absolutely no sense. I chose the hardest path with the greatest unknowns and the lowest probability of success in all aspects of my life. I now wonder how my life would have turned out if I had gone back home with him, if I had made what had seemed like the most logical and safe decision. He left that night and I never saw him again, but I keep his painting at my house with his handwriting on the back.

Another year and a half went by. I had taken all the math, chemistry, physics, and engineering courses that I could at the community college level. I was tutoring other college students in physics and Spanish, and I kept cleaning and doing babysitting jobs as much as I could. I was a straight-A student. Through hard work and discipline, I did well as a full-time international student, even in my least favorite non-science courses, such as history, philosophy, and English. I consistently managed to get the best scores. I studied nights and worked days. I remember when Mike would go out with Memel to dance clubs on the weekends, and they would come back to find me in Mike's bed with books and notes all over his bedroom. I was not interested in going out or having fun; studying became my obsession.

Early in our relationship, Mike left his stockbroker job and decided to pursue a career in the fitness industry. He was just holding on financially, transitioning to a new adventure while trying to maintain his image of wealth and success. He drove his Corvette to work as a fitness trainer at a local health club when at times he seemed to be struggling to pay for gas.

Mike was not able to help me with college expenses. Financially, all I could ask of him was an occasional meal at Italian restaurants. He shared whatever he had generously. He would even lend me his Corvette, allowing me to use it for babysitting jobs. I once babysat two Japanese boys in the afternoon. With Mike's Corvette, I became the coolest babysitter the boys ever had and even their father came out of the house one time to admire the car with disbelief. I loved those moments when the haves and have-nots surprised each other.

During these early years, I made a special friend, Gunilla, that has now lasted a lifetime. Originally from Denmark, she had spent years of her life in Marbella, Spain. She found love, at the age of 19, with an American, named Zak, who was traveling in Spain. Their love story was both beautiful and adventurous, a blend of cultures that fascinated me.

Gunilla would often cook dinner for me at their house in Burlingame, California. With her, I learned the art of savoring moments at a beautifully set table, with perfect lighting, flamenco music, and mostly Spanish dishes. Her embrace of the Spanish culture was deep-rooted, and her stories of Spain made me proud of my heritage. We both adored passionate dancer Joaquin Cortez and connected over our love of our roots in a foreign land. In a society so different from my own, Gunilla had a unique way of grounding me. She was the only person capable of slowing me down. She radiated tranquility. I was drawn to her unconventional thinking. Gunilla and Zak early in their relationship understood the meaning of living an authentic life. They followed no societal norms or imposed ways of thinking; they were free spirits. Many times, I adopted their perspective in life. With them, I learned about energy healing and other forms of alternative approaches to wellness. What's more, they were the rare friends who genuinely liked Mike.

Oftentimes, Gunilla and I adventured on city trips in San Francisco. Mostly lost, often amused, we navigated the city's streets, uncovering hidden gems in our exploration. Getting lost became a catalyst for finding the city's most charming secrets. I am now glad that GPS was nonexistent as we only relied on our little confusing map of the city. Those early memories in the US with Gunilla always bring a smile to my face.

After approximately two years of living in the US, first with my brother Chino and then with the Gilio family, I moved to San Jose to live and work for the Johnson family, who promised an unbelievable salary of $600 a month, while they also provided room and board. At this new job, I worked hard the entire day. I had to drive the kids to school and afternoon activities, clean and cook for the family and buy all the groceries, while still attending my classes at the community college. Every night after having dinner with the Johnson family and cleaning the kitchen, I would drive to Mike's house to avoid the complicated family dynamics that presented themselves every night. Yelling and insults were the norm at the Johnson's house. The dad seemed gentle, and the mom intimidated the entire family. This was quite new to me because I had never witnessed abuse coming from a mom instead of a dad. She had a demanding full-time job. I understood her stress, but it would make me furious to hear her screams every night. I never felt that the kids or the dad deserved such treatment. When the mom was home, there was nothing I could do for the kids. I would drive to Mike's house at about ten or eleven every night to study in Mike's bedroom, which became my safe place.

My Isuzu had died months earlier because I didn't know that oil changes were a thing, and I was driving a beat-up car, uninsured, that I'd borrowed from the Johnson family—a car that would randomly stop, sometimes while on the freeway, and require opening the front trunk and messing with the wires to get it to start again.

My brother Memel was in a situation much like mine, living in the US without work papers, and facing the challenges of earning a living. He worked as a nanny in a house a short distance from the Johnsons. His living quarters were in a trailer behind the family's house, and he cared for a nine-year-old girl—a super-cool girl who was proud to have a male nanny who was a kickboxing champion. Memel was the youngest person in Spain to receive his black belt in Shotokan and kickboxing at the of 17. Wherever he went, he was well-liked by everyone; he had and still has a charismatic personality, great looks, and the will to work tirelessly. At that time, Mike's roommate, a successful businessman, believed in Memel's abilities. He established a dojo for him to teach kickboxing and martial arts, resulting in an exciting adventure for all of us. I would drive to his dojo once a week in the evening. With red boxing gloves bigger than my head, I would spend hours practicing boxing and kicking. The dojo became my favorite place to be. I absolutely loved, and still do, punching and kicking, as long as I don't get hit back. Chino and Mike also joined in the fun. The dojo brought joy into our lives for many months.

After living with the Johnson family for about eight months, I left them without receiving the last three months of my salary. The dad every month would promise me that they would soon pay me. He explained how they were financially struggling for just a short time. He seemed nice and honest, but I couldn't continue staying with them. At that point, Mike suggested that I move with him, even though he had a roommate, and the agreement was no woman should be living in the apartment. I kept myself invisible, locked in his room as much as I could, quietly studying, until one night when Mike and his roommate were yelling at each other, on the brink of a fistfight. I came out of my bear cave, forced Mike into his bedroom, and gently sent his roommate into his own. I entered the roommate's bedroom, stared into his eyes, and begged him to let go of the incident, even though it originated from Mike's rudeness! He was kind enough to let go, perhaps because he had a strong friendship with my brother Memel and had always shown respect to me. Soon after, the roommate moved out and we kept the apartment to ourselves.

It was now the time to enter my fourth semester in community college. I was attending San Mateo College and running out of options to keep up with college expenses. Accumulating debt and constantly looking for babysitting, house-cleaning, and tutoring opportunities, my days were challenging and my future still uncertain.

Mike was trying to get his feet off the ground in the fitness industry. His goal was to achieve financial success. His image was very important to him. I thought that this was perhaps a result of growing up in California, a place where beauty, youth, straight white teeth, and money are of high importance. But the real root of his desires was the absence of parental love and guidance during his childhood years, and a need, similar to mine, to prove his value.

Only 17 months into our relationship, I asked Mike to marry me so I could get a work permit and continue my education by paying resident tuition. I thought it was a brilliant idea. I had excellent grades and the engineering skills to get a decent job. I believed marriage was my ticket to freedom, the only way to get out of my underdog situation.

In a low, sad voice, he replied, "No." I locked myself in the bathroom, upset, crying, telling him that this was the end of our relationship, the end of my dreams to get a college degree in the US, and that I was going back to Spain. I hated crying. I hated feeling weak. I hated feeling sorry for myself. I hated asking. I just wanted to keep moving forward. I didn't believe in marriage, but I needed help pursuing my goals. It was a means to an end. I don't think I understood what I was asking. In my mind, we were already living together, so why not sign *a silly contract* that would allow me to achieve success? Mike had a much more traditional mindset than me. He wanted to make sure he married the right woman at the right time and had an extravagant wedding.

As I was looking for options, tormenting myself, stubborn in not wanting to go back to Spain with another failure, Mike wrote on a piece of ripped paper, with the worst handwriting ever, *I will marry you! But I will marry you for love!* I opened the door, hugged him, and said, "Let's go! Let's do it! Let's do it *now!*"

The next day, January 22nd, we drove to Reno with my brother Memel and Mike's best friend. Mike scheduled a civil ceremony. The four of us in jeans showed up to the ceremony. I was having a hard time understanding the wedding officiant. "Do you, Almudena, take Michael to be your lawful wedded husband?" the officiant asked. I looked at Mike and replied, "I do you."

All I remember was three of them—Mike, Memel, and Mike's friend—laughing aloud as the officiant did her very best to keep her composure. I thought, *what am I missing here?* But I ignored the laughs until later when Mike explained the unusual answer I had given to the officiant.

In reality, the ceremony didn't mean anything to me. I was focused on getting the job done so I could apply for a work permit and go back to my books and my studies. At the time, this was the picture of a perfect honeymoon.

That night we went to the casinos, and I watched Mike, Memel, and Mike's friend play poker on my wedding night.

I was happy! Mission accomplished!

CHAPTER 10

A Glance of Reality

"Reality is created by the mind; we can change our reality by changing our mind." – *Plato*

MY MARRIAGE CERTIFICATE WAS ONE more step toward the possibility of individual power. A door to some type of financial freedom so I could make my own choices and help my mom and sisters. I always felt the strength of my brothers, Chino and Memel—their self-reliance and resilience were clear to me. They were both working hard on their own toward their own dreams. I never saw my brothers broken or with doubts about their futures. Unlike me, they seemed to be made of steel, only looking forward. I used to wonder how they were capable of such strength. On the other hand, when I thought of my mom and younger sisters, I perceived a different reality that tormented me with a burning desire to do something about it.

Unfortunately, Memel reached a point where he couldn't continue working at the dojo while pursuing an education without proper legal documentation. As a result, he made the decision to study and work in London. The night before he left, he stayed with us at Mike's apartment. I fell asleep crying like a young girl, devastated by the prospect of being separated from my big brother once again, admiring his willingness to start all over again in a different country. I felt devastated since he had been a strong arm of emotional support.

After our marriage ceremony, Mike and I immediately applied for my US residency. A few months later, I bought a plane ticket to see my family and friends in southern Spain for the summer. I borrowed some money from one of my college friends to help cover the ticket cost, and Mike paid for the rest. I had not seen my family in three years.

My mom, sisters, and father picked me up from the airport. I had missed the first three tremendously, but not the last. I was not looking forward to having to deal with him. Nevertheless, there he was waiting for me with plenty of hugs and kisses, regardless of my feelings. I hugged my mom, like I never did before. I could not stop hugging, kissing, and looking at my sisters, telling them how much I had missed them. Ana was 18 years old, and Carmen had just turned 17. They looked so different. My mom was as beautiful as always, and my father had not changed at all, though he pretended to care about me a bit more. His hope was that, at some point, all of his kids would take care of him financially. Perhaps he saw me as a potential for additional income in the future.

We drove back to a small new rental in the center of the town located right next to a nasty stinky river where my father continued to smoke day in, and day out. I would look into my parents' bedroom in the morning and find that the room was completely full of smoke. I worried about my mom's health. By now I understood the concept of secondhand smoke. The house felt like a large ashtray and still, he was the only voice, running the house like a tyrant.

Stories from Ana and Carmen made me really upset. I found Carmen in a bad place, upset at my dad, but unlike me at that age, she did not rebel; she still was able to bear a smile around him. She hurried to tell me that our father, that year, had punched her in the jaw with a closed fist, only because she spoke back to him with a clarification question: "Papa, I don't understand." Carmen considered taking her life forever that night. When I heard her words, I felt her pain, and I thought, *Papa, you can kill my soul, but you will not fuck with the ones I love.* Ana had been constantly insulted by my father for her *happy* feminine behavior. Ana told me stories—too many stories. While I was in the USA, my father once forced her to sleep under the bed for five consecutive days after slapping her face several times, demanding a smile. I felt deeply connected to Ana's experience. Out of frustration, Ana had left home at the age of 15 and had lived with a friend on a farm for about two years. She was now living back home. Ana never showed pain—she told me stories as if they were simply part of life, always with a mischievous smile and an *I-don't-care* attitude. My mom continued working as a teacher as my father lived off her salary, controlled my mom's income, and drank at the bar in front of the house daily.

I immediately started to feel the drive again to do something extreme. My desire to kill him came back. He disgusted me. I hated his guts. But I was not yet in a situation to help. I held my anger while observing the way I once lived.

I spent most of the summer buying food in the local market near the house and cooking lunch with my mom. In the afternoons I went with friends to the beach. Swimming and lying in the sun brought some peace to the still-disturbing reality.

On my way back to the US, my father decided that Ana would come with me. It was my father's assumption that Chino and I would take care of her. I had no place or money for Ana, so she stayed for a short time with Chino. On our arrival at San Francisco immigration, I was detained and stuffed into a room full of undocumented immigrants. They let Ana go with a tourist VISA. I told the immigration officers that I was married to a US citizen, and they replied, "You are married to an American, but you are bringing a little *girlfriend*," referring to my younger sister. Immigration officers, at least the ones I had communicated with, were far from polite. Two different ones interrogated me and made me feel less than human. They accused me of breaking the law. They said that I had no legal status since my tourist visa had expired six months after my arrival in the US. I really did not understand since I thought that I was on an international student visa. I didn't cry or show signs of intimidation, even though they were rude and threatening. I was concerned that they would send me to jail, but I kept my composure because I knew I deserved respect and that I had only had good intentions since I had first arrived in the US. But ignorance and sincerity are not good reasons for forgiveness when it comes to breaking the law. One more time in my life I had to rely on hope. I stayed detained for several hours until Mike figured out a way to get me out of there. Mike's persistence and assertiveness taught me that day to always fight for whatever I felt was right, regardless of rules or protocols. They took my passport and gave me an appointment on a later day to discuss my status in the US. On our ride home, Mike told me with conviction that he would not let anything happen to me. His confidence felt soothing and protective. It was so easy for me to trust his words and his ability to solve problems, but mostly his devotion to me.

The day I went to pick up my passport at the scheduled time, I sat in multiple rooms as they went through a detailed investigation of my status. The questions were draining, but I continued displaying confidence, something that was not natural to me. I kept telling the officers that I was an engineering student, that the university had issued the I-20 form, that I had been paying international high tuition fees, and that I was now married to a US citizen. I told them that and nothing more. Time went by and there was no resolution to my case. I was getting nowhere in convincing the officers, when I heard Mike talking to a woman officer next door, who seemed to be in charge. I heard his words: "She is a very smart student and soon she will be doing extraordinary work and paying lots of taxes." I thought that was clever. Mike later told me that he was knocking on doors looking for me, talking to people, until he found this woman. I could hear his reassuring voice through the walls, the same voice and tonality that had made me feel safe many times before. In the end, I recall sitting in the office with Mike and this officer. She was laughing at Mike's jokes, and they seemed connected through their own culture and impeccable American English language, while I was fuming inside, wishing I could call her out for being such a *bitch* to me just a few minutes earlier. Mike can be very persuasive, a natural-born salesman, always quick to react with a *plan B* and never defeated by the obstacles he encounters. After paying our immigration penalties, they let me go, informing me not to leave the country again until my still-in-process residency was approved.

At the end of the day, this had all been my fault, due to my lack of knowledge of immigration laws, my stubborn desire to continue my education in the US no matter what, and the excitement of seeing my mom and sisters again before I got my US residency. I had no one to blame but myself. Those rude immigration officers were only a reminder that the system didn't care about me, my family, my intention, or my value. I was just a number that needed to follow the rules. Without resources, I had no power anywhere in this world. I had to get my education. I had to turn my life around.

I was happy to be back, highly motivated to work taking advantage of my new legal resident status. The goal was to find a better-paid job that would allow me to continue my studies, but now paying California resident fees—insignificant compared to the international tuition fees that I had been paying. The concept of finding a job was intimidating since I didn't have good communication skills or much confidence in any of my abilities. Besides taking courses in community college, all I had done in the last three years was babysitting and cleaning houses.

Having Ana nearby gave me additional encouragement, making me feel more connected to my goals. I loved spending time with her, enriching my life with her positive, fearless, and adventurous teenage energy. She embraced the San Francisco life and became a social, fun-loving city girl.

Ana was quick at finding her first job selling fish in the Fish Market Restaurant in the city of San Mateo. I would visit the market just to see her working, full of confidence with hardly any English but looking sharp, immersed in her role, and enjoying every interaction with her customers. In a short time, she was able to afford living in San Francisco among other young and fun people. She did just fine surviving on her own. Her entire life has been an inspirational story. My father once called me: "Almudena, get your sister Ana out of the city life. There is nothing but faggots in the city. They all need a doctor to fix their sexuality." I was happy that day to speak to our homophobic father. I snapped back: "First let's find you a doctor who can fix you and your fucked-up head." The conversation continued for a while as each sentence became more and more offensive to each other. I recall being glad to have this conversation with my father, where I could express my opinion loudly and clearly without any hesitation, or fear of retaliation. On the other hand, Ana was happy, and her lifestyle was accepted by everyone in the family except him. He was now the only outcast in the family.

Bringing joy into our lives, Chino and Lina had their first child, Justin, who became my mom's first grandchild. We embraced Justin as the most precious gift. Lina was happy to include us in his life, allowing Mike and me to care for him on certain weekends when he was young. We enjoyed plenty of sleepovers and day trips with Justin.

My mom before marriage

My father

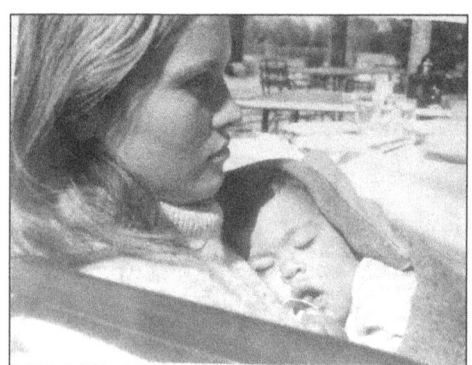

With my mom in Madrid

With my brothers in Madrid

Me at 15 years-old

The day I met Mike, I was 23 years-old

Mike was 28 years-old when we met

PART THREE

ACHIEVE

CHAPTER 11

The Beginning of Glory

"Everything you can imagine is real." – Pablo Picasso

THE HARD WORK DIDN'T END after my marriage but with a work permit and legal residency, I could take advantage of working opportunities in my field of study. The moment I got my residency, my Mexican friend Wendy's older sister, Isabel—a tenacious female engineer devoted to helping young immigrant women—took me under her wing. She helped me put together a resume and got me a job as an assistant engineer at the company where she worked: N. Marshall and Associates in San Carlos, California. Isabel was my first mentor in the world of engineering. My new name became Almi. Every day as I arrived at work before or after my classes, Isabel would greet me with a big smile, ready to teach me, and ready to make a difference in my life. I had so much to learn, so much to offer and even more to appreciate.

I mostly loved building surface-mount circuits and programming microcontrollers. However, my main project involved building the inventory database for the engineering activities. My coding skills were a little bit rusty, but Isabel gave me the space to study and review. I stayed in this job for one year as an assistant engineer, working on average 25 hours per week and earning a generous salary of $13 per hour while still attending community college as a full-time *resident* student. The founder and president of the company, Dr. Noel Marshall, wrote me a recommendation letter at the end of the year for me to use in the future whenever needed, which I have kept because this written page was much more than just a recommendation to go to college. It represented an accomplishment after years of sacrifices! Noel, with his kindness and his appreciation for my work, gave me the confidence I needed to continue in the field of electrical engineering. He took a chance to hire me, a woman with very little engineering knowledge and no work experience in the US other than cleaning and babysitting. He trusted Isabel's recommendation. I recall Noel sitting next to me in the lab once, observing my work as I built a surface mount circuit under the magnifier. I was not nervous; I was happy that he took the time to check on me. With a contagious smile, he told me that I was doing good work. He always made me feel that I belonged in his company.

Motivated by my experience at N. Marshalls, I applied to the University of California at Berkeley (UCB) to study electrical engineering (EE). At San Mateo College, my physics professor, Barbara Uchida, encouraged me to apply to UCB. She'd received her degree from there and spoke very highly of the university. As hard as it may be to believe, I'd never heard of UCB before, but she insisted that I apply. I followed her advice and with her guidance, I applied to UCB for a bachelor's degree in EE. I quickly learned from other students and professors how prestigious UCB was, but as I said in my application, *I was ready to rock and roll.* I wanted the challenge and the opportunity to compete academically with the best. I was blissfully unaware of the depth of the ocean.

I was accepted but had no idea what it meant to compete in academia. My first semester was a wake-up call. My let's-all-get-along personality didn't fit so well with the engineering department. To fit in, I stopped wearing red nail polish and gave myself a less feminine look. There were hardly any women in EE, and most male students would spend their nights in the labs working non-stop, eating pizzas, taking few showers, and using lots of vulgar language. I did not want to spend my nights in those stinky labs. But as much as I fought it, I didn't really have a choice. During those lab hours, my only hope was that Mike would show up as a surprise to take me out to dinner. My life had changed so much. I wrote letters to Mili reflecting on my life. Only three years before, I was spending my nights with her and friends dancing at the beach with a hopeless future, and now I was in one of the most competitive universities in the world studying one of the most challenging majors.

My undergraduate years at Berkeley were special because I had the luxury to study all the time without having financial concerns. I took on student loans and Mike took care of any extra expenses. I didn't have to work for the moment. I completely focused on my goals and dreams for the future. I also had the opportunity to get involved in doing research with different professors. I started to enjoy the world of digital systems and information theory, learning for the first time about the world of academic research.

In the final year of my bachelor's degree, Mike convinced me to apply to graduate schools and to the prestigious National Science Foundation's (NSF) graduate scholarship. Together, we worked on the lengthy application process. At the same time, I started a job search, just in case my graduate program application didn't go as planned. I was offered an interview with Cisco for a network engineer position. I was quite excited but very nervous. Days before the interview, I borrowed a professional-looking red suit and high heels from Lina. I loved the outfit, thinking that its striking colors would camouflage my low self-esteem in some way. However, on the day of the interview, I felt completely out of my element of those high heels and red lipstick. The world of network engineering didn't quite align with my elegant attire. I was not surprised that I never received a call back for a second interview. I've often wondered if the high heels deterred the hiring managers or if it was my struggle to convey confidence. Regardless, I didn't secure the job and proceeded with my pursuit of graduate studies.

We submitted a few applications, including one to UC Berkeley, and for months we impatiently waited for the letters of either acceptance or rejection. One evening, I was sitting at the phone booth on the lowest level of the engineering building, Cory Hall, trying to make a phone call to Mike. But he did not answer my calls. I was burnt out that day, with not a drop of energy left in my body, and I was ready to go home. Mike had gotten a printout of the awardees of the NSF scholarship, and my name was on the list! He drove to Berkeley and ran all over Cory Hall looking for me, eager to tell me the great news, carrying the printout in his hands. He found me deflated, sitting at the phone booth, with an expression of exhaustion spread across my face. He was gleaming, full of happiness, and running toward me. What could possibly have made him look like the happiest man on earth, especially when his wife was sitting miserably just a few feet away? He showed me the list of awardees, pointing at my name. I can still feel the shock and the joy, a special instant of time that I wanted to hold on to for as long as I lived. I remember staring at this long old piece of printed paper with holes on both sides and my name *Almudena Ordonez* etched into it, making sure that the moment was real. This meant that the NSF scholarship would completely pay for three years of graduate school, but its significance was much greater than that. It also meant that I had been recognized—that my name meant something to somebody. That was important to me. Nothing could stop me from continuing my higher education now. I ran through the building announcing the great news to my professors and leaving Mike behind. I went to the computer science building, Soda Hall, and found one of my professors, Prof. Shankar Sastry, in the elevator, and shared the news with him. I admired him for his extreme intelligence but mostly for his caring personality. He smiled, laughed, and was genuinely happy for me. I remember his reaction the most because of his sincerity.

Soon after, I received an admission letter from UCB. I had been accepted to their master's degree program in Electrical Engineering. Mike took me out for dinner to our special Il Fornaio restaurant, and there he asked me if I could be his wife forever. I was shocked by how our lives were turning around.

Our marriage had been kept secret from his relatives and most friends because Mike dreamt of a grand announcement and a glamorous celebration. But, at this point in our lives, we had become an inseparable team, making each other's goals our own and sharing a strong desire to reveal our reality to our family and friends. After Mike made the announcement, we celebrated not only our marriage but also my graduation, my NSF award, and my acceptance into the master's program at Arlene's house.

Before beginning the graduate program, one of my favorite electrical engineering professors, David Tse, offered me a summer research position working on Code Division Multiple Access (CDMA), a radio system channel access method. Prof. Tse's course was probably the most difficult course I ever took, but the material was fascinating, and his passion for his work was contagious.

One morning, I was enjoying my usual espresso at my favorite cafe when Prof. Tse walked in. He approached me and shared the inspiring story of Hedy Lamarr, a famous movie star. During World War II, Lamarr was married to an authoritarian Austrian munitions dealer associated with the Nazi party. Despite her unhappy marriage, she secretly learned about war strategies by eavesdropping on her husband's dinner conversations. Lamarr eventually escaped from her husband and became a renowned Hollywood actress, but her passion for innovation and deep concern about WWII was not hindered by the bright lights. Later in her life, she met George Antheil, a writer and music composer, with whom she shared her novel idea for a secret communication system that could guide torpedoes without enemy interference. George and Lamarr became lovers and together they developed a communication system known as Frequency Hopping Spread

Spectrum. She held the patent on CDMA, a spread spectrum technique used still today to mitigate radio frequency interference. This incredible story deepened my fascination with studying CDMA and intensified my appreciation for Prof. Tse. It also made me realize that women belong in this field, and Prof. Tse was offering me the opportunity to dig deeper into this fascinating subject of digital communications. I fell in love with CDMA technology. Later in my life as a professor, I taught spread spectrum in my computer networks course, passionately telling my students the story of Hedy Lamarr and her lover. These stories of women's accomplishments, passionate love, and struggle live in my heart and motivate me to keep going.

There was not one day in my years as a UCB student that I did not feel intimidated but inspired by the talented student population, the outstanding faculty, and UCB's long history of innovation and research excellence. I was probably one of the fastest walkers on campus. I would often ride my bike through the steep hills with my friend Lydia sitting on the back holding on to me, with my legs pedaling nonstop. I was physically strong, mentally determined, and always in a rush, accelerated by a desire to accomplish more. I studied day in and day out. On the weekends, Mike would drop me off at the library and pick me up at the end of the day. I would go back home with him to continue studying until late at night.

Mike had gotten his first job in sales in the software industry. Moving through several high-tech companies, he ended up as a senior regional manager at Oracle. This was the beginning of financial stability for both of us. He made the President's Club, a prestigious award given to the top sales performers, for several years in a row, achieving over a hundred percent of his sales quota every single year. He was driven by money, and I was obsessed with the academic world.

Through his success, Mike and I became explorers of fine resorts, visiting spas and dining in exclusive environments throughout California, Nevada, Arizona, and Utah. We enjoyed our alone time. Alone, we were perfect—without ever a fight or a doubt, we were present for each other. Those first resort adventures are still vivid because everything was new. Since I did not grow up in luxury, I could appreciate every single detail of these new experiences. At times, I wanted to keep it a little bit simpler, maybe with a sense of guilt that others who I loved could not experience the same, but Mike would always surprise me with the best room, the most amazing view and the perfect bathtub. All my trips were written in journals where I would describe the most minute details with passion, gratitude, and joy.

My life had taken a turn for the better. Doing the right thing through hard work felt right. But my mom all these years was still in Spain living as a prisoner of my father's wishes and temperament. My mom had inherited from her father a house in my hometown in Spain, and my father had borrowed a loan against the house under my mom's name. With that money, he decided to move to the US, leaving my mother in debt but with the possibility of starting a life of her own. The day that my father arrived in the US, he brought a *big* surprise: my sister, Carmen.

One of the greatest loves and partners of my life. In retrospect, this moment was the happiest surprise of my life. We hugged forever, putting on hold my mixed feelings about my father's arrival. Right before my father's departure to the US, my mom found the courage to tell him to find his own life and to use the money that he had taken from her to never go back. I had dreamt of this moment my entire life. I felt the beginning of my mom's freedom, but I wasn't sure of its meaning. I was nervous. I wish I could have been with her when she told him not to come back. I didn't think that she was letting go of the many years of abuse, and I didn't know if she would be able to find herself, the person my father tried so hard to destroy. I wonder if she would ever paint again, dance or read as much as she loved. Would she be able to smile at the possibility of a better future? I didn't know how she felt, but I was extremely happy that my father was away from her. Now my hope was that he would never return. In the afternoon after his arrival at Chino's house, I told him that I would help him stay in any way I could because I didn't want him to ever go back to my mom. Those were my words. I must admit many years later that I did not help my father in any way, financially or emotionally. I just couldn't find a drop of compassion. But he stayed away from my mom for the rest of his life.

He had received US residency through Chino at some point that I don't recall and moved to Fresno with Carmen to work as the maintenance manager in an apartment complex. I had to accept that my father was now living in the US. He was again part of my life, mostly because he found his way to be part of my siblings' life and Carmen still lived with him. I was stuck between my love for my siblings and my disgust for him. I was at times brutally sincere in my encounters with him and far from loving. Other times, however, I showed slight affection, by greeting him with two kisses and pretending that the past was gone. Even though I kept my interactions with him to a minimum, from now on, he was at all family gatherings. He complained to me once that my mom was asking to divorce him, to which I replied: "You are lucky that she left you; I would have rather killed you." He always thought I was capable of that.

My father played victim to all the new people whom he met, using his charming, manipulative personality to tell a new story of how his wife had kicked him out of the house after so many wonderful years of marriage. *He was such a good man*, these people must have thought. He played a new role with the ones he could. He didn't like Mike; he called him a *faggot* for not being a drinker and once insisted on having a boxing match with him, trying to provoke him into a fight. Mike and I left the family gathering feeling sorry for the lost soul.

I was relieved when my mom finalized her divorce. The Beast was now nearby, and acting like Beauty, but at least away from my mom.

Carmen's first few years in the US were also challenging, since she came on international student status with no work permit. At least she was on legal status. She had to live for a few months in Fresno with my father because the plan was to wait for my father to become a citizen so he could apply for her residency. Once again, Carmen and I were inseparable and constantly helping each other. As much as I disliked seeing my father, I often drove to

Fresno, 3 hours away, to spend weekends with Carmen. I knew she was bright, but the speed at which she adapted to the new environment was impressive. She learned English much quicker than I did, and in no time, she had a few jobs, including working as a waitress at several restaurants, getting paid under the table. She quickly understood jargon, idioms, and even Mike's jokes, which were still impossible for me to follow. Within five months, she found a live-in nanny situation and left my father. And soon after, she moved in with Mike and I. My life suddenly became much better, because every day my sister and I were together again. Carmen also joined some of our trips to nice resorts. My favorite one was the one to Arizona where Carmen and I rode horses in the wild and took hot baths at night.

Sometimes Carmen would come with me to the UC Berkeley campus. She would spend the day with me, walking through campus and sitting in on my classes.

At about a year after Carmen arrived, my mom visited the US for the first time. She was 50 years old, did not speak English, and had never left Spain other than her trip once to Africa right after she got married. Carmen and I were at the airport waiting for her with flowers. It was a happy summer; one I will never forget. Unfortunately, after the summer, when my mom left, Carmen followed her. "Mu, this world is not for me. I miss my mom, my people, and my culture." Just like that, I lost them both. I stayed close to Ana and Chino, but I missed Carmen, Memel, and Mom tremendously.

Since Mike and I were doing well financially, Mike had the idea to buy our first house: a brand-new, Mediterranean-style home with two floors, four bedrooms, and a large bathtub that I so much loved. The house was super spacious and beautiful to me. I felt proud living in my little palace. But in reality, the house was a common newly built residential family home and not a luxury one as I thought of it in those days. I had tons of dinner parties for friends and family as I continued working toward my graduate programs. My life seemed so perfect, but something was missing. I kept up daily phone conversations with my mom and Carmen, begging them to come to live in the US. I was being young and selfish with such a huge request. They both had a life and freedom from my father. My mom's job was enough income for them. But in my vision of the future, they were with me and the rest of my siblings here in the US.

CHAPTER 12

Facing to Conquer

"Failure is success in progress." – Albert Einstein

IN MY NEW HOUSE, I started grad school. I furnished one of
the upstairs rooms as my private office, so I no longer had to study
in bed. This became my sanctuary. In the first semester, I joined
a research team working under Prof. Joseph. Since I was taking
his wireless communication class and enjoying the lectures, I
approached him and asked him to be my research advisor. I
worked with him on a research project funded by the European
telecommunications company, Ericsson, that led to the heart of
my master's thesis, opening up new research opportunities.

I enjoyed doing research and my graduate courses were all
interesting. Hard work had been my magic formula, until I ran
into an unexpected brick wall. The willingness to work beyond
expectations was not working any longer. Everyone around me
seemed to have a much higher IQ. My peers working in my
research group were the smartest people I had ever known. Most
of them were outspoken and confident, while I felt like an
imposter, always overthinking my thinking. I admired them

mostly because I was not like them. I kept myself in the background, listening and learning from the best, observing the ease with which they would just get up and talk. But if I were to continue academic success in higher education, I had to find the courage to face my biggest personal challenge: the fear of public speaking. In graduate school, in addition to doing classroom project presentations, I was expected to present my research projects at conferences and in front of peers. During my first research presentation, I stood before a large blackboard in a big auditorium, scribbling mathematical equations, my heart racing, filled with dread at the thought of making eye contact with the audience. The situation felt incredibly embarrassing. The microphone felt threatening, possessed by some evil energy inside its circuitry. My irrational fear felt very real to me. *Universe, please send as much work my way as you want, but don't make me speak in front of people.* Those were my constant thoughts and prayers even though I knew this wasn't plausible in graduate school. Communicating the results of one's research was as important as getting results. Yet even in small groups with familiar faces, I feared public speaking. I became terrified of opening my mouth.

This fear spread beyond my understanding. My brain started to shut down at the simplest question from a professor or peer, leaving me feeling stupid, not good enough—a girl out of her depth. My career and years of effort were on the line. I thought perhaps I had reached my maximum potential and was facing something beyond my abilities.

The feelings I once experienced during my disastrous first interview back in Spain returned when I had to speak. I spent my days afraid of entering that state of mind, one where I couldn't be present in the moment, hear the people around me, interact and react, much less think about answering questions. This was no longer a language problem; it was rooted much deeper. Whatever it was, I had to face it and get over it. I had no other choice than to prove to myself that I could do it. I was only competing with myself.

I decided to join a Toastmasters group to get more comfortable with presenting my work. In these support groups, people with a fear of speaking meet on a regular basis and help each other to overcome the fear by doing presentations to each other. They strongly advised using notes during presentations, and even reading from notes, but I knew very well that I was not going to do so. I thought I would be judged by my inability to remember my words. But between the difficulty of the material, my strong and accelerated accent, my nervousness, my lack of lecturing skills, and my fears, I was not making sense to the Toastmasters group, and I ended up not getting much out of my time meeting with them.

I had to figure out a different way to overcome my fear. I started to video record my own presentations with just me in front of the camera at home. I remember being my worst critic as I watched my own recordings play back to me. *This is horrible*, I would say to myself. *I sound completely stupid.* This battle was personal. I couldn't share this challenge with Mike or anyone else because, maybe, they would stop believing in me. In the bookstore, I paid attention to self-help books and started to read lots of them on self-confidence, personal development, public speaking, and positive thinking. *Think Like a Winner* by Dr. Walter was the book that most helped me with my fears of public speaking. In it, I read for the first time the quote, "You are what you think." It became my motto.

I got into the habit of listening to self-help tapes and CDs in the car on my way to Berkeley. I started to meditate at night, practicing visualization and *artificial experiencing*. Basically, I would create a mental image of myself doing the thing I was afraid of while feeling a strong positive emotion as if it was a reality. At night, before going to bed, I would take hot baths while listening to classical music, doing relaxation exercises, and visualizing giving big lectures, small talks and having technical conversations with peers and strangers. I repeatedly imagined myself in front of an audience, being able to communicate technical topics perfectly without fear and with confidence. I also read Louise Hay's books on positive thinking and adopted the sentence, *in my life all is well*. I would repeat the statement over and over in my brain whenever I walked into a research group meeting or a presentation. I was eventually able to improve, to find moments when I could quiet my mind and stay present without the fear of being judged, making mistakes, or the constant concern of not being enough.

By the time I got my master's degree, I had contributed to great work in the area of wireless communication in the computer science department. Several research groups had yearly retreats in Tahoe, where all students and faculty presented their projects. In one of my first presentations there, a few minutes into my speech, I blacked out and lost the last few minutes of my memory. I recall feeling disconnected from my presentation, again in a different reality, by myself, immersed in discomfort, with an audience in front of me. I stopped, took a breath, and my rational self said to the audience, "I need to start from the beginning," while my compassionate-self kept repeating in my mind, *all is well, all is well, all is well.* I looked at the audience, and feeling connected to them, as I took a deep breath, I successfully delivered the presentation at a much slower pace. For once, I was able to momentarily disconnect from my struggles, center myself, and regain my composure. After the presentation, I immediately felt sick to my stomach, ran to the bathroom, and locked myself in a stall for a few minutes. I repeated affirmations and took a few deep breaths before going back into the auditorium with a renewed spirit. A few researchers surrounded me, asking questions about my project. I engaged in discussions comfortably and confidently with one person at a time. One of the North European researchers mentioned that it was the most entertaining presentation he had seen so far because he enjoyed the way I expressed myself using my hands. He said that I moved them like a flamenco dancer. He must have known that I was from the south of Spain. His comment was not common in a computer science retreat, but somehow the positive remark gave a good laugh. During our conversation, I felt I belonged, at least for a precious moment.

As I practiced my visualizations every night, my fear of public speaking lessened. In one of the Tahoe retreats, a researcher, in charge of the visiting research team, invited me to spend the summer continuing my work at Ericsson Research in Aachen, Germany. The trip started with a visit to Memel in London, where I met his future wife, Sarah, a beautiful woman from Melbourne, Australia. We did lots of sightseeing and enjoyed every moment of my short visit.

Our arrival at the Ericsson lab in Germany was fantastic—the engineers were welcoming, and the project exciting. After the summer in Germany, I was invited to present my research at their Stockholm headquarters. To my surprise, I was scheduled to give several research presentations to different research groups, all in one day. This was the first time that I ever engaged in my presentations without dissociating from reality, with confidence and finally with a sense of owning my audience. I so much enjoyed interacting and discussing their questions. That day was perfect. I felt competent for once in a world in which I still was trying to belong. I was not sure that my fears of public speaking were entirely gone, but that day I conquered them. As years have gone by, I continued having recurring dreams of facing an audience without anything to say, with a disconnection between my thoughts and the ability to express myself, and the need to hide. A reminder that, perhaps, some work is still ahead.

Memel's unexpected visit to beautiful Stockholm with Sarah became one of the most unforgettable weekends of my life. It was a time filled with pride in my achievements and a deep sense of connection as we both recognized that our paths were aligned for the first time toward the realization of our dreams.

I finished my trip visiting my mom, Carmen, all my friends, and my ocean in south Spain. Mili came to see me at my mom's house. I made coffee and bought delicious pastries. Mili was now the mother of a young toddler. He was as beautiful as she was, but much quieter and more reserved than his mom. There was a tremendous amount of love between them. She held him on her lap while we were telling each other our latest life stories, showering him with constant kisses and hugs, teasing him with affection. The kind of love that I could not comprehend. Even in her late 20s, she still looked too young to be a mother, still with a cigarette in her mouth and the same loud laughter that brought me back to memories of my teenage years. She asked me when I was going to have a baby with my handsome American husband. She teased me about the fact I had gotten married even though I'd promised her that I would never get married. And that even though I had told her years ago that my relationship wouldn't last, I was still married six years later. I told her that Mike and I were connected – "love" was a word Mili and I always avoided in our discussion of men and relationships, since in our unspoken understanding, love was weakness. "Mike and I share dreams and goals, but we will *never* have kids," I told her with strong conviction. I was 30 years old and still holding at least that promise. She replied: "You have changed a lot, *bichito*. You will have kids." With those words, we said goodbye by exchanging our rings as it was our tradition every time we saw each other, and by holding each other with a hug that neither of us could let go of. Separating from Mili was like leaving part of my childhood and teenage years behind.

On the way back to the US, after an entire summer away, I almost felt again like a stranger to my American life. The day that I arrived in the US, Mike had a surprise for me. He acted mysterious but loving and excited to share with me something he had been contemplating while we had been away from each other. He drove straight to a cozy resort in Napa, in the wine country in North California. We rushed straight to the room, showered together, and prepared to go out to eat at a restaurant where he was going to uncover the secret he was holding. During our dinner, he blurted out: "I have been thinking that we should have a baby. I know we will be great parents. The baby will be a girl and she will love math as much as you do." He had it *all* figured out. But he freaked me out! I hesitated even to think or process his words. Maybe the wrong time, the wrong day and emotions, or just one more fear that I was not ready to even consider for a split second. I was still trying to figure out my life as a graduate student, winning small battles at a time. Life as a mother was something I could not comprehend for a second. Mili's words were all over my mind, and my response to her was louder than ever: NEVER, NEVER, NEVER!

I had plenty of discussions with family and friends about how I was *not* going to raise children. The idea scared me to death. I remembered my days as a child. I didn't think it was easy to be a child, that misery could strike a family at any time. I had seen plenty of suffering from my friends, too, when they were children. I had friends who had been victims of sexual abuse, others had been hit by their parents, and, in my case, I had lived in constant fear. I didn't want to be responsible for bringing a child into this world. I expressed my concerns to Mike, hoping he would let me enjoy my dinner. But the conversation went on until we fell asleep that night.

After our night in Napa, there was not a day that Mike would not bring it up again. "We will be great parents. I can see a little girl. She will look just like you." He was using his best-selling techniques and his very persistent self. Meanwhile, I wrote plenty of entries in my journals reflecting on the meaning of being a mom. I wrote the pros and the cons. There was only one positive thing: *A baby will make Mike happy.* Some of my excuses in my journal were quite silly like, *my body will be destroyed*; others were practical: *I want to have a successful career*; and *the world can be cruel.* And one of the excuses was quite surprising to even myself: *I want a baby horse.*

Since my trip to Arizona with Carmen, I could not let go of the desire to ride my own horse. I had written in my journal years ago, in the present tense, *riding my own horse, riding my own horse, riding my own horse.* From now on, when Mike talked about having a human baby, I talked about having a baby horse. In the end, I won!

We ended up buying two purebred Arabs from a private owner, Alexandra Arabians in Santa Rosa, California—two young beauties, grandchildren of JK Spartan. Their names were Keziaa and Vincent. Mike's desire to extend the family was temporarily satisfied. We spent every evening of our new life with our new babies. Mike and I were completely in love with the horses! We already had three Persian cats at home, so he had proven to be an animal lover, making me think he would let go of the baby thing. The horses became our children.

Mike and I learned how to ride, English and Western style, and even practiced jumping. Fearless Mike, with his gentle horse, quickly became a better rider than me, and an excellent, sensitive horse owner. Keziaa became my greatest companion. I loved her from the moment I saw her. She was very young, elegant, and proud, with a golden coat, honey-colored eyes, and a magnetizing gaze. A few white tones on her light chestnut skin gave her touches of light, making her skin even more radiant. Her demeanor was that of a proud queen, and her movements were mesmerizing, as if she walked effortlessly in the air with powerful snort sounds. With her in my life, I had to push myself every day to match her level of energy. Her power and hot personality were constant reminders that I had to handle difficult moments with more confidence and trust, learning to use my breath to stay calm and present. Her strength pushed me to be stronger. The times I fell from Keziaa were my own fault. I would get tense, anticipating threats during our trail rides, causing Keziaa to bolt into a gallop, running out the trail in random directions and jumping over any obstacles in her way. These were teaching moments I could apply elsewhere in life. She was giving me great wisdom: *In the face of fear, relax.* The times that I was able to clear my mind and feel her power with total trust were heavenly and everlasting. Keziaa also taught me that relationships between animals and humans should not be different from those between humans. All relationships should center on trust and respect.

It was now the year 2000, I was 30 years old and starting the Ph.D. program at UCB. Our financial situation was stronger than ever, and the horses had brought a new level of happiness into our lives. I was having phone conversations back and forth with Mom, sharing my horse stories and hoping that her lifetime love of horses would get her excited about moving to the US. To my surprise, in one of these conversations she made the decision to come to California and live with us. She made it sound simple to me, but in reality, it was an immense life-changing decision. She was leaving a lot behind—her career, her culture, her language, her sister, her brother and father, and other family members at an age when life changes are not as easy as when one is young. Regardless, I was crazy happy, clueless of the sacrifices that she was making to be closer to her adult children.

The week of her arrival, Mike and I bought her two bearded dragon lizards and a Persian cat to make her welcome in our house. She brought her little dog and as soon as she settled, she attended classes to learn English. She was in her 50s and starting an entirely new life. I can only now understand what we'd asked of her. Months later, Carmen and her boyfriend at the time joined us too, leaving Spain and moving into our new home. Her boyfriend gave up after experiencing for a few months the struggles of an immigrant with no work permit in the US. Carmen stayed. She had a hard decision to make—her family or everything else. She chose us.

With Mom and Carmen in my life, I felt a stronger sense of support to complete my graduate work. But, despite my few successful research presentations, I was not free of my fear of speaking. As I worked toward my Ph.D. degree, one of the most challenging requirements was to take the qualifying exam. I wanted to study as hard as I could for a long enough time so that the knowledge I obtained would never go away. At least, that was my hope. I became obsessed and overprepared but held lots of fear. Unfortunately, the exam was oral and took place in front of a rather intimidating graduate council. I anticipated that this would be the greatest obstacle in pursuing my Ph.D. degree, and it was—not because of the difficulty of the exams, or my lack of effort, but because the thought of standing in front of the council was beyond frightening. On the day of the exam, as I had predicted, their questions turned me into a frozen block. I left the exam demoralized and wished that they had given me the option to take the exam in writing, but it was not possible because professors need to see graduate students thinking on their feet, a skill that years later I appreciated and encouraged with my own college students. I knew that I needed to overcome this challenge.

I had two chances to pass the qualifying oral exams and unfortunately, I failed both. Failing two times meant that I had to leave the Ph.D. program. I recall sitting on the stairs at our home. I was quiet and upset. No one was around but Mike. Standing in front of me, he said, "There must be a way. You won't be denied. Talk to the committee. Ask for one more chance. Please try." But I had run out of chances to take the exam—those were the rules. I couldn't understand why he was so persistent. "I already have two degrees, Mike, and many opportunities to make a good income," I responded with disappointment and the hope that he would encourage me to walk away from trying what seemed impossible to me. But he didn't. He continued: "You can do it. You are smarter than you think. You will find a way." He was a pain in my neck. The truth of the matter is that I wanted to continue in academia more than anything, but I felt that my doors had completely closed. But Mike has always believed that you are the only one who can completely close your own doors. So, with this mindset, he persisted.

The next day I went to my office, with my best friend and Ph.D. student Ben Zhao sitting next to me and feeling my pain.

To my surprise, I received an email from Prof. Joseph, my advisor: "You can take the preliminary exam again but in Computer Science (CS) and not in Electrical Engineering (EE)." The opportunity opened but not without additional work. I had to study a complete set of new material in CS, and the course requirement for the CS Ph.D. was quite different from EE. I was completely done with the EE course requirements, but nevertheless, I said yes! I spent months studying for the preliminary oral exams. For my own sanity, I could not fail again.

I visited my regular doctor and I explained to her how I felt anxious and unable to think on my feet with professors looking straight into my eyes. I told her perhaps I had some type of brain disorder; I was convinced of this. I was hoping that she would recommend a natural approach, but she prescribed a sedative drug. That was a scary concept to me! I have always been skeptical of taking meds unless convinced that there is no other alternative. But this was not the case. I believed that by taking pills I would not be facing my personal challenge or improve whatever condition I had and somehow it would set me on the wrong path. In my opinion, most prescription drugs can perhaps completely remove unwanted symptoms, but it is also true that they can open an entire can of worms, leaving the body with new symptoms and in need of other medications. My apprehension toward prescription drugs and my stubborn ways to heal naturally perhaps come from my own mom. For one reason or another, I did not take a pill, and instead, continued doing my night-time meditations, visualizations, slow breathing techniques, and studying as hard as I could.

I remember the morning of the exam. I took a shot of espresso and right at the door of the exam room I found one of my research mentors from Ericsson, Reiner. He gave me a kiss on my forehead, similar to how a dad would treat a daughter, and said, "You got this."

Inside the exam room that day, a confident version of myself could not stop talking. Maybe the espresso kicked in; for one reason or another on that particular day, my brain decided to cooperate. Days later, Prof. Joseph gave me the great news that I had passed the qualifying exam. I felt incredibly proud—such a sense of accomplishment. I wanted to yell to the world that my dad was dead wrong and that I was not stupid! I was now in the Ph.D. program. I spent the next years taking the CS course requirements.

Working under the continued supervision of Prof. Joseph, I published great research work and attended high-ranking conferences. In the summer of 2001, I presented my recently developed wireless mathematical models at the Association of Computing Machinery (ACM) International Workshop on Modeling, Analysis, and Simulation of Wireless and Mobile Systems which was held in Rome, Italy. On the day of the presentation, I felt powerful. I remember that day like it was yesterday. I had the right outfit and the perfect mindset. After my presentation, there was a line of researchers waiting to meet with me to discuss my research. I was enjoying the entire experience and felt I was born to live that moment. On the day of the award ceremony, I had arrived late to the announcement and snuck in quietly, finding a seat in the back of the room. I patiently sat in the last row of the conference room, hearing some of the awards. The awardees would come to the podium and at the microphone they all had something nice to say, about their research and their collaborators. I paid attention to how easy it was for other researchers to get up and eloquently share a few words. I felt safe in my last row until the next announcement: "The best paper award for the ACM International Workshop on Modeling, Analysis, and Simulation of Wireless and Mobile Systems goes to … Almudena Konrad." I suddenly fell into a different reality—I wasn't safe anymore. The thought of my getting an award was far from what I had expected. I could only hear my heart palpitations. I walked through the hall with chairs full of people on my right and on my left, feeling the weight of hundreds of eyes on me, all the way to the podium. I took the plated award, said thank you, and left as fast as I could go, looking down, running for my life. Somehow, I felt immersed in an alternate reality, feeling undeserving and consumed in discomfort. The audience's applause brought me back to the present moment. This was more than I could have dreamed of. I felt humbled, unsure of what to make out of this unique accomplishment. I had worked passionately and fiercely for this unexpected moment, but I somehow felt like it did not belong to me. I didn't know at the time that this was going to be the climax of my professional existence, at least the way my life stands now and without knowledge of my future. The level of intense recognition was unbelievable to me. A time when, outside of myself, everything seemed perfect. I was young, accomplished, and recognized, but new to this reality. I only shared this accomplishment with Mike, my mom, and my sisters. I chose humility as my stance. Sharing or bragging would only lead to isolation and torturous thoughts.

The year ended with Memel and Sarah celebrating their grand wedding at the Pan Pacific Hotel in San Francisco. Memel hired a flamenco singer and guitar player. It was the best and biggest party of my life. We had family and friends coming from London, Spain, Australia, and other countries. We spent the entire night dancing flamenco and enjoying everyone's company. At the beginning of the night, my mom, driven by a passion that had been bottled up inside her for years, unleashed her fervor into a solo flamenco performance—one to never forget. I loved her attitude and stamina that night dressed in the traditional flamenco male outfit with a red rose in her hair, black boots, and a black *mantilla* (shawl) over her shoulders. Flamenco to us is not just a dance, but an expression of who we are—a way of life that calls for courage, an embodiment of an attitude, a shout-out to our Andalucian roots.

My father was also at the wedding celebration with his new wife, Jessica. She was my age, with innocent green eyes that revealed her captivation by her troubled husband. I looked at them from a distance, as they were sitting at a table far from mine, wondering if my father was capable of change—of really loving her.

The next day, our house had friends and family sleeping or resting in every available space, occupying beds, couches, and floor, while the flamenco music was still playing softly in the background. That morning perfectly represented how I like to live my life, with family and friends connected, sharing, and celebrating life.

That same year, Mike received several sales awards, with tremendous financial bonuses, outstanding commissions, company presents, and upscale president club trips. We decided to sell *our* house to move to a ranch so we could live with our horses.

We bought a home in Alamo, an affluent town, twenty minutes from UCB, on a one-and-a-half-acre horse property so we could have our horses in our backyard. I recall the day that we brought them to the property. I will never forget seeing them run for the first time to their new arena. We had lots of family and friends at our house that day. We continued to host big parties and family gatherings there in our new property for many years. The house was quite large, with a cute cottage unit in the backyard that became my mom's sanctuary.

CHAPTER 13

Unexpected Decisions

"Life whispers to you all the time ... from the time you wake up in the morning and with every single experience." – Oprah Winfrey

FOLLOWING MY PERSONAL VICTORY over my fear of public speaking, I made considerable strides toward completing my Ph.D. program. In many ways, my life appeared to be ideal. For the first time in my existence, I had no financial worries. I could purchase any type of food that I desired and dine out without restraint. Yet, my reality felt different. My fixation on the possibility of food scarcity persisted just as strongly as before. I found myself hiding items such as strawberries, yogurt, and chocolate in the refrigerator, ensuring that only I could consume them. These were foods that I loved, but my mother had been unable to afford them during my childhood.

Once in a restaurant dining out with Mike's family and Carmen, I ordered a shrimp appetizer. As soon as the dish was put in front of me, Mike reached over and took one of the shrimps from my plate. I immediately transformed into a possessed creature and sternly shouted, "Do not eat my shrimp!" in front of numerous family members. My face displayed such a fury that

I felt as if my father's distorted expression were being channeled through me. My table and the surrounding ones fell silent. Carmen attempted to calm me down in Spanish by suggesting that we order more. But I could hardly hear Carmen's suggestion. I couldn't understand my rude behavior and internal anger. No one ever questioned it, and no one tried to understand it. But in my quiet hours, I could not let go of my lunatic moment. The incident eventually became a family joke that haunts me to this day. In my reality, it wasn't amusing. I struggled with controlling my eating habits, unable to stop once I was full or share food.

It was now the final semester of my Ph.D., almost three years after our first conversation about becoming parents. Mike had not let go of his strong desire to have a child, not even for a split second, during all this time. I was well aware that he would never let go. It was becoming a sensitive conversation. I felt it was selfish of him to insist on something I felt so afraid of; on the other hand, it was breaking my heart that he'd never experienced a healthy parent-child relationship as I did with my mom. He never fully understood my connection to my mom and siblings. He wanted a family. He begged me for one.

Frustrated with my lack of enthusiasm toward the prospect of being parents, Mike made the conscious decision to take my mom and me to watch *The Phantom of the Opera* in San Francisco. My mom and I were both lovers of operas on TV, and I had been infatuated with the original film since I was a little girl. I empathized with the Phantom's disfigured face and admired his tenderness toward Christine Daae, the young woman he loved. I enjoyed the musical so much that we ended up watching it three times during the same season. Mike and I became obsessed with the music, but mostly with the character Christine. In my mind, this had been Mike's hidden agenda; he was planting a seed in my head: "Almoodin, our daughter will be just like Christine," followed by, "and of course, she will love math." At home, we played the Phantom music over and over. Eventually I embraced the idea of having a girl. I decided to commit to bringing Cristina into our lives. I had also tasted some level of success and started to believe, mostly encouraged by Mike, that maybe we could do things differently. In a way, for the first time in my life, I felt fortunate and unstoppable.

This year, Chino and Lina welcomed their second child, a daughter named Olivia. She was tiny and incredibly adorable. On the day of the delivery, I arrived with my video camera, ready to capture the momentous event. Alongside Carmen and our cousin Aruca, who was visiting from Spain and living with me that year, we witnessed the entire delivery—a truly profound experience. Strangely, I didn't perceive Lina undergoing excruciating pain, promoting the thought that perhaps giving birth didn't have to be as dramatic or terrifying as it is often portrayed. I spent the entire day in the hospital with Olivia, cradling and showering her with affection, intending to provide her with a beautiful and loving start to life. I vividly recall the first weekend Olivia spent overnight with Mike and me. I cried when I had to say goodbye and drive her back home.

As time went by, after Mike and I made the commitment to pursue having a daughter, we realized that becoming pregnant was not as easy or romantic as it sounded, at least for us. After trying a few methods for over a year, we ended up doing In Vitro Fertilization (IVF). I still remember Mike's favorite words replaying in my head: *We won't be denied.* Getting pregnant became a slow painful process with lots of medical procedures.

Just as I was going to quit after my body rejected several embryos, a strong little one stuck to my uterus and did not let go.

I was sitting with my mom and Mike at the table in my house in Alamo when the doctor from the IVF treatment at Stanford called me to share the news that my pregnancy test was positive. As I said it aloud, my mom and Mike got up from the table, and hugged each other, jumping in circles around the dining room. I enjoyed how much they cared for each other and their happiness for the special moment brought me joy. Looking at my mom, now living with us, hugging my husband, was a dream come true.

There was a significant internal shift from the moment that I became pregnant. My biggest personal transformation. Prior to my first pregnancy, I was living a fast pace of professional and personal growth, with a single-minded focus and dedication. Nothing would distract me from my goals and no obstacle had been big enough to get in the way of my CRAZY determination. At the time, obtaining a Ph.D. and preparing myself to be highly competitive in the world of engineering and computer science was not just my main purpose but what I believed to be my ticket, my contribution, to financial freedom for me and my loved ones.

The pregnancy brought a significant transformation in me. In just a matter of days, my journal entries shifted their focus to one thing: my baby. Without moving away from my core career goals, I was adding new dreams from the perspective of a mom, shaping our approaching life. I found myself already planning for a future where I could successfully do it all. It was Mike's and my opportunity to do it right, to have what we thought could be a perfect family with love at the center. I took my pregnancy and approaching new role as a mother to an extreme. I surrounded myself with lots of psychology books on how to raise a child and made plenty of notes. I didn't hesitate to share my knowledge with Mike.

"Mike, we need to change our words in our conversations because the baby can feel our energy. Sorry, but no more cursing for you. And we need to have daily conversations with the belly to connect with her," I said once. "Yes, of course, Almoodin, why didn't I think of that?" he replied, rolling his eyes. My hormones were causing changes in me that I could hardly recognize. Mike felt my transformation from the moment I learned I was pregnant. He wondered how a woman's thinking could shift so rapidly from *"I don't want to have children"* to *"Everything I do, think, or say is for my baby."*

Mike and I were dreamers, beginners, almost completely ignorant about parenting, slightly overconfident in how we would face and manage the challenges of parenting. We were about to blindly enter the land of endless rollercoaster rides, with ups and downs, and with extreme moments of intensity—moments that would bring all kinds of emotions like joy and panic without hardly any time to process.

Sitting at a lunch table across from parents of teenagers at a neighbor's party, a wise mother expressed her feelings about being a parent and its difficulties, especially with parents as career driven as we were. Mike, with a sense of we-have-it-all-figured-out, replied arrogantly, "We will hire as much help as we need." These words bring us the loudest laughs now as somehow enlightened parents and extremely humbled by the lessons our kids have taught us from day one. On certain occasions, ignorance is bliss, especially when it comes to making the decision to be a parent.

In my first trimester of pregnancy, the gynecologist found growing uterine fibroids, one the size of an apple. Already an anxious soon-to-be mother who saw her doctor weekly, this news didn't calm any nerves. Doctors must tell you the facts. In this case, the message was that fibroids can lead to miscarriage during early pregnancy. That was enough for me. After a few visits, I told my gynecologist that I didn't want to hear anything about the fibroids or statistics any longer, and that I only wanted to hear the sound of my baby's heartbeat. It became my obsession. Nothing else in the world mattered as much as my baby's heartbeat. My gynecologist understood my emotional request, and he obliged. Even though percentages and real science were extremely important in my career, in my personal life, I wanted nothing to do with them. My new *religion* was the power within me – *the ability to create my own perception and even my own reality.* I went back to books that speak of the power of the mind, and how we can change our realities with our thought choices and meditation practices.

In the evenings, I started my visualizations again, but this time I was doing a simple body scan, sending light and healthy energy to my uterus to support the growth of my baby. In my second trimester, the baby had conquered the space in my wound and the fibroids were kind enough to become insignificant. I will never know if my visualizations made a difference, but it doesn't hurt to believe that they did. I spent the rest of the pregnancy daydreaming and writing in my personal journal but mostly working on my Ph.D. dissertation and doing a job search.

The Universe always seemed to be on my side in the end, but it didn't make the journey easy. I had to work hard for anything I wanted. And it didn't always bring the outcome I'd predicted.

After months of buying tons of pink outfits and shoes for baby Cristina, Mike suggested that there was a possibility that the baby was a boy. To his insinuation, I responded: "Do I look like I can be the mom of a boy?" I reminded him that he was the one who'd insisted over and over that I would be the mother of a girl. I started to question whether he really cared about having a daughter—after all, the lack of a father-son relationship in his life was extremely painful. He never discussed any feelings or thoughts about his father who had walked away from him when he was a little boy. This topic was taboo. I noticed during movies that any sensitive interaction between a father and a son would bring not anger but extreme pain and sadness to Mike. At times, he would walk away from sensitive movie scenes. Any question I ever had about his father, he would reply with: "I don't have feelings for him—he chose a different family."

Together we were making a dream happen, but maybe a different dream. A few weeks later, in the next sonogram, we were told that the baby was a *boy*. I was shocked without words to describe how foolish I felt. I had been in love with an idea—the possibility to love and care for a girl who only lived in my mind. At times I felt that girl could have been a younger version of me so I could make it right for her. But my baby was a new being in this world with its own personality traits and unique future. *Who was I to decide who my baby was?* This new life that I was carrying was a new beginning and not someone for me to heal the part of me that still was upset or frightened. I will never give up on that dream—the possibility to love Cristina. But that dream could just be a dream. This was my very first lesson in motherhood: *We bring a life we can't control.*

Mike was thrilled and he quickly thought of a name for our son: Michael Jr. I chose the middle name David, thinking of Michelangelo's sculpture. My son Michael, my little Kiki as I always called him, was born in the midst of finishing writing my dissertation while still going through my job search. We had scheduled a C-section since little Michael was breached, ready to come to the world feet first, and I was not willing to go through the procedure to turn the baby around. The morning of the delivery, my mom, Ana, Carmen, and Mike were all ready to drive to the hospital. It looked like the preparation a family would do to go on a fun vacation. I even bought a sexy, white silk nightgown, size small, thinking my belly would immediately be flat again. Nothing could have been further from the truth. We were all super excited. This was a family event. At the hospital, I felt terrified. The moment they put in an IV, I started to cry. I felt overwhelmed by the thought of giving birth. Nothing I did really prepared me for the emotions I was having. Carmen and Mike were by my side in the delivery room. Carmen was next to my face while I was throwing up—a side effect of the epidural anesthesia. Mike was happy but nervous recording the delivery.

My mind goes to the moment I first held little Michael on my chest making soft baby noises. The last 33 years of my life became insignificant compared to the intensity of that moment. And any thoughts about myself or any other family member became nonexistent. The only thing that mattered was my son. To comfort him. To love him. He felt so tiny and fragile, but at the same time so powerful—with big cheeks, big eyes, big lips and a strong temper. I became a devoted mother, with an immense amount of love for him and always obsessing over his well-being. The rocking chair while listening to classical, opera, and baby music became my happy place. Mike once asked, "Will you ever love me again?" With his words, he woke me up to the fact that other parts of my life needed some attention.

Just a week before Michael's birth, my father and Jessica welcomed their son named Jefferson into the world. While I had exchanged only a handful of conversations with Jessica and already liked her a lot, a sense of sadness made me maintain a slight distance from her and Jefferson, to avoid my father. I felt terrible because I remembered how my father's extended family had chosen to distance themselves from us, my siblings and me, due to our father's temper. I could empathize with their choice, understanding the complexity of such a decision.

Seven months after Michael and Jefferson's birth, Carmen added to the excitement by giving birth to her own son, Dani. When Dani was only four years old, Carmen's marriage ended, and both moved in with us. Dani quickly became another son to us. He and Michael grew up as close as twins. Although Dani had a father, Angelo, who was present and actively involved in his upbringing, Mike also took on a fatherly role and was affectionately called "daddy" by Dani.

Since Mike and I did IVF, we had a few embryos waiting to come out of the frozen daycare. We lost most of them since my body kept rejecting them, but eventually, we had another success. And that is how we conceived our second son, Brandon, who was born two years and three months after Michael. Brandon was a big baby, with big hands and feet, and the loveliest disposition from day one. On the day of his birth, Mike, holding baby Brandon, asked: "Will you be able to love him as much as you love Michael?" to which I replied: "I love my sons equally. How can you question my love for him?" A mother's love is blind, illogical, and unconditional. It cannot be measured. It cannot be questioned.

Since there were no more embryos left, I mentally closed the chapter on my pregnancies. I gave away all baby items and maternity clothes. To my surprise, my body decided to get pregnant *naturally*, and that is how my last son, Dylan, came into our lives, twenty-two months after Brandon's birth. Dylan was my youngest and bravest—he came to the world with loving parents, big brothers, and lots of quick learning to do. I was now the mom of boys, and I blindly adored them. There were hardly ever three boys at the house or in my family pictures, but four. Four mountains of Christmas presents, four boys in the car on their way to piano classes on Wednesdays, four pairs of stinky feet coming out of my bedsheets in the morning, and four boys at the dinner table. Dani has always been part of our life as a son. I can't ever say "sons" without him in the mix.

Perfect Cristina with big brown eyes and ponytails did not happen for me, instead, we were blessed with strong-willed sons. Carmen and I teamed up to raise our boys with our mom on the throne, and Mike by our side. Ana also found ways to be involved in raising the boys, between her travels to New York, Los Angeles, and San Francisco working as a hairstylist and makeup artist. Even though she lived a glamorous life, when she was at home, she was a loving mama.

During these same years, Memel and Sarah had moved to the US. Memel secured a prominent position as the Director of Market Credit Sales at an American company, Standard & Poor's. They purchased a house just minutes away from mine and extended their family with the arrival of two children: a son named Ruben, followed by a daughter named Lola, who was born just after Brandon. With Ruben and Lola, our family count grew to seven boys and two girls. Life took on a vibrant pace as we all embraced the responsibilities of parenthood. Carmen took a significant step as well, enrolling at Mills College and achieving a bachelor's degree in molecular biology. The trajectory seemed to be clear; each of us was on a course toward prosperity and accomplishment.

Ana made an unexpected decision. She begged me to drive her to Lake Tahoe, where she would undergo plastic surgeries. I was eager to embrace my new super sexy sister, but the process demanded more courage than I had anticipated. The surgeries took place at a house and not in a hospital. A minor detail that she forgot to mention to me. It was too late for me to complain, as Ana does what she wants and listens to no one —a trait I both admire and fear. Alone with her during her recovery that night at a hotel, I found it difficult to close my eyes. I was already missing my sassy fearless sister Ana, and instead felt concerned as I heard her moaning in pain from the surgeries. We had no nurses or doctors around.

After her recovery, Ana transformed into the striking woman she was always meant to be —a nightlife dancer who shines like a star wherever she goes. Her unbeatable spirit continues to inspire and give courage to everyone around her, including me.

CHAPTER 14

Work-Life Balance

"You gain strength, courage, and confidence by doing the thing which you think you cannot do." – Eleanor Roosevelt

AS A WORKING MOM, I would be doing an injustice if I didn't address how difficult it was to pursue a work-life balance. It was hard—very hard! Being a parent was becoming absolutely the most difficult job I had ever done and having a career on top added to the insanity. With little boys in my life and a new career, I was setting myself up for a rough adventure. I could only hope to be able to achieve to some extent a sense of work-life balance. As the kids were getting older, I didn't see a break as I had expected, but escalating concerns. Despite many workshops, talks, faculty retreats, and books on work-life balance, I realized that I was working toward the impossible.

I was naive to the concept of being a working mom. My first attempt to balance my career and family started while I was looking for a job while still finishing my Ph.D. The interview process couldn't have started at a more difficult time. My first in-person interview was at the Lawrence Berkeley National Laboratory. I wanted a research position since I had experienced success as a graduate researcher and found the work enjoyable. However, my belly was quite large, and still growing by the day. A pregnant graduating woman in computer science from UCB was not an everyday sight. On the morning of my interview, I walked from my office in Soda Hall on the UCB campus to Shattuck Avenue in Berkeley. From there, I took a bus and walked up a hill to the lab. I arrived at my interview overheated and out of breath, looking like I was ready to give birth. The interviewer was more concerned about my pregnancy than my research. I felt confident and ready to talk about my projects. But I immediately knew that there was not going to be an opportunity for me there. I felt like a fish out of water, completely disconnected from the interview process. But I didn't become discouraged. I had other prospective interviews.

Prof. Joseph, my research advisor, suggested that I investigate becoming a tenure track computer science professor. He had spoken to an MIT graduate who was a friend of his, a tenured professor now at Mills College, and gave her a recommendation on my behalf for a current open tenure track position. For some reason, he thought I was capable of such a job, something I had not ever considered or imagined in my wildest dreams. It had been my goal to work in a research lab, but somehow, I decided to explore the academic path despite my shaky history of public speaking. After the application process, I went through an extensive interview process with Mills College and quickly fell in love with the institution and the idea of becoming a professor. I was impressed and introduced for the first time to the concept and benefits of teaching and learning at a private liberal arts college. It became clear to me how much Mills valued teacher-student connections, small classroom environments, interactive learning, and social justice in the classroom and at an institutional level. This was all super cool and completely new to me.

During my first interview at Mills College, close to my delivery day, my belly had grown out of proportion. I delivered an overprepared lecture on one of my weakest areas, Operating Systems, but I did well—at least that is how I felt. Practice, practice, practice! By then, I knew what I had to do. I felt connected to the students, the faculty, and the community. No one seemed bothered by my belly, my slow walking, or my out-of-breath moments. My first visit was embracing and welcoming. I must admit that when I first applied to Mills, I didn't know that it was a women's college since I didn't understand its concept or purpose. In Spain, universities are all co-ed and my experience with single-sex private institutions was only connected to the Catholic schools I grew up with. This was new to me, but I quickly became immersed in the culture of women's empowerment, and that was fun. Mills also had a strong co-ed grad student population, especially in computer science, that I very much enjoyed. During my interview lecture, the kind audience with mostly women was uplifting and quite different from my previous experiences at UC Berkeley or my previous research talks. I felt comfortable. I remember mostly their smiles and a strong feeling of belonging. The students' questions were genuine. No one tried to impress anyone. At UC Berkeley, I was used to students who would only ask questions when they knew the answers or were quite familiar with the topic of discussion so they could engage in intelligent conversations and somehow get their professors' attention. I didn't blame them because many were competing for research positions. And a few were genuinely interested in advanced conversations.

UC Berkeley, in the classroom environment, was all about survival of the fittest. As I remember it, students compete with one another without understanding *humility*. At Mills, the students' disposition was different. I felt kindness and a strong sense of inclusion. Mills students were not just eager to learn but also to connect and grow as a community—I'd never understood this concept before.

When Michael was about four months old, I scheduled my second interview with Mills College. I was not yet mentally ready to transition from a loving mom, completely dedicated to my son, to again, a go-getter—*Where did all my ambition and desires for career success go? I only wanted to be with my son.*

Nevertheless, the day of my second interview arrived. As soon as I got there, I used the public bathroom to pump breast milk. This was my first experience of being a professor as a mom. The bathroom stall was tiny and the Medela pumping equipment at the time was large and made an embarrassing hissing sound that made me look like a cow milking herself.

A couple of months after the interview process, the chair of the department called me to share the great news. The college was offering me the position. I was thrilled! Especially since my mom had decided to take care of baby Michael during the week so I could work. Before my first son was born, my mom was living with my sister Ana and working with her in hair salons in San

Francisco having the time of her life. Living with Ana, she always looked beautiful with perfect makeup and fashionable outfits. But as soon as Michael was born, my mom stopped working in salons, and made the decision to stay with us Mondays through Fridays, to help raise Michael. I promised to pay for all her expenses including her apartment in San Francisco so she could continue her fun life on Fridays and weekends. I loved seeing my mom for the first time ever really enjoying life. She didn't hold back or play at being the victim of her past. It felt for a while that she had erased the last 30 years. She went back to painting, reading, and dancing flamenco at family gatherings. She even dated and glowed with happiness. Her spirit was back! She was fully alive! But for her, being a mom and a grandma was the first thing in line, so she made the commitment to me to help me raise Michael so I could follow my career goals. I was lucky, very lucky, and I knew that.

I took the job offer even though the salary in academia was significantly less than what I would be making in industry, but it didn't seem to bother me at the time. And the fear of speaking seemed like it faded away. I had spent years visualizing myself giving lectures, finally breaking my silence. Now, in my new job, I had the opportunity to confront my greatest fear on a regular basis. I followed my intuition—my desire to pursue something unique, unknown, and exciting. It wasn't part of the plan and was outside my comfort zone, but it felt right. A few friends in the computer science Ph.D. program at UCB and some family members discouraged and questioned my ability to express myself, given my strong accent.

One friend told me that being a professor was not something

to take lightly, and she was concerned that I was jumping into something beyond my abilities. Maybe I was, but I had to try. It was much later in my career as a professor that I read the book *Mindset* by Carol S. Dweck, which helped me understand my students, my sons, and my own approach to life challenges. An individual with a fixed mindset believes that they are not intelligent enough to learn a specific skill, while with a growth mindset, we believe that we are capable of learning through effort and time. The latter was my mindset!

I had the tendency to make challenges out of other people's negative opinions of me since I had never appreciated it when others had questioned my abilities, perhaps because I had worked too hard to conquer my own thoughts of self-doubt. I wanted to live life to its fullest by taking on opportunities regardless of others' opinions. In those days, someone's doubt about my abilities would motivate me to work even harder to prove to myself that I could accomplish things beyond expectations.

A professor at UC Berkeley, a father of daughters, called me into his office once. We were discussing my research project from a mathematical standpoint. In the middle of our conversation, he changed his tone of voice from professional to personal, and asked, "What did your parents do to motivate you to pursue a career in computer science?" I openly responded, "I enjoy math and engineering. My parents were not part of the decision. My father told me that I was stupid, and my mom's hard life gave me the strength to never quit trying." I felt comfortable having this type of personal conversation with him. It was not common for me to talk about my feelings with anyone, even less with a professor. But somehow, we ended up talking about my mom and avoided any further conversation about my father. I expressed my concern about the suffering of so many women in the world who were not allowed to have an education or even a voice. I felt lucky to have these opportunities.

I was ready for my new life as a computer science professor and a mother. With an I-can-do-it mindset and lots of excitement, I embarked on a long journey in academia, a journey that evolved and went in many unexpected directions.

My first semester was the hardest. My first lecture was supposed to be one hour and 15 minutes, but even after lots of practicing, I got through it in only 30 minutes. My presentations were dry, fast, stuffed with concepts, and lacked interaction. My students were patient as I frequently apologized and observed, and they saw my struggle and ongoing efforts to improve. I completely overestimated my teaching skills, but I was determined to do better—I felt I could. I spent long hours preparing the curriculum and rehearsing my lectures at home for better timing. I even drafted potential questions that students might ask, and if they didn't, I would say, "Perhaps you are wondering how to …" It may be that no one was actually thinking those questions, but it made the class much more engaging.

Caring for my little one, Michael, was the highlight of my days. Since breastfeeding was important to me, I bought a mini fridge for my work office so I could pump breast milk between classes and meetings. Students would knock at my door, and I had to pretend that I was not there despite the hisses of the machine to insist otherwise. Eventually, I put a Do Not Disturb note at the door. My students knew what I was doing and respected my privacy.

With three of my babies, I followed the same breastfeeding routine. Pumping at work, labeling, and freezing the milk, and bringing home the little milk packages for my mom to feed the babies the next day while I was teaching. I persisted in breastfeeding during the first year of life, even though my large breasts with constant milk dripping did not fit so well in my role as a young driven computer science professor. At night-time, I mostly felt compassion for all working moms. I knew I was not the only one in this situation. My babies slept next to me the entire night so I could easily breastfeed, and because at night-time I wanted them to feel my connection to them. We slept as a family in the same bed for too many years until they decided to move into their own space.

My working days were challenging. When the kids were babies and young toddlers, I did not sleep well at night. But regardless of how tired I felt, on lecture days, I had students waiting for me in the classroom eager to hear and learn from me. I woke up every morning to my mom's espresso before going to work—a coffee so strong that it could awaken an entire zombie village. And that is how I did it. I powered through my days at work with coffee and dark chocolate. And plenty of food that I would take to work from home.

During my three pregnancies, I experienced horrendous morning sickness, a term that is misleading because for most women it is an all-day feeling. There were times when I couldn't bring myself to eat at all, and others when I consumed large amounts only to find myself rushing to a bathroom, my head hung over the toilet. Memories bring me back to when I was pregnant with Dylan and had two toddlers to care for at home. That semester, I was teaching the computer language JavaScript at 8:30am. During one lecture, I suddenly stopped, rushed out of Stern Hall's lab feeling sick to my stomach, and sat on a bench outside the classroom. From my pocket, I took out a Ziploc bag full of grapes, and ate just one. Almost instantly, I found myself vomiting in a small garden just in front of me. I quickly cleaned up and returned to the classroom, my face pale, with nothing in my mind but the topic in my PowerPoint. Days like these were not uncommon during Dylan's pregnancy. Many evenings, worn out from battling morning sickness all day, I would drive home and find myself shedding tears of fatigue. Upon arriving home, my mom would be there, seeking her own solace after spending the day with the lively superheroes, as she lovingly referred to the toddlers. She would dedicate her evenings to taking care of herself. The cottage where she stayed was surrounded by beautiful roses and trees with a view of the horses—the perfect cozy environment for her to decompress. She was determined to do her daily workouts. I was proud of her dedication to her health and wellbeing. And there I was every evening alone with my toddlers and my struggles.

Mike worked long hours. And he absolutely had to work out at the gym at the end of his workday. Sometimes that brought some fights into the marriage. I never said that during the first few years of being a mom what bothered me the most was that he still had the time to exercise while I didn't anymore. His body was perfectly in shape, and mine was not! I gave up on protesting. I recall locking myself in the bathroom with three-year-old Michael

and one-year-old Brandon, again with my face in the toilet, waiting
for Mike to come home. As soon as he walked through the door
in the late evenings, he was in a great mood and still had plenty of
energy to play with the little rascals. Unlike other American
families, our bedtime was ridiculously late for young boys. At
10pm, I was still trying to get those boys and Mike to bed.

Mike showed love and admiration for my strength to hold on
to both my family and career demands. I believe that his
appreciation for my sacrifices as a mom kept growing over time.
He took joy in observing my deep adoration and care for our sons.
Since he didn't grow up with parents next to him, unity was a
priority. He had no reference to what it was like to be a parent.
At times I wonder if he was just another boy without any sense of
family structure, or discipline. His energy was childish, and he
had no boundaries or rules with our sons. Our evenings ran wild!

❋ ❋ ❋

I did it all together; I could hardly separate being a mom from
being a professor. My office at Mills had a kids' table and plenty
of toys for whenever I had to bring them to work when they were
young. At home, my kitchen and kids' playroom had a computer
with access to my documents and emails. My lecture notes had
my kids' drawings, and my kids' coloring books had notes with
my academic thinking.

I made my home office near the kids' play area, where I could
work and still be present for them. I will keep this habit as long
as I have any of my sons living at home, regardless of their age.

My mom stayed with me during the week for eight years until she turned 65 and four-year-old Dylan started preschool. At that time, Michael and Dani were eight years old, and Brandon was six years old. Carmen—a working, and single-mom, full-time student—and Dani lived with us. Without my mom, my work-life balance suddenly became a lot harder. *Why didn't I hire a babysitter?* I tried and I failed to find one with a flexible schedule and willing to handle four boys. Our only babysitter lasted just a few weeks, after Brandon found many ways to torture her with his mischief. I came home after work to angry Brandon fighting with the babysitter, because he refused to eat her rice or listen to her.

During spring break and on a few other occasions, when the kids were off school, I had to take the boys to work. They enjoyed interacting with my students and causing trouble around campus. Brandon once jumped into a fountain of water in the middle of winter! Completely soaked, we drove back home at the end of my workday.

For years of being a mother, coming home from work brought the most exciting moments of my life. My little ones made me feel profoundly loved. When they were babies, they would quickly latch onto me to breastfeed, staring at me with their tiny hands holding on, as if they never wanted to let go. I would keep them attached to my body one way or another until bedtime and during the night. As they grew older, they would run to me, kiss me, tell me stories, and be ready for Lego time. We built every single Lego model available at the stores. Dani, Brandon, and Dylan followed instructions to the detail. Michael used his creativity to build something new every time. I came home once to find that they had made an entire Lego home simulating our lives. I lived for those moments when chaos was taking a break, and I could enjoy my life as a mom.

Figuring out solutions for sick days and dealing with hospital visits added another layer of stress, as it does for all working parents.

Once Michael had to spend the night at the hospital because we could not stop his fever and vomiting. I stayed all night next to him in a chair, staring at his beautiful cheeks. On a piece of paper with hardly any light, I wrote my thoughts: "*If you make it through the night, I promise to stand by you for the rest of my entire life. I will always be right by your side.*" That night I prayed to the Universe, to my grandma, and to all divine powers. In the morning, he woke up strong. Early that morning, Mike showed up at the hospital with an espresso, fully prepared to take over. Despite not having had a minute of sleep, I headed to teach my Computer Networks class at 9am.

Another big struggle as a working mom was figuring out a schedule to drive back and forth from the kids' school, figuring out a solution for sick days, and dealing with holidays, staff development days, and other nonsense non-school days where parents still work but kids are at home. Not to mention the crazy school schedules in our district with different grades and different days of the week having specific, but different, starting and ending times. The educational system has *not* been designed with working parents in mind!

Parents' classroom involvement was another challenge. The schools use parent volunteers to help with the classroom and other activities. Our kids would ask me to volunteer as other moms did. As a professor, I had to work seven days a week to keep my lectures and curriculum up to date. Not to mention research and the many other obligations at the department and institution level. I did all my volunteer work at my kids' schools at the end of May when I no longer needed to teach at Mills, since college classes end before public schools. I offered to teach in the classroom and drive on school trips for just a few weeks out of the year. I loved seeing my boys' faces, proud to have me helping in their classrooms. Once I came to school and read *Pippi Long Stockings*, my absolute favorite kids' book. Another time I gave a talk about coding for kids to the parents. And multiple times I helped in their math classes.

The overinvolvement of some parents, and the high expectations of parents' participation from the teachers, made me think that I was not doing my job as a mom. Especially when so many parents were doing (unrealistically good) school projects for their kids. Maybe I was jealous of the moms with the time to work on their kids' projects! At home, I supervised certain assignments and projects, but I encouraged my boys to use their own creativity and put their own effort into it. To me, practicing their creativity and the ability to think was much more important than the look of their final projects or the score that they got on an assignment, especially at this early age. At the end of the year, the parents would come to the classroom and the kids would show their projects on the walls. It really bothered me that my boys' feathers for the Thanksgiving Turkey Art project were the simplest non-artistic work on the walls. I still think about it.

Despite my friendly nature and love for conversation, I felt that

I never truly connected with most moms at my kids' schools. Perhaps it was something about me, or perhaps my situation. I was always in a hurry. Some mornings, I would drop off the kids at school and observe the moms engaging in conversations, dressed in workout outfits and cute hats, holding their Starbucks coffees, and getting ready for group walks. At times, these gatherings reminded me of scenes from Hollywood movies where high school girls chatted and competed to be the cutest. I was lucky to have my good friend Bonnie. I met her on a Halloween night while walking through the neighborhood, and from that day on, we became best friends. She was my only friend in Alamo during the kids' elementary school years. But one good friend makes all the difference in the world. I constantly asked her questions to keep up with the school news. We went together to all school events; we even dressed together for Halloween with the kids. I would have appreciated a stronger community of moms, but this didn't happen for me. Bonnie was my community.

On days when I had meetings or college events and Mike was traveling, I had to ask my boys to walk home alone. Sometimes, they would walk in the heat or the rain or the cold, and call me as soon as they got home. Brandon always took care of Dylan. I knew I could trust him. Even though Brandon has always been mischievous, he also had the strongest sense of responsibility when I was not around. Michael was more interested in chatting with friends and didn't always head home directly. Even from a young age, he had a unique approach to tasks, and looking back, I can recognize how this trait could lead to tremendous success.

The boys, especially Brandon, learned to cook a few things. At times, I found the kitchen ceiling full of chocolate. But Brandon was proud of his chocolate cake recipes. He was only eight years old and already independent. During the kids' home-alone times, my heart would beat hard, and my thoughts would go wild with worries, hoping that they didn't get in trouble and that Mike would make it home at a decent time before me. I know I wasn't the only working mom having these experiences.

Mike did a lot of driving, too. But on those days, the kids were mostly late. A few times he dropped off Dylan wearing unmatched pajamas. My boys liked to dress themselves from an early age, putting together outfits as they pleased. And Mike never thought this was an issue.

Dylan, as a young boy, didn't seem interested in changing his pajamas in the morning. Seeing him in pajamas when I picked him up from school would drive me completely insane, but Mike was doing his best managing school runs, household errands, and taking the kids to sports activities while juggling work calls. Once during his first-grade year, I picked up Dylan from school in his unmatched pajamas. As he hugged me, I remarked, "My poor little boy is at school in pajamas." He responded, "Mom, I am not poor, and nobody cares about my pajamas but you." It was a clear reminder of what truly matters—a lesson from my little one. Mike and I both managed multiple responsibilities. He did all the groceries and nighttime dishes that had accumulated since breakfast, while I took care of cooking and school responsibilities.

My boys were beyond mischievous little boys. They often took videos of one another doing dares. They would find the most creative ways to get in trouble. But I believed that their own playing and mischief was part of their healthy development. I didn't enjoy or encourage this behavior, but for the most part, I let them be. I recall the boys competing with one another to see who could jump over a large couch in the living room with a side table next to it as an extra obstacle, without touching the objects and landing on their feet without falling. The worst thing about this dangerous goal was that Mike joined the competition while I prayed that none of them would get seriously hurt.

Over the years, Brandon had multiple stitches, broken bones, and concussions. Michael and Dylan had just a few broken bones. Dylan broke his foot once jumping from the top of our minivan and Michael once had to have stitches in his forehead. Dani could climb anything and everything with extreme accuracy and agility. I had a better chance of finding my kids by looking up at trees than around our backyard. Now, as teenagers and young adults, they continue to look for opportunities to climb trees, now up to dangerous heights. Dani's always at the highest point of the tree, followed by Brandon, then Michael, and finally Dylan.

I shared plenty of stories about my boys with my students at Mills, and I would often ask about their childhood hoping to learn something that I could integrate into my parenting strategies. My boys have had a wild spirit from day one—a need to question all authority, provoke a reaction, trigger the environment, doubt society's rules and etiquette, test new ideas, take revenge into their own hands without parental advice, and always had an answer for everything. Once we took the boys to a dinner at a restaurant in San Francisco where Ana was performing as a dancer. The boys were her most devoted fans. During the evening, one of the owners of the restaurant asked 10-year-old Brandon how it was possible for a young boy to have social media accounts, to which he answered: "Oh, that is not a problem. On Facebook, I am 21 years old."

Their witty responses would often make me laugh, but their tendency to seek their own form of revenge or their lack of communication about their intentions were a source of frustration to me.

Once, on a plane traveling back from Maui, I found myself sandwiched in the middle seat between Brandon and Dylan, with both leaning on me. To add to the discomfort, I noticed two feet with dirty, stinky socks dangling over my head from a kid sitting behind me. The feet alternated between kicking the back of my seat and resting on top of it, just above my head. It occurred to me that perhaps I was being punished for the countless times that my boys had bothered someone else. That is when I came up with a splendid idea. Without mentioning anything to Brandon, I asked him to switch seats with me so he could be next to Dylan. In reality, I wanted to test Brandon's ability to handle the situation. "Perhaps boys are more tolerant," I thought. The teenage boy in the back seat decided to put his feet down but kept kicking Brandon's seat on and off. I was proud of Brandon because it looked like he fell asleep and ignored the boy. On our way out of the airplane, I asked Brandon about the boy and his kicking. I was curious how his mind was able to block such a bothersome event. To my surprise, Brandon casually replied, "I took his shoes from under the seat and spat on them. That made me feel better."

Before bedtime was the best. We would all go to my big bed,

Dani with us too during the years that he lived with us. I would bring my box of books and read, while they mostly jumped in the bed, doing somersaults, and fighting on top of each other like the way puppies play. If I got their attention on my reading for just a minute, I would feel fulfilled as a mom. Then time to brush their teeth. I was intense in brushing their teeth. I did it myself for years, always worried that they would miss cleaning a tooth. In bed, I told them pirate stories, while touching their hair or their soft skin. Then I would close my eyes, without a thought, exhausted. I have plenty of memories of the four boys in the morning, sleeping together, entangled, with their heads pointing in completely different directions before waking up.

Despite the many working-mom challenges and the mischievous spirit of my boys, I have always felt an uncontrollably strong maternal love for my sons, inexplicable from the moment I knew of their existence. They were presents from the Universe to teach Mike and me the perfect lessons so we could evolve through hardship and love. Mike learned quickly to be humble and extremely patient. I learned about the world of boys and young men, their brains and drives, and their unique way of accomplishing goals. My sons have shattered most of our core beliefs, and they have proven us wrong hundreds of times. They show us infinite love, loyalty, and patience, and have taught us to live outside our comfort zone every minute of our lives. Mike and I soon surrendered to the power of their love and to their wild nature. Being the mother of my boys has been and will always be the best part of my life!

CHAPTER 15

Being Me

"If someone ever says you're weird, say thank you."
– Ellen DeGeneres

THROUGH HARD WORK AND PERSEVERANCE, my destiny seemed to be written in stone. With no doubts about my future, I believed that with effort—working as hard as I possibly could, and with the right mindset, writing down my goals, visualizing, and meditating—I would keep achieving goals. I had to exceed expectations, and I had to believe and feel my future. It had worked!

For the first time in my life, I was financially on the side of the privileged. I had the means to provide for my family and live with the freedom of having choices. The choice to live in safe low-crime neighborhoods to raise my boys, to work or to be a stay-at-home mom, to buy high-quality organic foods, to travel for fun, to put my kids in strong academic programs such as piano, violin, or math, and finally the choice to choose my professional environment with a variety of financial opportunities. To me, this was the perfect picture of personal and professional success.

Regardless of how great I felt about my accomplishments in my professional and personal life in my 30s, however, the world around me did not have a similar perception. The incidents were too many to count, too many to write and painful to tell. Subtle or ruthless, the messages were the same: *You don't belong to this social stratum.*

In front of my toddler boys, Mr. Cranky, a man doing his own shopping at a grocery store near my house, insisted in a rather demanding tone that I should speak English if I intended to live in the US, and that I should communicate with my sons in English instead of Spanish, as he had overheard me doing. On a different day, Mr. Frustrated yelled at me that foreigners *kill babies* while I was taking money out of the ATM machine also near my home. At the gym, Mrs. Ignorant, an American lady who seemed to be of my age, asked me if she could hire me to work as her nanny. Years later, at the grocery store, in the same town in Alamo, Mrs. Nosey with a sarcastic laugh made the comment that my son Michael had expensive taste since I was buying sushi, ending with the question, *Doesn't he like Mexican burritos?* These incidents were the result of living in a bubble where not even the wind dares to bother their people.

In my professional life, the assumptions were laughable but not shocking. Once, at a wireless communication conference in Denver, one of the attendees, another Ph.D. researcher, asked me if I could add more coffee to the coffee pot, assuming that I was helping set up the conference. At a cybersecurity conference in San Jose, another attendee asked me to work on his reimbursement paperwork. On many occasions, during conferences, I was asked questions directed to the organizers because in their minds I did not look like a computer scientist. I once attended a conference on women's leadership, and at the end of the talk, I asked the speaker how I could portray a professional, respectable look as a woman engineer. Her answer was discouraging and unexpected: "Cut your hair and get some tattoos." That really bothered me. She had short hair and tattoos, and I was already jealous of her muscular body. I have always admired women with strong presences, but with my question, I'd been hoping that she would have advice on how to address diversity and women's leadership, especially in my engineering field. But when I think about diversity in the engineering field, I mean acceptance of all women, regardless of their looks. If I have to wear tattoos to be respected, then I don't want to belong to that group. That was the point! Groups at times have the tendency to close the doors to others who are not like them. In this case, as open-minded and cool as she seemed to be speaking as a woman's advocate, she closed her doors to me. My father had shamed me during my teenage years for being a woman, and now I would not let anyone shame me for not following a certain look, whatever that was. I have, during my career, met extremely intelligent women who look like Barbie dolls. While I neither possess this kind of objective beauty nor is it my goal, I understand the struggles that these women go through. There are countless women with Marylin Monroe bodies and Whitney Houston faces who should never be—but have been—discouraged from pursuing careers in male-dominated fields.

All of which led to a battle with my true identity. In my personal life, I wondered at first how I could create a community for my boys, to connect with other moms, without having to reinvent myself in ways that I would not even know how to do. In my professional life I could stop wearing high-heeled boots or painting my nails, but would this really make a difference? Did I have a label on my forehead advertising, *I don't belong—treat me differently?*

I had to make a choice: I could let things be while hiding behind anger and complaints, or I could use these moments to break barriers and dispel ignorance. I realized that I was in a lucky place— that I was unique in a way that for many was a threat. Once I changed my perception of the situation, the message seemed to look different. The message they were really sending was: *If you don't look like me, you cannot be part of my group.* That realization made all the difference in the world for me. I was not the problem; they were the problem because they could not see beyond their own limited beliefs and experiences. I started to put my effort into working on myself, in having a voice when these incidents happened.

Amy Cuddy, an American social psychologist, and her work on power posing helped me to be more aware of how I was presenting myself to the world. In her TED talk "Your Body language may shape who you are," she emphasizes that putting yourself in a power pose, similar to Wonder Woman, will give anyone an automatic boost in confidence. I often carry a soft, humble disposition to the world, at times opening opportunities to be a target of others' hatred, misery, or desires. I won't say that I brought those incidents onto myself since no matter what I do, I cannot change others' opinions and biases. But it helped in making me aware of my own strengths.

I stopped the battle with my identity, accepting all aspects of myself. I started to wear my hair unruly and wild, with its natural curls, many times frizzy, as I always had before I started going to hair salons, and I became more comfortable speaking with my strong Spanish accent. I realized that I had been struggling with my voice and my image, and that I was making changes that were pushing me away from the authentic me. I must admit that this realization was not as simple as it sounds; it took more than a decade. When I was in my late 40s, I realized that I was slowly walking away from my roots and from myself, from the person who had achieved goals and dreams beyond expectations. My strength and resilience came from me and not from the person that perhaps others wanted to see.

I often visit a little alley in Walnut Creek, a town near my house in Alamo. This alley is very tiny and charming, with restaurant tables outside and water fountains by the side. At the end of the alley, there is a large strong oak tree that captures my imagination. One of the branches comes out of the tree in a random direction, naturally following down, almost to the level of the ground, but still strongly connected to its root. The other ones are perfect but not so interesting to look at. They are where they are supposed to be. Exactly as one would expect them to be. But the falling branch has so much more beauty—she is different from the rest, struggling to belong. She will keep living unless humans cut her because she doesn't look like the other ones. In a way, she may disrupt the comfort of the people who use the street. I worry about her.

Like the falling branch, looking at the part of us that does not belong, gives us the opportunity to see how special we are. The courage to be different comes with battles we have to fight. But it is also the ability to accept and love who we are that will bring peace into our hearts.

CHAPTER 16

My Tenure Process

"Successful mothers are not the ones who have never struggled.
They are the ones that never give up despite the struggles."
– Sharon Jaynes

I CONTINUED TO NAVIGATE the delicate balance between being a mother to my highly energetic boys and working toward tenure as a professor at Mills College. The tenure review process is undeniably stressful, demanding faculty to demonstrate excellence in research, teaching, service to the college, and professional contributions—all within a span of about six years. At the end of this period, faculty members present a lengthy detailed report including items such as publications, research statement, written grants, curriculum vitae, course syllabus, and analysis of all course evaluations, teaching statement, and professional services. The tenured decision involves numerous parties, including tenured faculty in the department, the tenure committee at the college, the provost, the president, the board of trustees, and external reviewers. Based on this evaluation, the faculty member either advances to the position of associate professor or is required to leave the college.

During these early career-defining years, I encountered a lack of support from some faculty members, which added complexity to my tenure process. Balancing responsibilities at both the departmental and institutional levels, along with a heavy teaching load and my research, while worrying about the lack of support, became the norm. I never blamed the ones who did not believe me capable of achieving tenure, instead, I took it to heart, because at times I could hardly believe in myself. But regardless of my own perceptions, it hurt to have some of my peers doubt my abilities.

In my first four years as teaching professor, I was tasked with developing and teaching six different computer science courses, some of which were well outside my area of expertise. In academia, this level of commitment during the tenure process is unusual, to say the least. Despite my reservations, I did not voice objections.

As many women must do to achieve professional success—especially mothers—I concealed my personal battles and became as versatile and adaptable as possible. This meant expanding the range of courses I could teach to fulfill the department's needs. The college, facing financial constraints, couldn't always hire additional faculty to cover courses outside my expertise. Eventually, I couldn't continue saying yes to every demand that came my way, which led to arguments and tension the moment I expressed my concerns. A fellow colleague once told me, "As a junior faculty member, you should not refuse to take on extra-departmental tasks if you're ever going to achieve tenure." I felt I was already taking on more than I'd signed up for. Nevertheless, my tenure track was at risk, and it was clear that I was not fully appreciated by *all* the faculty, which bothered me.

To stay focused and motivated, I listened to self-help

audiobooks during my drives to and from work. *The Secret* by Rhonda Byrne became particularly helpful. These CDs taught me how to use the power of the mind to change my reality. It refers to this concept as the law of attraction–we attract things we think about, especially in our relationships, financial situations, and professional success. I also read the book and watched the film made about the book. My favorite quotes are "*Energy flows where attention goes*" and "*What you resist persists.*" Basically, the more we focus on our problems, the bigger they get. Instead, the author suggests that it is wiser to accept our circumstances as they are while keeping our thoughts on prosperity and growth. This was the perfect time in my life to implement what I had learned, to test the law of attraction in my professional life.

If I wanted tenure, I needed to concentrate my thinking on making it happen, and not on the obstacles coming my way. I was committed to doing the work. Every day I visualized achieving tenure, focusing on my goal rather than the challenges, and working to cultivate confidence that would persist regardless of others' opinions of me. As I interacted with the members of the faculty not so fond of me, I would tell myself, "*I'm OK—You're OK*"[1], to remember that regardless of their titles or status or the possibility of them writing a negative review, we were equal.

Despite my best efforts, the ongoing stress of daily life began to take a toll on my physical health. I developed persistent throat pain and intermittent ringing in my ears. One morning, on my way to attend meetings before the semester started, I found myself overwhelmed with emotions and broke down in tears. Over the weekend, I pulled a muscle in my lower back while lifting

Brandon and I had been in excruciating pain with a lack of sleep. On my drive to work, I called Mike and he panicked when he heard the exhaustion in my voice. He asked me to come back home, but I didn't. I went to work and glued a smile on my face. That evening, when I finally returned home, Mike suggested that I take a break from work. At that moment, I didn't have the energy to question his idea, instead, I saw light at the end of the tunnel—the possibility that life could just slow down a bit. The truth was, my academic salary didn't adequately justify the countless hours I was dedicating to my job, the relentless demands, and the stress it was creating—not to mention the time I spent away from my children.

Without much reflection, on that night of Monday, January 19th, 2009, I found the strength to compose and send an email to the provost of Mills College, addressing the entire faculty within my department—announcing that I was, without reservation, resigning from my tenure track position, basically abandoning my job. With my sons next to me, I went to bed that night dreaming of a life free from the weight of work responsibilities—a life devoted to the care and nurturing of my boys.

The next morning, I woke up to a phone that would not stop ringing. The voices of many of my colleagues were on the other line making their support clear. I was happy to hear that they cared, that they valued me, and that they did not want to see me quitting. If I were to leave, it would not be because I did not have a strong united team fighting for me. While I appreciated them tremendously, and their gesture of support would always stay with me, I could not find the energy to continue working at that same pace. Carrying the words of my caring colleagues with me, I took my boys to the park, and for a few hours, I tasted sweet freedom. I was just a mom. I still remember that feeling of relief.

When I returned home, I sat down with Mike and my mom to watch President Obama's inauguration. Although I hardly involved myself in politics or followed the news closely, Obama's speech left a profound impression on me that day. His words had a remarkable way of lifting people's spirits. Phrases like *hope over fear* and *unity of purpose over conflict and discord*, resonated deeply. Together with the encouragement from my colleagues, this moment sparked a radical shift in my thinking. I suddenly realized that I had worked too hard with extreme determination in my career to give up on my goals so hastily. Even the slightest chance of achieving tenure was worth the struggle. When I shared this change of mind with the department chair and the provost, they were genuinely pleased to hear that I had decided not to follow through with my resignation, marking the end of my 24-hour experience as a stay-at-home mom.

Holding onto my identity as an independent woman meant a lot to me. I loved my job, but not the politics or complex relationships that often came with it. I was dedicated to my students and enjoyed my academic career. Sitting with a cup of coffee or tea in front of my computer to think and create was, still is, and probably always will be one of the most fulfilling parts of my life. I wanted to work; I needed to work. But how could I balance motherhood and work without burning myself out? I was a loving dedicated mother—I know I was. I was a caring professor—I also know I was. *But what about myself? Was I being great to myself?*

My obsession with achieving personal and professional goals, the support from most of the faculty, the provost, my family and friends, and my love for the students, with plenty of espresso shots, gave me the strength to pull through. Regardless of the challenges I was facing during my tenure process as a mother of young boys, there wasn't a day in my academic career when I didn't bring a smile to my students, project my passion for teaching, and give hours of preparation and dedication to my lectures. Entering through the door of a classroom full of students still brings a unique sense of happiness and fulfillment. In front of my students, I always kept my head up and my spirit alive regardless of my circumstances. Professor Konrad was always happy, uplifting, and ready to do the work!

CHAPTER 17

Financial Adversity

"Success is not the absence of failure; it's the persistence through failure." – Aisha Tyler

FINANCIALLY, MIKE WAS AT THE TOP of his game, and paired with my contributions, we were doing very well. Taking advantage of our financial opportunities to perhaps achieve a new level of comfort and luxury, we decided to remodel our home. We remodeled the kitchen and bathrooms with custom wood cabinets and granite countertops, and installed maple hardwood floors throughout the entire house. We also took what seemed to be a safety risk in real estate. We invested a large amount of money in a few acres of land in Lafayette, a nearby town.

Mike then decided to take a chance with a startup, leaving his well-established position in sales at Oracle Corporation, with the promise of earning a higher income while enjoying the flexibility of a startup. At the same time, after my career struggle that almost left me without a job, I took a one-semester leave of absence from Mills to focus on my research and the upcoming publication on a project in which I implemented a wireless simulator. This meant that for a year I would receive just half of my salary, which did not look like a problem since my salary did not seem to be terribly needed. In other words, Mike and I both simultaneously decided to take risks in our careers while extending our investment strategies.

Memel, in response to his wife Sarah's desire to be closer to her family and home country, Australia, made the decision to pack up and leave. I felt incredibly distressed! The idea of separating not just from my brother but also from toddler Ruben and baby Lola was truly heart-wrenching.

Soon after Memel and his family moved, right in the midst of our career changes, the 2008 Global Financial Crisis knocked on our door. Within a short span, Mike's new company was stuck in a financial downturn, leaving Mike without a job and our family with just half of my income for nearly a year. I don't think I ever valued my career and salary as much as I did in those days. Our investments in real estate went south due to the housing market crash. We lived off our savings like many other families who were also affected. As time went on, though, our savings accounts were drained and we could no longer afford our mortgage, our investment property, and our monthly expenses.

Mike and I panicked, and my magic formula of (effort + mindset = dreams) didn't balance anymore. I hardly had time to react. We looked for opportunities, thought hard, consulted with friends and family, and accomplished nothing. We put our home up for sale in a rush and under pressure. The stress kept going up as months went by without even a single person making an offer on our house. The value of the house had appreciated to over two million dollars just months before the global financial crash, and now, we could not even sell for pennies. We were so desperate that we allowed our real estate agent to bring potential buyers to our home at random times during the days with little notice. These visits were disruptive and caused additional daily stress. My mom, the boys, our yellow lab Charlie and I would pile up in our minivan and drive around until they were finished. I felt exhausted all the time! While still in the middle of trying to sell the house, Mike found a job as director of sales with Utopy, a growing startup. But in his new position, he needed to build a sales pipeline from scratch before he'd be able to cover our monthly expenses. Despite his best efforts, the financial damage was too great to recover.

Mike could not imagine losing our house, but I gave up on it and, without consulting with Mike, started searching for a rental on my own. For a long time, Mike seemed numb to our new financial reality; I, on the other hand, could not wait to move away from our daily stress. I was looking for rentals outside Alamo to move to a more affordable neighborhood, when I heard from a school mom about a rental home near the kids' school. The house was much smaller (three bedrooms and three bathrooms) and the property perhaps one fourth the size, but I loved it right away, especially the backyard with four giant redwood trees, and a giant one just in front of the house. In a week, Mike followed in my steps for the first time without hesitation or questions, and together we signed the contract to rent the house, while keeping our beautiful home on the market.

While Mike was on a business trip with Utopy, I surprised him by moving into the rental with the help of my mom and Carmen. The three of us did most of the work over a weekend through the chaos of having four little boys under our care. The situation felt familiar. Back in Spain, my siblings, my mom, and I had grown resilient and strong during changes far more drastic than this. My upbringing had prepared me for this situation just like a soldier is ready for the battlefield. The three of us knew exactly what to do. Carmen would bring constant jokes to make fun out of misery—my only tears were tears of laughter. My mom told me to protect myself from unhealthy, unnecessary stress by focusing on my boys: "Come on, Almudena, don't waste your precious life with events that you can't control. These kids need a strong healthy mom." And she was right, focusing on my four boys kept me busy in the present moment and my dreams for their future. When my mom worries about me, she still brings up the fact that my boys will always need me. She is clever; she knows well that a mom may sacrifice and neglect herself, but not if it is hurting her children.

In a short time, we lost our house to the bank, the investment property, and all our savings.

Leaving the house was painful, but separating from the horses was devastating. We moved them to a ranch about an hour away. I could no longer look through the window to see their beauty or feel their power. I could not see them so often anymore. Their physical distance created a separation that still hurts.

As hard as it was, I had to focus my attention on the future. I could no longer hold on to the one-acre horse property that I'd lived on and absolutely loved for ten years. Great memories of my children, fun parties, my horses in the backyard, the boys rolling down the mountain of horse manure, and the most healthy-looking vegetable garden, which the boys and I cared for—all of it had to be left behind. I let go and did not look back.

It took Mike years to accept our new financial situation. We had been financially responsible, worked hard, saved as much as we could, and made sure that we didn't accumulate debt. But, during this crisis, we found ourselves with more debt than we could have ever imagined. For Mike, it was more difficult to accept. He felt ashamed! And I understood, imagining how I would feel if I had lost my degrees and had to do it all over again.

We didn't have the luxury to process our emotions. We had jobs and little boys constantly demanding our attention and love. I was concerned about Mike since I recognized the value he placed on money and success. Looking back, we could have kept what we had without taking unnecessary risks, but that is not who Mike is; financially he will always strive for more.

The kids were as happy as ever. They continued having the same friends and going to the same school. I felt grateful that their perception of reality did not change much. I recalled my childhood and how I moved to new homes almost every year and had to deal with constant changes in school and friends. I was afraid of changes until one day it became the norm. As a child, I couldn't make sense of the pain of letting go. The memories and emotions during those transitions seemed so vivid and painful. As soon as I became an adult, I accepted that things and even people come and go, that only difficult experiences make us grow, and that the ones I most care about will give me the strength to endure.

Mike and I were now in our new downsized rental, depleted of savings and investments. We coped by doing what we knew how to do best: working to exceed expectations. I found my magic formula again. By then, through all my reading, I understood the dangers of negative thoughts and the power of the mind. Losing all our assets could have been only the beginning of a much more detrimental situation. I could not feel sorry for our losses. I strongly believed that the stories I would tell myself and others, the thoughts that I would hold on to, and my own perception of my reality would redefine the next trajectory in my life. Life moved on. In my journal, I quoted John Lennon: "*Life is what happens to you while you are busy making other plans.*"

CHAPTER 18

A New Reality

"A woman is like a tea bag – you can't tell how strong she is until you put her in hot water." – Eleanor Roosevelt

THAT SUMMER, I STARTED my new beginning in my rental home. This would be the first year we didn't have the money to enroll our boys in summer camps. During previous summers, the boys had been part of team sports, swimming, music, and engineering camps. There was a sense of wrong, a feeling that my kids would not be OK if I let them spend the entire summer without making progress toward learning new skills or developing academic strength. I felt the pressure to find a creative solution. Ironically, this is not something the boys ever asked for or cared about, but somehow, I imposed on myself this unnecessary pressure. Maybe without much awareness, I was comparing my family to other families around me and feeling that I could not keep up with whatever everyone else appeared to be doing and that somehow my boys would fall behind if I did things differently. Completely wrong thinking, but nevertheless, persisting in finding ways to provide an affordable learning summer camp environment for my kids, I designed an ultimate learning experience.

I developed a new academic curriculum to teach computer coding and problem-solving to kids, not just my kids but to other elementary school kids, too. The motivation for this project soon became twofold: to create an educational summer experience for my boys and to test effective coding and problem-solving teaching strategies on a diverse youth population. I focused on five technologies: Lego Mindstorm and Arduino robotics (to teach how to build and program robots and digital circuits); Alice programming (an easy-to-learn block-based programming environment for computer animations); processing programming (to program visual designs); and my favorite multipurpose computer language, Python. I created a variety of beginner, intermediate, and advanced lessons to accommodate kids with different backgrounds and learning styles. I called my program *KidsLogic* and I loved it from the very beginning.

Mike secured a business license and took care of marketing and any other aspects of the business. He also negotiated with Seven Hills, a prestigious private school in Walnut Creek, to use their modern recreational and computing facilities. We offered free tuition to students who could not afford summer camp, worked on building diverse classrooms, and reached out to girls less interested in coding, inviting them to join the camp for free to achieve a balanced boy/girl ratio. The camps ran for six consecutive years, and to meet the demand we started providing winter camps.

My brother Chino happily took on the role of an instructor, dedicating every day of his summer vacation to coming along with my niece Olivia to teach coding. It was easy for him to connect with the kids, matching their high energy level with creative games, basketball breaks, and his gift of mimicking animal sounds. Occasionally, he would playfully imitate a cricket's chirping in the classroom, nailing the sound with precision and showing his most mischievous smile. After all, he is not just a funny adult with a youthful spirit but also possesses a sharp software engineering mind! He was a key component to the success of the program.

As time went on, my curriculum extended to high school and first-year college students. In the sixth year, a professor from the Education department at Mills College and I conducted a comprehensive formal assessment of my methods and curriculum. We evaluated acquired knowledge and skills, but what stood out most was our ability to inspire students who had previously held negative misconceptions about computer science. The project proved to be an ideal opportunity to ignite a passion for computational thinking and computer programming among young students.

I also taught my curriculum to Mills College students in a traditional undergraduate classroom, and to a group of *Summer Academic Workshop* students, a program designed for first-generation college women students. I published the results of this study, sharing the process of how we taught complex computational thinking to the youth, at the 51st ACM (Association for Computing Machinery) Technical Symposium on Computer Science Education in 2020.

I turned a financial crisis into academic research success. I gave my boys and many other kids the gift of learning coding and technology through engaging and effective techniques. I felt accomplished. I was working all year round, and my thinking was driven and accelerated in multiple directions. But I was enjoying what I was doing regardless of putting in extensive work hours. I was also working on other research projects while still creating new courses and curricula for my undergraduate and graduate students at Mills.

At the end of the summer of our first *KidsLogic* camp, Mike started a new tradition for the family that we continued for many years: camping! The perfect way to explore nature with my savage-spirited little ones without having to spend a crazy amount of money on summer traveling. The boys loved jumping in lakes from rocks, climbing trees, hiking mountains, looking for wild animals, and catching water snakes. On several occasions, they were thrilled to encounter black bears. Young Dani once took a stick and ran after a brown bear, with the other boys following, while Mike and I stopped the adventurous fun in a matter of seconds. The night before, the camp ranger had told the boys that they didn't need to be afraid of brown bears, and he even imitated the chicken sound to show the boys that bears were scared of humans. Not great advice for young boys. To imitate our way of life, my boys and Mike made sure that we never followed the hiking trail signs. Instead, they challenged our hikes by finding the most interesting off-trail paths. We often got lost and we had scary moments, but we always ended up with a delicious dinner, eating food with dirt all over us and big smiles on our faces. We did camping trips in Yosemite, Kings Canyon, Calaveras Big Trees, Crystal Basin, Graeagle, and many other California camping grounds.

The memories of hiking up to the Vernal Falls in Yosemite still give me chills. This is a four-mile round-trip hike all uphill on the way to the top, rated as difficult and challenging for even adults in good shape. Mike and I took the challenge and brought the four boys on the hike. Mike carried two-year-old Dylan in his arms with Michael and Dani, both six years old, following right behind. Four-year Brandon did not leave my side, and we held the back of the line. Climbing up cliffs made me realize that I had a terrible fear of heights, but I felt mostly nauseous as I saw my boys, Michael and Dani, at a distance in front of me walking on a narrow dirt path with only a weak railing separating them from the side of the cliff. I suddenly could see in my mind their little bodies rolling down the cliff and losing them forever. I yelled as loud as I could at the boys, "STOP! STOP RIGHT NOW! We are going back. This is too dangerous. We can't do this." I wanted to cry, hold my boys, and run with them down the hill to a safe place. The boys, slowly followed by Mike and Dylan, walked down toward me. They came close to me held tight to my legs, and insisted on continuing, begging me to let them go to the top with Dad. Mike, holding Dylan, looked at me with a please-let-us-do-it expression on his face, waiting for my decision. *How could Mike and the boys be so reckless? How could they put us all in this situation? Why did I have to be the bad guy ruining the fun? We are all going to die in this crazy nonsense adventure.* Those were my thoughts. A sudden feeling of strong discomfort ran through my entire body. It felt familiar. I had faced many difficult times in my life as a mother, moments when fears or concerns for my kids seemed unreasonable to Mike and the boys but so real to me, as real as if they were putting me in front of a hungry wild tiger. At that moment, I wasn't sure if I was being delusional or if we were in real danger. The boys and Mike promised me that they were going to be careful and that they were going to walk very slowly on the left, as far as they could from the right cliff. I wanted to get mad and run down with all of them but instead, I said: "OK, let's go, but if one of you falls down the cliff, I will jump too." They continued going up, again at a fast pace, leaving Brandon and me trailing behind. As we continued climbing, Brandon got a stomachache. We sat on a rock probably half the way up to the top. I lost sight of Mike, Dylan, Dani, and Michael. I wanted to cry again, feeling powerless, with no control of the situation, but masking my feelings I showed no worries to young Brandon sitting next to me. He was a funny boy. Brandon loved making jokes and always ended them with the sentence, "I just joking." I enjoyed the time we spent sitting together on the rock; it was one of the most precious moments of my life. Brandon reminded me how much he loved me and discussed the fact that he was four and I was 40, a very special year for both of us. His conversation kept me focused on the moment and quite entertained. Finally, after a lot of convincing on my part, we turned around. He felt bad about not reaching the top with his brothers, but he understood that, with his stomachache, it wouldn't have been possible. I felt heartbroken leaving my other boys behind with Mike. And I was furious with Mike! As we reached the ground, Brandon and I waited for what seemed like an eternity—in reality, a couple of hours. I kept asking people as they came back if they'd seen a crazy white man carrying a toddler with two six-year-old boys. Anxiety built as the minutes ticked by. A lady finally said, "Yes, they are happy swimming by the falls at the top." I was so relieved. Now I knew that they'd made it safely to the top, but they still had to make it all the way down. Brandon waited patiently; I sat in agony. It was one of those moments when a mother can only cry silently inside. I played with Brandon, reassuring him (but mostly reassuring myself) that his brothers were fine and that soon they would be back to play with him. When we finally saw them coming down, we both ran toward them. Brandon ran to Dylan, I hugged Michael and Dani, and gave a look of death to Mike for having a daredevil spirit like our boys. I was happy but exhausted. Brandon had lots of questions about the adventure he had missed.

I continued getting myself into trouble on adventures with Mike and the boys for years. Part of me wanted to overcome my fears so I could enjoy what Mike and the boys seemed to love so much: heights, cliffs, lakes, wildlife and exploring new mountains. But I never did. I had similar panicking experiences hiking in Zion National Park, Bryce Canyon, and the Grand Canyon. My obsession was not to enjoy the views but to make sure that the boys stayed away from the edge of the canyons.

During our drive through Zion National Park in Utah, after several days of adventures and with no more energy or courage to hike any longer, Mike stopped at the Overlook Zion hike. It was a really hot day, over 100 degrees Fahrenheit. As soon as we started to get close to the cliff, I panicked. This hike was not less or more dangerous than previous ones, but for reasons that I cannot explain, fear overtook logic and reasoning. I turned around, walking away from Mike, the boys, and the cliff. Nine-year-old Dylan didn't want to leave me alone, so he held my hand and followed me to the car. Those minutes in the car were not spent happily. Dylan was serious and mad, and he didn't say anything until I asked if he was okay. "Do you want the truth, or should I lie, mom?" he asked. Knowing how Dylan easily gets into deep conversations, I wish I had responded differently, but I asked for the truth. He continued, "I understand that you were scared but you always tell me to face my fears. So why are you not facing yours? I wanted to go with my brothers, but I couldn't leave you alone. I think we should go back when you feel better." I felt wrong staying in the car and denying Dylan the experience. I felt that I had no choice but to put my hat and shoes back on and follow Dylan to the top of the hike so I could show him how I do face my fears. The entire time he used words to reassure us that we were safe, and at one point he said, "Your mind is strong, Mom. Imagine that if you fall, Dad will catch you in the air like Superman." We made it to the top. Mike and the older boys were shocked! I felt so proud for showing Dylan that I had the strength to fight my fears and that he had the power to help others overcome challenging moments. And of course, the view at the top of the hike was breathtaking and worth the effort.

CHAPTER 19

A Trip to the Past

"Those who forget the past are condemned to repeat it."
– Chuck Palahniuk

A YEAR AFTER WE MOVED to our rental home after our financial crisis, I received tenure at Mills College. I had pushed myself as hard as I could to achieve the status of Associate Professor while maintaining strong relationships with my boys, but I hadn't paid much attention to my health, my spiritual life, and the purpose of it all. My tenure review report, which took me about a year to write, did not mention my kids or life struggles. It was a piece of art, portraying a driven woman who had no other focus but dedication to her career. It represented less than half the story. But I got tenured! My salary increased and I now had job security for life. In a way, it felt like a life sentence; I observed how some professors were still working in their 80s, entering a classroom and playing similar roles for many decades. I wondered if this was going to be me. I accepted that there was a possibility that my destiny had signed a contract. Yet being rejected from my tenure could perhaps have been devastating.

At the time I got tenure, Mike's company Utopy had been

acquired by Genesys, and he continued as director of sales, selling speech and text analytics to call centers but now at a more established company, bringing home with him a higher salary again. Right after tenure, I was given half-year paid sabbatical, I spent most of my time learning a new software engineering platform called Ruby on Rails, and a new way of building software, the agile development process. But since our financial situation was taking a turn, I wanted to celebrate by taking Mike and the boys to Spain on an adventure of learning about the first 22 years of my life. I planned a trip for the entire month of September with Mike and the boys (ages between nine and five). We first stopped in Paris and visited the Eiffel Tower, the Arc de Triomphe, and a charming French cafe where we all had the best-ever hot chocolate. This was our first time outside the USA with our boys. From France, we flew directly to Madrid, my birthplace. We stayed there with uncle Jesus (my dad's brother), and my cousin Aruca for a few days. I showed the boys and Mike the historic city of Madrid. We visited the Prado Museum, Almudena Cathedral, El Retiro Park, the Royal Palace, the Plaza Mayor, and the Puerta del Sol. My favorite activity was hanging out at the San Miguel Market eating Spanish tapas. We also visited the nearby town of Segovia, which has an ancient Roman aqueduct known as *El Acueducto de Segovia*. We parked near the aqueduct and walked to the Cathedral of Segovia, the second biggest in all of Spain. We had lunch in the main square right next to the cathedral, famous for its pigs. I honestly felt sad for the pigs, even though my Spanish heritage took over. Delicious meals and, even better, delicious coffee. We drove to a medieval castle, the Alcázar de Segovia. I learned that this huge castle was the inspiration for Walt Disney's design of the Disney Castle. The boys became medieval soldiers playing with swords and crossbows during the rest of the trip. We also toured La Granja Palace, walked the grounds doing our best not to get lost, and learned some of the history while the boys kept fighting with their new weapons.

My cousins, uncles, and aunts in Madrid organized an elegant get-together lunch at a winery. For the first time, the boys learned about my country, my language, my culture, and my extended family. Dylan woke up every morning asking if we were in the English world or still in the Spanish one. They quickly had to get used to the kisses and hugs from family members and the friendliness of strangers. Once in the train station, a young woman kissed Brandon and called him handsome. A waiter at a cafe with a big smile pinched Dylan's cheeks and called him *bonito* (cute). This unfamiliar world embraced my boys in a way they hadn't experienced before. Most Spaniards are affectionate in nature and don't have a sense of personal space boundaries as Americans do. Dylan after just a few days told me that he needed a break, and that we needed to go back to fewer kisses, more English, and mac and cheese. He was having a hard time adjusting. I was in heaven!

We continued our trip going south, visiting Jaen, and ending up in *Granada*. In Jaen, Mike and the boys experienced the *ferias*—week-long flamenco festivals featuring flamenco dresses, flamenco music, horses, parades, great food, carnival amusements, and fascinating nightlife. Mike could not believe his eyes when he saw entire families, even babies in strollers, celebrating late into the night. I recall with pleasure going to the *ferias* as a girl, wearing my red polka-dot fancy flamenco dress, a red flower in my hair, and matching necklace and bracelets to dance *sevillanas* (a type of flamenco dancing). I was never shy to dance flamenco as a girl or even later as a grown-up woman. I'd join a *tablao*, or dancing floor, at the first opportunity. The *feria* brought back memories—some great and almost forgotten, but some not so great or easy to forget.

When I was about six years old, I remember an evening when my father drove me to the *ferias* while my mom and siblings stayed at home. I remember being happy wearing my beautiful flamenco dress. My father was drinking with friends, while I danced *sevillanas* with others on the *tablao*. I came back to him and asked him to take me to the bathroom. He got mad at me for asking, even though he seemed to be in a happy mood. I wet myself. I wanted to go home. In front of his friends, he pulled my dress up, took my underwear, threw it on the dirt floor, and asked me to keep dancing. I stayed in the *tablao*, standing without the ability to move, feeling embarrassed because even though no one could tell, I had on a wet dress and no underwear. I so badly wanted to run away, feeling the eyes of many staring right at me, judging me. But while my thoughts were betraying me and working against me, everyone else kept dancing.

I didn't tell my boys this story, but I thought about it.

We arrived in *Granada* late at night after a day in the *feria*, with the boys sleeping in the back of the car. We realized that we had left our passports in Madrid at my uncle's house, but after a lengthy conversation with the receptionist, they let us stay at the hotel without proper identification. In *Granada*, we visited *Albaicín* and *La Alhambra*, two places that I had most enjoyed when I lived there. Memories of Juan, the laughter of my girlfriends Lola and Antonia, the innocence of little Carmen, and the troubled thoughts of my younger self briefly rushed me back to my past and into a storm of emotions. The boys and Mike quickly brought me back to my new reality. In *Albaicín*, we walked up to *La Plaza de San Nicolas* and enjoyed the magnificent views of the city. There were, as there often are, two gypsy men singing flamenco and playing the guitar. I enjoyed dancing next to them, surrounded by tourists while Mike was video recording and the boys quietly watching their mom dancing with the spirit of a gypsy woman. Flamenco brings me back to my core, my center, my peace. We ended our day eating a delicious meal at Bar Kiki.

Our next destinations were Marbella and Algeciras, where I was able to connect with friends from a distant past when we were living in *Villa Coca* and *El Escorpion*. We spent a fabulous day with them having a lengthy lunch and walking through town while remembering stories. I was carrying some pictures in my purse of my early years that my mom had given me. My friends drove us to my old house, *Villa Coca*, which now lay in ruins. No one had ever lived in that house after we left. The reasons remain unknown— maybe the snakes. As Mike, the boys, and I stepped inside, memories of every room flooded back. I could almost feel myself holding Ana and Carmen as babies, see my older brothers racing around, and sense my father's lingering presence within the walls.

El Scorpion brought me different memories. Our backyard full of strangers playing guitar, smoking pot and drinking. My father's young lover, homeless chef, and the naked female statue by the pool. It felt good having Mike and the boys with me as I remembered my childhood.

The next day we drove to a farmhouse to visit friends of my parents. My mom's best friend cried when she saw me; she said that I looked as beautiful as my mom. It brought tears to my eyes. Her husband, embracing me closely, told me how much they both had cared about my mom. I was hoping that he had forgotten the incident when I'd stabbed him with a pencil. I am not sure that he did, but he treated me with a lot of affection. Their family had grown huge. There were many people and children of different ages whom I did not recognize. During lunch, the men sat at one table and the women at a different one. I saw the men holding Mike with their arms around his shoulders, giving him no physical space to breathe, talking quickly in Spanish, cigarettes in hand, and then Mike, somehow, using a few Spanish words, responding and laughing loudly. He was having a great time, feeling for the first time the love of the older men of Spain. Mike doesn't drink or smoke or speak Spanish. But that day he experienced it all.

The trip to *Algeciras* was enjoyable, but it also brought back many painful memories from my childhood years that I'd kept buried. We then headed to my hometown, *Chiclana*. After visiting family and friends, and enjoying a few days at the beach, I drove Mike and the boys to *Villa Lichi*. This was the place where I'd endured years of misery as a teenager and ultimately walked away from at the age of 18. We sat outside in the car for a while looking at the old house. Mike and the boys had a hard time believing that I'd lived there in a poor house, but to make things better, I told them how much I loved riding my *Vespa* to the beach.

Later that night, I told Mike some stories I never thought I'd be ready to share. I believe this was the first time that Mike truly felt the cruelty of my father.

We ended our trip by enjoying some of the more touristy adventures in *Jerez, Puerto de Santa Maria, Sevilla, Cordoba, Gibraltar*, and Morocco, driving down the Atlantic coast to visit my favorite beach towns.

After our road trip through Spain and a successful tenure review, I felt a new sense of career growth and financial stability. The struggles of being a working mom continued but being tenured gave me the extra strength and willingness to push forward. I was also highly motivated to travel with my family back to Spain at some point not too far in the future.

I started to accept that I was doing my best job raising my kids, trusting their nature and inner strength, but mostly starting to see that there was a lot I could not control. I tried to stop overthinking my concerns and blaming myself for their behavior or the consequences of their actions. I started to laugh at the chaos of my life while sharing anecdotes with family and friends—stories like losing my phone inside the fridge, picking up my boys from school at the wrong hour, forgetting doctor's appointments, or the constant burning of my cooking. My working mom situation definitely gave me a lot to tell and write. As the kids got older, the chaos and the inability to keep up with my daily responsibilities continued.

A memorable incident was Michael's back-to-school night. Determined to attend and be part of his high school experience from day one, I drove to school with the schedule he had given me. I joined the classes, only realizing at the end that I had been following his friend Max's schedule. My mix-up left me feeling unable to get things right with my kids' school events, giving my friend Bonnie and me a good laugh and another tale.

My constant absent-minded behavior was accepted by my close friends, family, and students.

CHAPTER 20

Breaking Down

*"Let food be thy medicine and medicine
be thy food." – Hippocrates*

TO MY SURPRISE, MY OVERALL health deteriorated. I was
in my 40s and had spent the last two decades drinking plenty of
coffee and still eating all the delicious food that came my way. I
became the kitchen vacuum, eating any leftovers from the kids'
dinners and stimulating my brain with plenty of *Manchego* and
other high-quality cheeses, a variety of exquisite chocolates, and
plenty of French bread with butter or olive oil. I didn't gain
weight, maybe because I kept myself moving either at work giving
lectures, running between buildings or at home caring for the boys
and the house. I thought being thin meant being healthy, but
nothing could be far from the truth.

Following my trip to Spain, at the start of the semester, the
ringing in my ears became more frequent, accompanied by vertigo
and daily fatigue. My left shoulder and lower back were also
causing pain mostly at night, and I had difficulty digesting many
of my meals. My doctor found slightly elevated cholesterol and
concerns about low blood pressure. My vertigo and fatigue were

awful—at times, I had to sit during my lectures, pretending to be thinking or letting the students work on a problem to avoid the sensation of fainting. I spent most of my winter breaks, spring breaks, and the beginning of my summers sick with some form of the flu. My time off from teaching was dedicated to feeling ill. During the semester, my body was driven by adrenaline and caffeine, with always something to do to the point of exhaustion. But as soon as the semesters were over, I had the opportunity to slow down, allowing my body to get sick. At times I wondered how my brain was able to choose so well the times when my body could afford to be sick without impacting my teaching responsibilities.

To address my symptoms my doctor kept prescribing different medicines that I never took for headaches and vertigo. I went to my doctor so she could help me find the reasons for my symptoms, but I was not willing to take medication to hide the problem without solving it. My doctor encouraged me to introduce some type of exercise to my daily routine—other than rushing after my kids or running around the Mills campus. Yet any attempt at working out weakened my immune system and resulted in sore throats that would last for weeks. To add to my health struggle, after dinner I often experienced stomach pains and poor digestion—at bedtime, I would often have to drink Pepto-Bismol. What a disgusting, unhealthy habit that was, even though I enjoyed the taste. I believed that Pepto-Bismol was damaging my body, providing temporary relief while hurting in the long term. I was only adding fuel to the fire because I didn't know what else to do.

My friend Bonnie and I would sometimes go on a bike ride

on the Iron Horse Trail—a never-ending walking, running, and biking path crossing our town. Those rides were fun but, unfortunately, followed by sore throats and headaches the next day. My energy to exercise was just not there!

Mike put on his thinking cap: *Almudena is skeptical (or afraid) of the healthcare industry; she believes unnecessary drugs are overprescribed, but SHE IS A MESS. How can I help her?*

Thinking outside the box, he found an Ayurveda wellness center, without even understanding the meaning of Ayurveda but holding on to the word *wellness*. Without consulting me, he made an appointment with the main doctor in the clinic, Dr. Jain. I spent the next year visiting her office and learning about Ayurveda—a holistic Hindu philosophy that defines health as a state of balance between the body, the mind, and the spirit. I initially found the spiritual aspect of Ayurveda intriguing. During my appointments with Dr. Jain, I listened intensively, took notes, and followed most of her advice. She made me believe from day one that I didn't have any diseases. *But if nothing was wrong with my body, then what was wrong? I was definitely not feeling well!*

I still remember one of Dr. Jain's early pieces of advice. She spoke of the role of great-grandmothers in Eastern cultures. They are present and make a difference even though they're not always involved. She asked me to take breaks every day at home and play the role of a great grandma, maybe by sitting outside, breathing for just a few minutes. She insisted that it was critical that I spend every day some time relaxing and being at peace with myself. I took this advice very seriously, trying to relax and walk away from stressful situations. It was not something I accomplished right away, but over time I got better. I was able to integrate this practice during some, but not all, chaotic moments. Today, I still at times play the role of the great-grandma, effortlessly and powerfully present.

As part of the wellness plan, Dr. Jain asked me to see the psychotherapist at her clinic. I made an appointment hoping for an interesting conversation or to learn something new about the mind—a topic that had caught my attention for years. She asked me how I was doing, and I replied that I was struggling with health issues but that my mind was not too bad. We first briefly exchanged a few words about my life, my feelings, and my childhood. She asked me to close my eyes. I felt comfortable, with very little idea of where she was about to take me. With my eyes closed, she asked me to remember a time in my childhood when I was not happy. Thinking I was safe inside my head with my own thoughts, I traveled to the time I lived in *El Escorpion*. She asked me to go back to a moment or incident during that time associated with negative emotions. My mind went right back to sitting in the car with my dad driving and his lover in the passenger seat. She asked me to describe the details (still inside my head)—everything I could recall. To my surprise, I started to cry, letting lots of pain come out, but also feeling a tremendous amount of shame for crying in front of her, feeling weak and emotionally vulnerable. I apologized for crying, and with anger I told myself to STOP. I wonder why I had no compassion for myself, when I had never asked anyone, not even my kids, to ever stop crying. She gave me tissues, and after my short but painful story, she asked me to go back to that moment as the adult I was now, taking me on a beautiful but powerful mental journey. I, as grown-up Almudena, went back to the event and sat next to little me holding her tiny hand. I looked into her big, distressed eyes, and told her that never again did she have to feel alone because I was here for her, to love and protect her forever.

My session with the psychologist was unexpected and left me with thoughts I didn't know I had. Somehow, I was still upset that my dad and his lover made fun of me, and in my 40s I was still feeling the pain. It really bothered me, because I never wanted to give my dad and his lover that kind of power over me. Accepting my pain was hard. At the time I could not understand how critical it was for me to finally conquer the pain of the past in order to have a truly healthy life. I walked away from the psychologist's office with the understanding that in moments of fear or hatred, I could always hold my own hand to make myself feel better. It became my little secret. I learned that I could always go back in my mind to love and protect the child and the teenager in me. With this technique, I moved on and did not return to see the psychologist. Now with my understanding of the power of psychotherapy, I wish I had!

Dr. Jain's office team also advised me to make dietary changes like quitting cheese and cutting back on chocolate and caffeine. These suggestions were difficult to hear. I resisted most dietary advice because of my strong relationship with food and my stubborn mindset. I strongly believed in my homemade Mediterranean diet with fresh and organic ingredients, and I could not see the negative side of my eating habits. But Dr. Jain had a uniquely gentle way to get her philosophy into my head, so I trusted some of her advice and made a change, starting my days with warm water with lemon for hydration and salt to help my low blood pressure instead of my regular shot of espresso. I learned Kundalini Yoga and breathing techniques, and slowly improved my understanding of mindfulness and meditation. The health improvements were significant, and what I was learning was exciting and promising.

I understood the changes that I needed to make, but I was having a difficult time integrating them into my busy life. I didn't think I had the time or discipline to commit to any big changes. Avocado instead of cheese, lentil soups instead of lamb, mushrooms rather than chicken, green tea instead of espresso, cumin water during the day, almonds or walnuts as snacks, and the introduction of so many new-to-me healthy substances such as turmeric, ashwagandha, ginger, and seeds—this advice was challenging enough on its own. Add to it the struggle of removing sugar and toxic chemicals from my diet, which are included in most products today at grocery stores. I felt overwhelmed.

During one of my winter breaks, I had a sore throat that lasted six weeks even though I took, against my wishes, a full course of antibiotics prescribed by my regular doctor with her very best intentions. Regardless, my sore throat continued. I visited Dr. Jain's office again, this time extremely concerned and believing that something was irreparably wrong with my health. I told Dr. Jain about my sore throat and all of the other recurring symptoms. "I think I may have a very serious health condition," I concluded, waiting for her to give me some nasty news or send me to a lab for a bunch of blood tests. But instead, she said confidently, "Almudena, we need to change the foods you eat." And immediately, without a doubt in her mind, she signed me up with a chef for plant-based cooking lessons. Initially, I faced a dilemma: on one hand, skeptical of traditional medicine, but, on the other hand, not sure that I had the discipline to switch completely to a plant-based diet. With this hesitation, I started my cooking lessons.

On my first day, I told Chef Eddie that *Manchego* cheese was at the core of my eating values. We shared stories of European positive attitudes toward cheese, referring mostly to the French, Italians, and Spaniards. I mentioned how good-quality cheeses were a critical part of my diet for their calcium and protein content. But also, most importantly, for their dopamine effect on the brain. I used to think, *If a piece of cheese doesn't make me happy, nothing will.*

Chef Eddie asked me to dedicate just a week of my life to following his cooking advice. Stubborn in my ways but deeply concerned about my health, I agreed, but then I said, "I love to eat. Food is my happy place. If I get hungry or I don't enjoy the food, I may have to quit." This was obviously not his problem, but mine, and somehow, I was turning it into his challenge.

Every day for the next week I came to Dr. Jain's office to the kitchen room with my notebook and an empty belly. Chef Eddie and I would cook together and eat whatever we made. He told me miracle stories of how a plant-based diet could heal the bodies of people with worse health problems than mine. I so much enjoyed his stories of healing. I learned that, when given the right nutrients, the body has the wisdom to heal itself from some chronic lifestyle diseases like the ones I was experiencing. Besides being a charming muscular black man with tons of wisdom to share, I must say that there was something special about Chef Eddie that made his beliefs convincing. I wanted to learn from him. After a few days of following his cooking methods, I felt completely different, with all my unhealthy symptoms completely gone. All gone—sore throat, fatigue, and low blood pressure.

I stopped consuming all animal products except for free-range eggs and stopped eating sugar—one of the biggest silent killers in the life of most humans today. I started reading all the nutrition labels, shocked to see sugar in almost all tomato sauce at the stores and integrated a variety of fresh new vegetables and grains into my diet. His recipes were full of flavor, colors, and nutrients. I could not have done this transition on my own. I realized that I was stuck eating a variety of brain-stimulating foods like sugar, plenty of bread and unhealthy fats, and I could not see beyond my busy daily life.

With this radical change in diet, I gained a tremendous amount of energy. In a couple of months, my blood lab work went from dismal to outstanding. But most importantly, I felt great. I attended a lecture in Dr. Jain's office by Dr. Raymond Francis and followed his advice in *Never Get Sick Again*. I also read and followed *Healing with Whole Foods* by Paul Pitchford (a great recommendation from my mom), *How Not to Die* by Dr. Michael Greger, and *Conscious Eating* by Dr. Gabriel Cousens. I spent the next six years of my life enjoying great health without experiencing even a simple cold. I went back to the basics—whole grains, a variety of vegetables, and the bean and legume recipes that I grew up eating at home.

I was feeling healthier again when my friend Bonnie asked me to start playing tennis with her. She was more advanced than me; I was at level zero. But right away I joined a class that she suggested for beginners. For the next five years, I ate the way Chef Eddie taught me, read lots of books based on similar philosophies, and played lots of tennis. I joined the Crow Canyon Country Club in Danville, and I even did USTA competitions in recreational leagues.

Tennis became a big part of my life—I studied tennis, dreamt of tennis, and practiced almost every day of the week. First thing in the morning, right after waking up, I would move my arms simulating a back end shot still in a state of half-sleep, visualizing the tennis ball hitting the racket in the perfect spot. I could hear the sound and feel the excitement of the shot. I became obsessed with tennis, putting in lots of hours of practice and lessons. Serving took great dedication and patience. I'd never played sports in my life, so it took me many lessons and practices over the years to learn how to serve decently. My instructor spent hours working with me—I thought to myself to be his greatest challenge. He once came to the lesson holding a football in one of his hands. He threw it softly at me and yelled, "Catch it." I barely did, pretending to be a cool American mom. He then asked me to throw it back to him. "Well," I told him, "I have never thrown a non-round ball." We both laughed. The goal was to teach me how to use my body to throw an American football. According to him, this movement would help with my tennis serve. I was determined to be the best tennis player I could be. I had a folder with notes where I had drawn detailed diagrams of the rules involved in a tiebreak. I studied and became good at following the steps. I might have thought about it so much that I manifested my first single USTA match to end on a tiebreak. My opponent was obviously better, much taller, and stronger than me. The speed of her balls caught me by surprise. But in that game, I gave it my all, pushed myself to my max, and won the game! I still remember that day as being one of the best of my life. Because I was able to accomplish something special, I proved to myself that hard work pays off and that the sky's the limit. I felt empowered!

That Sunday, I went back home after my early morning triumph, and after feeding the boys, naturally went back to work. I was writing computer code on a software cloud solution called Cloud9. A club instructor, Mick, texted me later in the afternoon. "You must be on cloud nine," he said. "How do you know?" I replied. I had not heard that expression outside of my technical world. But yes, I was both working on Cloud9, preparing my code to teach during lectures, and feeling on cloud nine. My tennis partner, Nikki, and I did many double USTA matches afterward. We won sometimes, we lost other times, but we always had the best time.

On weekdays, after my full days of work, I would spend time with the kids, helping them with homework and making sure that they had a proper healthy dinner, and once I finished with my responsibilities, I would drive late in the evenings to the country club to meet with friends for practice. On Saturdays, I joined the club group lesson and stayed afterward to play with friends, ending with Nikki, and at times other friends, having brunch at the club cafe. I would often give my friends unsolicited tips on conscious eating during our brunch hour—even though I still seemed to be the only one overeating. On Sundays, Mike, the boys, and I took lessons with our excellent tennis instructor, who demonstrated a tremendous amount of patience with all of us, especially with me.

My new life chapter was great! I felt healthy, strong, efficient at work, full of energy, and better able to enjoy being a mom. We continued doing lots of traveling and camping. I gained the strength to hike for hours with Mike and the boys, to bike with my friend Bonnie, and to keep my busy work schedule and life demands somehow under control. My work life was still busy, but I felt much more confident doing my job and accepting my future in academia.

Toward the end of my 40s, at the age of 48, I was given a promotion and a semester of sabbatical—basically, seven months of paid leave to work on my own projects and research.

During the summer of my sabbatical, to celebrate years of great health and academic success, I traveled to Spain, but this time for eight weeks with five adolescent boys: my three sons, Michael, Brandon, and Dylan; my nephew, Dani, whom I'd rather also call my son, and my young brother Jefferson. It had been several years since Jessica had left my father, and both Jessica and Jefferson had become part of my life. Jessica and I developed a close relationship and Jefferson joined the boys' crew. Michael, Dani, and Jefferson were 15 years old, Brandon 13, and Dylan 11. We rented a big house by the ocean. They all fell in love with southern Spain, my hometown *Chiclana*, my friends, and my family.

This was my second time in Spain with boys. They were older and could appreciate the chilled lifestyle, the long fun nights, the beach life, the food, the freedom that teenagers experience, and the relaxed environment. Michael was only 15 and already planning for early retirement in southern Spain, while Jeffersson was planning ahead in his young mind a semester in Spain during college. The memories of that summer will live with all of us forever. As soon as I arrived in Madrid, I drove with the boys through the crazy Madrid traffic. The boys trusted me, relying on the fact that it was my country, and I was supposed to know what to do and how to drive. The reality was quite different, I was completely lost, and cars were driving too fast and too close for me to even think when to take the right turns. I yelled a few times thinking we were crashing, and we spent quite some time missing turns unable to follow the rental car navigational system. We finally got to the hotel, but between my jetlag, the adrenaline rushing through my veins, my impatience to wait for the morning to drink Spanish coffee, and the excitement to drive to the south the next day, I did not sleep for the entire night. In the morning I had another coffee and a few slices of Spanish ham and cheese with plenty of bread, breaking my over five years of a consistent plant-based diet and turning back to my old eating habits.

I drove the boys safely out of Madrid down to the south straight for six hours to *Chiclana*. Our first stop was near the beach, at the house of my high school friends, Ana Mari and Alfonso. She made me a delicious cup of coffee with plenty of white sugar. I forgot about my no-sugar rule and enjoyed sitting next to them, feeling as if I were a teenager again. We drove to our summer rental gorgeous Mediterranean Spanish villa and walked to my ocean, just a couple of minutes from the house.

Looking at *La Barrosa* Beach felt as if I had just arrived at the only place I belonged.

The next day I drove to a cafe to drop off Michael—my friend Alfonso had invited him to the end-of-the-school-year trip at the high school where he worked as the principal. This was the same high school that I'd attended as a teenager, and I was super excited for Michael to have that experience. The moment they left, I sat at the cafe alone reflecting on how happy I was feeling, even though I'd had very little sleep the last few nights.

After my cup of coffee, I walked outside, and to my surprise, I could not find my rental car. I could not make sense of the situation. It was early in the morning and the street was completely quiet. I immediately saw one car—just *one* car—and from far away, it looked like my rental car. It was far down the hilly street and crashed into a wall at the very end near the ocean. A view to never forget. Apparently, my rental car had rolled on its own down the hilly street, crashing at the end into a white cement wall. For a second, I didn't want to believe what my eyes were looking at. I had forgotten to pull up the manual brake and left it in neutral! I went back to the rental place and asked for an automatic car. *Thank goodness for insurance!*

Michael that day made tons of friends, marking the beginning of a summer of fun, especially for the older boys.

Gina visited us for a few weeks. With her, the fun reached another level. We visited my cousin Aruca in Marbella, where we enjoyed dancing to flamenco and reggaeton music at the *chiringuitos* while eating delicious tapas. During the drive, Gina and the boys played plenty of American rap music, dancing in the car, bouncing up and down, while I carefully drove them safely from town to town late at night.

Mike arrived in the last two weeks. This had been the longest time we had ever been away from each other. I picked him up at the train station in Jerez. My hair was curly—in natural voluminous beachy curls that he had never seen before on me—and my skin was very tanned. He looked at me as if he had just seen me for the first time—with eyes of passion and curiosity. We felt a strong attraction and love for each other and were happy to be back together.

We ended the trip traveling from south to north up the coast of Portugal—Mike, the five boys, and me. Then drive east from Porto, Portugal back to Madrid through charming towns and cities like Salamanca.

PART FOUR

SURRENDER

CHAPTER 21

Loving is Painful

"Our dead are never dead to us until
we have forgotten them."– George Eliot

MY HEALTHY TRANSITION to a plant-based diet together
with my passion and dedication to tennis brought years of positive
mental and physical changes. I was at the peak of my health. My
circle of family and friends was unbreakable. I had a deep
appreciation for everyone in my life, both in the US and Spain.

While I was traveling in Spain, my mom experienced kidney
failure, something she and my siblings hid from me until I was
back in the US. When I got back, I saw my mom fragile and
debilitated. She had lost too much weight and was pale. I
immediately became concerned, but without the time to
understand her health situation. In a matter of months, she had
a stroke.

I received a call from the hospital without much detail about
the situation. I immediately drove to the hospital. She was
sleeping, and breathing well, with all vital signs under control.
When she woke up and first spoke, late in the evening, I could
hardly recognize her. She wasn't making any sense. She believed

she was a mermaid. I tried logic with her. She asked me to take her to the bathroom to see the baby girl she'd just given birth to. She was sweet, like a mother of a newborn, to the invisible baby and spoke soft words to her, breaking every little part of my heart into the smallest possible pieces. The nurse came, and my mom called her *pequeño diablo*, little devil. I spoke to my mom as I would to a child. "Mama, I am Almudena, your daughter. How are you?"

I called my siblings. I cried on the phone, looking away from my mom. In front of my mom, I swallowed my tears and smiled reassuringly, looking into her eyes, pretending at that moment that everything was fine. The fear of losing my mom became real. I hadn't experienced the fear of losing a loved one since I was a teenager when I'd lost my *abuelita*. I hadn't thought much about the concept of mortality either. But now I felt my mom's life was on the line. *Would she ever come back to me, to be my mom?*

After our strange conversation, she fell asleep happy about her new reality. I stayed with her that night watching her sleep waiting for her to wake up to maybe more crazy talking. The doctor said to me that we needed to wait to see how the brain had been affected and that it was too early to tell. I felt my heart dying holding onto hope. I wouldn't know how to live without my mom. I begged her in her sleep to stay alive. I told her that whatever the situation was, I would take care of her with the same love and affection that I would for one of my sons. She had to live!

She woke up in less than 24 hours, mostly back to being herself. She called me by my name and told me that she could only see well with one of her eyes. I felt as though a miracle had just happened. She was back to being my mom, at least mentally.

The final diagnosis was that she had lost vision in one eye, her balance, part of her speech, and coordination in her right hand. But my mom understood the situation. Carmen and I alternated staying at her house, but this arrangement only lasted a few days. My mom insisted on working on her own recovery. She had the knowledge and practice of working back in Spain with special-ed children in physical therapy, and she seemed to know exactly what to do. She spent entire days doing her physical exercises, and in a matter of months, she was able to read again. "The day that I cannot read a book will be the day that I will feel dead," I remember her saying. I paid attention to her stubbornness and admired her persistence, but mostly her pride. My brothers, sisters, and I were shocked by her recovery and inner strength.

Over the course of just a few months, she recovered from the stroke with a strong spirit, superb resilience, and extreme determination. But she has continued to have arrhythmia episodes and other heart conditions like tachycardias and bradycardias, which often brought her back to the hospital. No one, no matter how much we love her, can control her health and how long she will be in our lives. I believe that her years of high-intensity stress living under the abuse of my father caused permanent physical and emotional damage. I will always blame him for that. My mom is tough. I can only rely on that. While she is still struggling with her heart condition, she still makes sure to do some type of exercise every day. Her mind is strong as steel. Her visits to the hospital and doctors' appointments continue to be our battles. I often visualize my mom as a very old but happy woman playing the role of the great-grandmother.

Some of my precious friends have had different destinies.

During the time that my mom was recovering from her stroke, my friend Mario was suddenly admitted to the hospital in Buenos Aires under intensive care for a heart and pulmonary condition. Mario was my colleague at Mills College, a professor of Hispanic Studies, and a very dear friend. Our teaching schedules would overlap so that our paths crossed in the same building every Tuesday and Thursday. We would give each other a hug and two kisses while exchanging a few words in Spanish as we ran to our own lecture halls.

For years, Mario and I would meet every few months for lunch and spend hours talking about life, sometimes about work, and a few times about my boys. He had also become a great friend of Carmen, who was once a student in one of his classes, Hispanic Cinema, while she was studying for her Molecular Biology degree at Mills. And Mario was also fond of my mom. Many times, we would all get together. He was a good listener and one of the most beautiful souls I ever had as a friend. Our time together involved a lot of laughter and left me with new wisdom and ways of thinking. He told me once that when we grow older our happiness comes from our ability to love others, even if we were not loved back. That statement, in his unique Argentinian accent, still stays with me as I practice unconditional love.

On a sad afternoon, Mario passed away. I don't recall much else except the many days of tears and anguish that followed that conversation. Walking by the entrance of our shared building every Tuesday and Thursday left a painful sadness deep in my heart for a long time. I miss his hugs, his smiles, our long conversations, our lunches, and his everlasting love for life.

In that same year, my incredible and courageous friend Gunilla lost the love of her life to cancer. Zak and Gunilla both had been part of my entire American life. They'd witnessed the best and the worst, always providing love and support. We shared unforgettable moments of traveling, and parties by the ocean near their home in the beach town of Half Moon Bay. Zak carried a special light within him, a light that will continue to shine in the hearts of those he touched. I will always miss his words of encouragement. For him, nothing ever seemed to be a challenge. His confident and peaceful but strong nature will always remain alive in the souls of his son Joaquin and younger daughter Isabeau. Gunilla will remain by my side as long as I live, for she has been an integral part of my life for over three decades. As a single mom working and caring for her children, she became a hero to me. Friends like her become cherished treasures as time goes on.

Just a few months later, I lost another of my dearest friends and colleagues from Mills College, Steve. He passed away after a battle with pancreatic cancer. I will forever feel the emptiness that he left behind. He gave me a huge amount of strength in my academic career, always pushing me to be authentic at work while loving my family.

While these losses and events made me question the meaning of life and the fragility of our existence, my life kept quickly moving on, regardless of my feelings and without giving me time to process and grieve the loss of my friends.

Worsening my sadness, our rental home's landlord made the cruel and selfish decision of cutting five massive healthy redwood trees in the back and front yard of the property. Without thinking twice or consulting with us, he killed 100-year-old powerful, giant trees. The house became a sad place that was constantly reminding me of the lives, friends, and trees that were gone. I could no longer live there!

Mike, the boys, and I decided to move to another home. Brandon and I did the work of searching for a new property in Alamo. We found a much larger home in Alamo within walking distance from the Monte Vista High School which Brandon wanted to attend. The new home was spacious, had a more traditional style, and was perfectly set up for a family with teenagers. I made the upstairs the teenage cave, with Brandon occupying the much larger room, and it was my intention to make the downstairs a peaceful temple with my music playing in the background and figures of my travels decorating the bar area and living room.

As soon as I moved in, I unsuccessfully tried to connect with my neighbors. I knocked on doors and introduced myself, but there was zero reciprocation and clearly no intention on their part to keep in touch. On a hot evening in early summer, a month after we moved in, Mike started a conversation with a neighbor while doing his daily walk around the neighborhood. Mike invited him inside the house, and in a matter of minutes, we became friends. Our new friend Arin invited Mike and me over to his spectacular Spanish architectural house with palm trees, a few doors up our street. This meant a lot to me because I was dying to broaden my neighborhood circle in Alamo. I am the kind of person who wants to say hi to almost everyone I encounter, whether that be while I'm driving on the freeway or taking a simple walk. My new friend was, in my mind, an opportunity to temporarily satisfy the need to connect and interact with new people. I have always enjoyed meeting new people: it gives me the chance to experience life through the lenses of others. I love to hear their stories.

At the time, I was planning another quick trip to Spain to attend a conference in *Barcelona*. I was communicating on video calls with Mili, my best friend since childhood in Spain. She had been fighting cancer for several years, and we were both counting the days until we could see each other again, most likely for the last time. We texted each other every day. "*Bichito* (little bug), hurry up, my body is dying. I need to see you one more time," she would insist. Her body was holding on to a thread of life. She called me on a WhatsApp video call, and we talked for hours. Her smile was as beautiful and inviting as it was when we were five. We planned our special reunion: We would sit on *La Barrosa* Beach one more time to watch the sunset together as we did as teenagers, smoking our cigarettes and planning a future together that never happened. We both laughed! I had so much to share with her, idea after idea of how we could still make a difference in each other's lives. We had not done our best to stay connected during my years in the US. In a way, I needed her more than she needed me; she was always the strong one, even at this most vulnerable moment in her life. Her spirit was tougher than any life struggle and her personality was joyous under the worst circumstances. Her mind was sharp and unbreakable, filled with memories that I hardly remember. We recalled how as teenagers we laughed all the time at the world and even our own shadows. I hadn't wanted a husband or a family; she'd wanted both. I didn't believe in marriage, but she did. She never got married but she had her son whom she loved tremendously.

Her body could not hold on any longer, and I couldn't fulfill her dying wish; she left this world just a couple of days after our conversation. The last thing she said in our last conversation in a strong Andalusian accent similar to mine was, "You made it, *bichito*. All your dreams came true for you. And you deserve it all." Her words have tormented me ever since. *Did I deserve a better life than her?* I'm not sure. What I do know is that she deserved much more.

I felt empty. I'd let years pass by, too concerned with my own life and struggles to realize that I was losing my best friend to cancer. There wasn't a tomorrow anymore, just memories and guilt. So much guilt. My best friend's death put my life on pause. I couldn't see the meaning in my own life. I just wanted to be next to her one more time.

Arin, my new neighbor friend, sent me a text the day that Mili passed away, asking if I wanted to get together before my trip. Deflated, I told him about Mili. He texted back words that I can't remember, but they were about the meaning of life and death. It seemed to me that he had an understanding of death that I couldn't comprehend, but his text could not get me out of my sadness. Maybe Mili was in a better place now that the suffering of her cancer battle had stopped. When I think of her, I still tell her, *I am sorry.* Then I breathe, take a second, and try to remember our time together. Sometimes I wish I could go back and ride life's roller coaster next to her. I find myself daydreaming about what that would have been like. But dwelling on regrets brings nothing but pain.

I went to Spain for my conference, but first I went to see Milli's mom in the south. So many times, she had also been a mom to me. Her house was full of many memories that Mili had left for me to keep. Among them was my favorite Spanish doll that we'd played with when we were girls, the jewelry we made and sold together as teenagers, and all the letters I had written to her while I lived in the US—letters describing my early struggles and how much I missed her.

I have asked myself for forgiveness for not being by her side during her most difficult years. We were once inseparable, but destiny kept us apart when we needed to be together the most.

As soon as I came back from Spain, Mike and I were invited to a neighborhood street gathering. Mike and I went to be polite and look for opportunities to socialize and connect with the neighbors. My energy was low, and I wasn't my normal upbeat self. I sent a text to my neighbor/friend Arin, but he did not reply, which was unusual.

Except for a couple of friendly faces, I did not feel welcome. Mike did most of the talking, but I saw a change in his expression toward the end of the evening, and I knew something was wrong.

On our way home, he said that he had bad news for me. At the gathering, he heard that our dear neighborhood friend Arin had had a heart attack while we were traveling and passed away during the night. My heart shattered one more time.

By the end of this summer, I was angry and very disturbed. I had to face emotional confusion, pain, and anger for many months. I'd lost friends, others were currently battling their health, and I saw my mom on the line between life and death. My journey through these moments made me realize how fragile our lives are, how quickly we can vanish, and how precious everyone is. I wondered if I was spending enough time with my friends and family. I started to look at everyone around me differently, understanding that tomorrow is not a guarantee but a hope.

With each friend I lost, I had to let go of a piece of me. The precious, happy moments and my dreams with them in my life became wounds in my heart. These friends are no longer there, and there is nothing we can share with each other anymore. They only live in my thoughts, in my memories, and in my writing. I can't connect with their needs and desires. I can't tell them about my challenges, despair, or accomplishments.

Letting them go is a lifetime endeavor. Their lives are an important part of my story.

In America, so far, I had been able to face difficult circumstances with energy and courage, without letting anything ever reduce me to a feeling of powerlessness, but losing people whom I loved caused a sadness I could not overcome. With a broken heart, I continued my life.

CHAPTER 22

When It Rains, It Pours

"I believe in the sun, even when it rains." – Anne Frank

MY 40S DID NOT END as expected! The suffering of friends and seeing my mom dealing with the unpredictability of her heart struggles was a reality beyond my control.

My travels through southern Spain had been special and enjoyable, but they'd brought back nostalgic memories. I paid close attention to the way I'd once lived: morning and afternoon coffee by the beach, late dinners by the ocean with friends and laughter. Daily walks and swimming in the ocean. A taste of coffee that I could not find in any other place in the world. And the nightlife with friends, tapas, music and dancing. A culture that values connections with family members and friends more than anything else. And Sundays, everyone's favorite day of the week, a time when families get together, present in the moment to eat and connect without rushing to sit in front of a computer. I enjoyed having lunch with my high school friend Ana Mari and her family on Sundays. After lunch or nap time, we would all sit around the pool, with friends, siblings, parents, grandparents, and grandchildren, enjoying hours of just being together. There was no rush or intensity or the need to work. I marveled at how my friends, burdened with responsibilities, managed to remain immersed in the present, unbothered by obligations, and free to savor each passing moment. I admired their ability to wholeheartedly enjoy the company of one another, giving undivided attention. These observations led me to question whether I had made the best choice raising a family in my current American environment.

Living in the busy Bay Area of California meant adhering to work commitments and scheduled activities almost every day of our lives. Countless family gatherings were hosted at my home, where I constantly juggled work with the festivities. Life in California had been rather chaotic, characterized by ceaseless multitasking and constantly giving more than I had.

Returning to my hometown of *Chiclana* in southern Spain served as a powerful reminder that alternative ways of living existed. In this serene environment, my friends and the surroundings left me with no choice but to embrace a slower pace. During the post-lunch hours, while the boys and I would embark on explorations of nearby towns, our friends would indulge in siestas or simply rest. Initially, we clung to our ingrained American mentality of maximizing every moment. After a week or so, however, we surrendered to the rhythm of the new life, allowing ourselves to adapt and embrace the art of napping. While I dozed, the boys would engage in lively conversations around the table on the patio, thoroughly enjoying their time.

Each day brought me immense happiness and a profound sense

of contentment. My projects, research endeavors, publications, and course preparations gradually took a backseat to the importance of connecting with friends, cherishing family moments, and simply having fun.

In southern Spain, the concept of time takes on a different meaning. During the evenings, my friends would casually gather at the beach without the need for scheduled meetings. It worked like magic! I vividly recall my attempts to establish specific meeting times with my friends, but those plans never materialized. All it took was a simple declaration: "I'll see you tonight at …" followed by the name of the beach area or bar. Miraculously, after dinner, we always managed to find one another. I was the sole individual preoccupied with the notion of time, burdened by the pressure of being late or missing out on something. This used to be the only way I knew how to live. But over the past 27 years, my ability to embrace a laid-back mindset had faded away.

I enjoyed the food, the beach, the slow pace, the people, and the entire culture more than ever before. Yet I appreciated the job and academic opportunities that the Bay Area offers, the diverse thinking, and the efficiency with which things can get done. I was torn between two worlds without fully belonging to either of them anymore.

After six years of enjoying a strong healthy body and mind, I found myself facing new health issues. My neck had been hurting for over a year, which I had been treating with holistic approaches such as acupuncture and chiropractic treatments. Since it was getting gradually worse, I finally decided to see my regular doctor who recommended an MRI scanner. The test result showed an irritated disc bulge that was painfully pinching the nerve on my upper spinal cord—mostly due to long hours of sitting at my desk but also aggravated by my tennis playing. I tried physical therapy and bought an ergometric standing desk, before making one tough decision: to stop playing tennis. I could have continued playing if I were willing to take cortisone shots and painkillers, but I had no intention of taking those approaches which in my opinion are short-term solutions with long-term negative ramifications for the body. My neck was relieved when I finally gave it a break and stopped playing tennis. The pain was gone but I felt devastated. I found myself lacking the motivation to do any other exercise. Tennis was more than just a workout to me. The country club brought friends, laughter, and happy moments into my stressful life. It was my happy drug. I missed tennis every single day tremendously!

Only a few weeks after completely quitting tennis, my body rapidly became debilitated with anemia, according to my doctor, due to hormonal changes possibly marking the beginning of menopause. A very scary word for any woman! I definitely did not want to associate myself with that condition at a time when I still felt young. But whether I liked it or not, it was not my choice. I found out that I also had several large fibroid growths in my uterus and absolutely no breaks between periods. Following four months of pursuing holistic methods to restore hormone balance and combat anemia, I ultimately underwent a partial hysterectomy. This outcome left me feeling frustrated with myself, as I had hoped to regain control over my health without the need to remove my uterus. Even my holistic doctor recommended surgery. I was furious!

Forgetting everything I had learned about meditation, visualization, and ayurvedic healing approaches, I proceeded with the removal of my uterus without preparing myself mentally or physically. The recovery was painful, much more painful than my three C-sections and emotionally a lot more difficult. I started to wonder if during surgery the doctor had also removed part of my brain. Immediately after my recovery I felt lost with a new perception of myself and my reality. I could hardly identify with my new feelings and emotions. One moment I wanted to cry and die, and the next I wanted to be on top of a mountain dancing naked with the world watching. I started to develop a strong desire to walk away from my current life, alone without anyone in my present life following my steps. *How could I want to push everyone away?* That thought tormented my nights. I kept it all to myself for a long time without understanding what was happening to me.

A month after my surgery my doctor's office sent me a note: "Hi Dena, your hormone levels are on the higher side, suggestive of a perimenopausal state." I quickly did a Google search. Perimenopause means "around menopause," a time when women's hormones go haywire leading to a variety of emotional responses such as mood swings, irritability, and anxiety. A high FSH or Follicle Stimulating Hormone means that the body is starving for estrogen, the hormone associated with youth in women. The solution was Hormone Replacement Therapy (HRT) or going through the changes while holding tight through the madness. Since I hardly understood the concept of HRT and I wasn't convinced that all my internal drama was linked to hormone changes, I chose madness.

This woman's life transition, menopause, is a silent struggle that most do not discuss because we fear that it means losing touch with our youth. We may throw around silly jokes about menopause and getting older, but real conversations are not common. Not only the physical but the mental ramifications of this stage are not well received or understood by the ones around us, not even by ourselves. My menopause symptoms perhaps triggered my internal crisis, which years later I better understood and started to call by its name: a midlife crisis.

I tried storing away my personal struggles without discussing them with anyone and quickly started working on writing my next publication. Back on the grind and swallowing my emotions, I entered a much deeper, sadder, nostalgic state. Internalizing a massive amount of uncomfortable feelings, I spent most of my days writing research results and creating new curriculum.

As I continued achieving success in academia, my inner world was crumbling more and more. Without a clear explanation, my feelings of sadness brought anger and rebellion. My rebellious teenage self-reappeared, but now, I had no reason to fight anyone except my own thoughts. After decades of striving to do what seemed to be right with dedication and discipline, both for myself and for others, I found myself in a state where my thoughts didn't seem to belong to me anymore. I started to question all the decisions that I had ever made, including my relationship with

Mike. I pushed him away as hard as I could. I once yelled at him, "I will never have sex with you again." I didn't want to hurt him, but I did. I needed him to stay away from me, even though my love for him was still there, buried under many layers of confusion. I felt trapped by all the choices I had made! They all become noise in my head. The struggles as a working mom, the incessant battle with my health, the friends I had suddenly lost, my mom's fragile heart, and my sons turning into teenagers along with my thoughts about menopause resulted in a turbulent and agonized mind. I was losing control of my emotions, and I felt I was running out of time in my life, getting older more quickly than I wanted.

Ana had been living with us in those days when my mind was working against me. She was very connected to my sons—her teenage nephews. She was the cool aunt who, even in her early 40s, still behaved like a 15-year-old. Nevertheless, she was exactly what my boys and I needed. She helped drive the kids to school on the days that she wasn't working, and in the evenings, she spent time talking to me while I cooked a meal for her. I never told her that I was struggling myself, but her daily stories brought laughter and gave me a different perspective on my troubles. She was the only person who could make me feel normal again, even if it was just momentarily. I used to tell her the concerns I had with my teenagers, and she always responded, "You have nothing to worry about. Those kids have it all figured out. They are just like me." I am not sure that I felt so relieved about the last statement, but somehow, she made me feel better.

Ana has always had a great attitude about life, always looking at the glass half full even when she encountered tough situations. I don't think that I would survive a day in her shoes. She chooses to live life constantly seeking excitement, on the edge between safety and danger, never holding back, and fearless of the world. I felt her truly free spirit, as I felt mine restricted and restrained. I have chosen to live in the opposite way from her. My heart had been tamed over the years. I was once a spirited teenager, broken but free, and now I was a wife and a mother, and I kept myself as safe as I could and out of trouble adhering to societal norms and what I believe to be the right path. Ana has lived a life that surpasses the wildest dreams of many women. Her story is one that no novel could ever recreate, and her experiences are unlike any other. But regardless of our choices, on those evenings, our spirits were the same.

CHAPTER 23

The Internal Storm

"I think that somehow, we learn who we really are and then live with that decision." – Eleanor Roosevelt

AS I WAS LEAVING MY 40S, my internal world became troubled. I tried to escape from my strong emotions through writing, similar to the way I wrote during my teenage years—staying really present with my emotions while addressing my feelings without doing much reflection or putting any thinking into the future. My journal entries continued to get more and more intense. I wrote continuously, never lifting my pen from the paper, with thoughts jumping too quickly for me to even end my sentences.

I questioned everything about my present. *Why don't I have more research publications? Why have I not yet created a successful software business? Why am I not doing more volunteer work? Why don't I make more money? Why is my house always a mess? Why are my kids so mischievous? Why am I not spending more quality time with my mom? Why can't she be healthy? Why am I always in a rush? Why can't I feel passion anymore? Why don't I go out more often with my sisters and girlfriends?*

I felt empty, overwhelmed, and agonized with thoughts of running away from everything that I had worked for. Suffering in my own accomplishments and dreams, I sensed failure. Nothing made sense anymore. Even the most precious parts of my life were making me feel trapped. I grew concerned about losing everything, all because of my brain and my uncontrollable, exhausting thoughts. I felt dead inside, overwhelmed by desperation and a great sense of loneliness. I could no longer play my flamenco music without bringing myself down with sad thoughts for reasons I could not understand.

My writing became full of dots, and I could not stop myself from constantly writing the word FUCKING. Never until then was I fond of using this word. But during this time, I grew a new appreciation for expanding my vocabulary to express my inner turmoil.

As I sit here writing my feelings about the word FUCKING, I recall a female student who, during class, right after I quickly fixed her computer code, expressed gratitude loudly and in front of the entire class, "You saved my FUCKING life!" I was shocked but, because of my own internal turbulence, I did appreciate her honesty and passion. She seemed so real. I almost wanted to be her. Another female student in a different class also started to use the same word to express her feelings. And suddenly my appreciation for such a word grew. I found an article mentioning studies concluding that swearing is a sign of more intelligence, and since my boys were great at it, I joined the club!

I forced myself to a nighttime practice of gratitude for all the things I should be grateful for, all the good things I had in my life: *I am so FUCKING fortunate to have a family and many friends, a uniquely FUCKING successful career, a fulfilling FUCKING job, and a dream husband who constantly shows me appreciation that is so FUCKING nice it is making me sick with guilt for not being able to show him love anymore.* Finally, Carmen bought me a personal journal titled "Zen as FUCK." And Bonnie got me a wooden display: "FRIDAY my second favorite F-word." They understood my pain.

I was rebelling against myself and everything I was. I felt sad because nothing seemed to make sense anymore, completely stuck in my roles as a wife, a mother, and a professor, while not getting any younger. My 50s were around the corner, waiting for me with no mercy, ready to steal my youth. *"The dots are here again ... sadness is taking over ... unbelievable ... unbelievable ... and there I go ... the FUCKING word again. FUCK, FUCK, FUCK, I am turning fifty. Can somebody help me?"* I wrote in my journal at the age of 49.

There is nothing I have ever loved more than my boys, and now for the first time, I felt disconnected from them. That, perhaps, was more painful than anything. I had very little control over them anymore. My boys were changing fast—too fast. They were not boys anymore but teenagers with their own opinions and agendas. I had to let go of making decisions for them since I felt a strong pushback. I slowly and painfully learned to stay in my lane to avoid their wrath.

One of the mistakes I made as a mother was trying to shape my little ones into something they were not. To control their destinies in ways that were not meant to be. I tried it all: piano and violin lessons, meditation classes, yoga, advanced math curriculums at the prestigious Math Berkeley Circle, coding lessons, and lots of extra summer learning. None of these activities were pleasant experiences for anyone because my boys never liked structured activities. The worst of all was my ridiculous proposition that my young teenagers put their electronics in the kitchen in my charging station at 9pm before bedtime, when in reality no one ever went to sleep before at least midnight. Every single time they won the battle, since I was the first to run out of energy. I would fall asleep much earlier than they did, exhausted, with only one thought: *I hope they brush their teeth.*

Staying in my lane with my teenagers meant not forcing control over their choices, as long as they were not destructive; knowing when to give advice; choosing to be quiet when it was not the right time to say something; and realizing that not letting them fail on their own could be my biggest failure.

The books written by Dr. Daniel Siegel became my anchor to my sanity. I learned the concept of co-regulation—basically the importance of being centered and calm whenever the teenagers were acting up, like when they refused to wear seatbelts or wouldn't get up to go to school. When they were little, I was not too bothered by their mischievous behavior unless they were dangerous like walking near the cliff of canyons; it was physically tiring, but I embraced and enjoyed who they were. And in a way, I still was making most of the choices. As they became teenagers, they would easily upset me. They'd tell me, "You're triggered, Mom ..." I was not doing a good job understanding teenage boys.

Michael was at the heart of his rebellious teenage years between the ages of fifteen and sixteen, and he brought home with him daily challenges that led to extreme conversations and resulted in unconventional resolutions, completely different from the plans that we had for him. I was driving him to his high school one morning and noticed that he was wearing pajama bottoms and had a hoodie pulled over his head. We listened to rap on the way. I wrote a journal entry that day: *How many times in my life would I be able to sit next to my wild-spirited teenager, my oldest one, dressed in pajamas driving to high school and listening to rap?* "Toosie Slide" became one of my favorite songs. He reminded me of my teenage years. I was not conventional either. Now, as a young adult, he no longer lives at home. I miss my troubled teenager, his mischievous laughs, and his brilliant mind. I knew those days were special, as they quickly slipped through my fingers.

During the weekdays, after work, my routine used to be first say hi to the boys, then cook with music and an apron, feed the boys, help them with homework, end the evening with a strong intense workout, and at last check my emails and respond to some of them before bed. During my workouts at the gym, I started to listen to loud reggaeton using headphones and I noticed that I started to run as fast as I could—faster than ever—to the point where I could no longer breathe. I experienced a strange high level of energy and an unbearable state of being all day long. The treadmill became a good friend.

To add some excitement to my life and distract my mind, I decided to take Zumba classes, a healthy way to burn my excess energy in a fun, safe environment. But soon, I took it to the next level and signed up to get a Zumba teaching license. On the day I was being tested for my certification, I danced and followed choreography with a fun group of young Latin dancers. I was not as coordinated or young or knowledgeable about the many different Latin dance styles. *What is the difference between salsa, cumbia, or merengue?* I still don't know. I could not even do the popular body wave Zumba move. Like an odd bird, I was completely confused but looking for something exciting. The girls in the training dreamt of dancing careers and wanted to teach Zumba to make a little bit of money. I, on the other hand, already had a successful career, but desperately needed to find a new passion.

I paid $300 and got my license. I was suddenly a *certified* Zumba instructor! I hung the certificate next to my three UC Berkeley degrees. Within a few months, I created a one-hour Zumba routine by watching other Zumba videos at home. And once I felt comfortable enough with my routine, I danced it with my students at Mills, some faculty, and at times with my friends in our backyards. This routine required a great amount of work since I tend to dance freestyle and have never been able to follow choreographies. This was a fun accomplishment for me, and for a while, it brought relief and passion, and it quieted some of my extra energy. I still dance my routine at times in my garage if I need to raise my spirit.

Mike was willing to do whatever it took to match my level of intensity in my search for passion. I wanted to make sure that I had plenty of fun before I turned 50, thinking that my 50s would be a life sentence. To add some fun to my life, I bought a wetsuit and went swimming a few times in the frozen Pacific Ocean of northern California. *If this experience doesn't awaken and center my mind, nothing will,* I thought. But my feelings of sadness and obsessive-compulsive thinking continued to haunt me. I felt trapped no matter what I did.

As the thought of running away kept getting stronger, I recalled the night at the hospital when I made the promise to Michael when he was a baby that I would always be by his side, regardless of and especially through hardship. I knew well that, contrary to how it may be perceived, teenagers need their moms as much as they do when they are little or babies. Mostly for my sons, I needed to find the strength to survive my personal storm.

After a normal Thursday of teaching, full of positive interactions with my students as always, enjoying my drive from work and listening to music, I arrived home to follow my normal after-work routine. But that day was different. Mike was away traveling, and while cooking, I choked in agony and felt tears coming down my face. It was sudden and unexpected. I felt a sharp pain in my throat and my chest while losing the ability to breathe. I ran to the bathroom. I thought for a moment that I was dying. I had never experienced anything like this before. I wanted to run far away to a place where no one could ever find me, a place where I could no feel pain any longer. I felt like I didn't belong in this world, afraid that I wouldn't be able to do the right thing not even one more time in my life as a mom, wife, professor, mentor, daughter, sister, or friend. I was overwhelmed by a feeling of inadequacy and tiredness from overthinking my thinking. I wondered if the overwhelming feeling stemmed from buried shame resulting from unresolved childhood trauma, a sense of inauthenticity as if I were an imposter in the world, or perhaps I was simply losing my sanity. The true root cause was unknown to me. But I know what I did. I wiped my tears, waited a little bit, sat in the bathroom doing breathing exercises, and texted my friends Bonnie and Trish without sharing my reality. I remember the text: "*Does anyone want to come and drink a glass of wine with me?*" They would—even though they know I don't usually drink or keep wine at the house—but they couldn't. Texting something silly pretending that I was in a great mood somehow put a smile on my face for a minute. I left the bathroom and went back to cooking. Brandon came down from his room and showed me a gun that he had built with straws and other simple materials. With a proud smile, he explained how it worked. He brought me back to the present. He, without knowing, saved me from my inexplicable moment of pure panic.

After dinner, I sat next to Dylan as he did his math, pretending to be happy. I waited by the window for Michael to come home. I gave Michael a hug and kiss and went to bed. The light was off when Dylan came in to say goodnight: "Mom, your favorite kid is here. I know this is your favorite part of the day. I love you." Another son to my rescue.

When Mike came home the next day, I told him how I was feeling. I was losing the desire to live. I was experiencing physical pain from stress and overthinking and felt confused about my life. I was having an existential crisis. Mike was supportive but very scared of my words. He was determined to work with me to get me back to feeling well. He asked me not to push him away. I saw fear on his face.

Next day, I reached out to Carmen and told her how I was mentally collapsing in a way I could not help myself. Carmen, younger than me but many times wiser and stronger, responded by constantly texting, calling, and having in-person conversations with me. "Anything that gets into your brain, you text me or call me immediately" were her daily words. I spent my days constantly telling myself to do the right thing, to separate my feelings and thoughts from my behavior, to keep those as disconnected as possible, as if they were two different versions of myself—*I am not my thoughts; I am better than them*—I would often repeat in my mind. For years I have told myself that we are what we think, but now I could not believe any longer that I was the person with the uncontrollable destructive thoughts. That was not me! But then, who was I?

Carmen and I spent a few days with my brother Memel and his wife, Sarah, in Cancun, Mexico. I felt free and at peace for that short period of time. During the plane ride back home, I told Carmen that I had to stop the way I was living my life, but that I didn't know how or what exactly to change, that I had the need to go back and repeat my life. My life had been rushed. Even the books that I had read, I'd read in a rush, always feeling like I had to be productive and efficient. I told her that I wanted to re-read many books that I'd already read on personal development, nutrition, meditation, and even technology and science. The pace of my life felt too fast, and I needed to go back to many moments, to reflect and make sense of them. I didn't want to continue moving forward in a rush. Carmen listened, never questioning my desires, trying her best to support my crisis.

Mike, determined to bring me back from this dark place, surprised me with a trip to Puerto Vallarta, Mexico to celebrate our 25th anniversary. He was hoping that my connection to the ocean would soothe my turbulence. During the trip, I found relief by connecting with the ocean and dancing at the club resort at night. The DJ was not very busy since the dance floor was mostly empty, so he played all my Spanish song requests while Mike and I made sure to keep the dance floor alive. In a way, I was trying to connect to my young years in south Spain, to those days when only the ocean and dancing would quiet my mind.

Every year for our anniversary I would write Mike lovely cards. He never cared about presents, just cards written in my own words. My cards would reflect our lives and my feelings for him.

On our 25th anniversary, I had no words. I sat in front of an empty page several times, and nothing would come out. I thought I loved him, but I didn't feel love—not for him or myself. I was empty with anger and an enemy to myself. Gunilla who had herself gone through a tremendous amount of adversity, fighting with the spirit of a Viking warrior, suggested a book on healing, *Code to Joy*. While reading this book, my writing for the first time reflected childhood pain. Some of my childhood stories came out in the writing, but encoded in ways that only I could interpret the words. I took those painful journal pages and folded them into tiny pieces so I would not easily go back to read them. But I made a connection between my unresolved long-ignored childhood trauma with the pain I was externalizing. I realized that my past was the shadow that Mike had blocked for years with love and acceptance. I felt the need to push him away so I could finally face it on my own. My internal fight with my own feelings and thoughts were hurting both of us. For the first time, I understood.

Growing up embracing my sexuality could attract the wrong attention and even lead to punishment. The lingering effects of my father's inappropriate comments during my teenage years haunted me for an extended period. Engaging in sex evoked at times a subtle sense of guilt, while love was perceived as a vulnerability. Now, it was imperative for me to eliminate any remnants of deeply ingrained shame. The profound sensation of loving without any emotional barriers became a formidable goal, one that I could no longer postpone.

At last, I took a seat and began composing his anniversary card:

We started our relationship almost twenty-seven years ago; I'd just turned twenty-three and you were twenty-eight. At the time, I was just surviving day by day: a new country, a new language, no money, and no papers. You seemed to have it all —mmmmm, strong, and financially fine you were. Arrogant but deeply pulled to me. I was quiet and humble, yet mysteriously connected to you as well. The couple that would not last!

Things just happened for us; you believed in me even more than I believed in myself. You bandaged the part of me that felt hurt. I hated and loved the dysfunctional you. Our love was there but under a foggy cloud of fights and dysfunctionalities.

Twenty-seven years later, the picture is quite different. The cloud has slowly passed, and a new us arose.

You are still handsome and strong – I would never take that from you – but you are also sensitive, compassionate, caring, loving, patient, eager to listen, willing to learn and change, generous to the world, positive, confident, and a hot lover. The best father I could ever have dreamt of for my kids.

And me? I am hitting the feisty fifties, insensitive, impatient, and rude, but real. I enjoy saying the word FUCKING a lot, and I just want to feel passion… I need to feel that I am still living and not just going through life.

Nothing is the same. The only thing that remains intact is our connection that never made sense but was always there. It is like a gravitational force. Our minds can go wild, our stories can change overnight, our financial situation will never stay the same, and the kids surprise us every day, but the force is always there. It has been there with us for twenty-seven years every single second.

❊ ❊ ❊

Our trip to Mexico was wonderful and, as always, our travels added magic to our lives, allowing us to experience different realities and the feeling of passion that I so much needed. But as soon as I got back, I continued to experience a high level of internal uncontrollable dissatisfaction and stress.

I realized that my internal world could not be fixed with the solutions I had been trying. Nothing was working, and my anxious thoughts were getting worse by the day.

Mike, without one more drop of energy left in his mind, insisted for the first time that I seek professional help. Carmen had already been pressing this recommendation. And Gunilla advised me not to feel shame about healing. I stayed at Gunilla's home for a few nights, nestled by the ocean in Half Moon Bay. While I couldn't articulate the depths of my thoughts, her presence provided solace, and our walks along the shoreline acted as a natural balm for my soul. I recalled explaining to Gunilla over dinner at her house that I had spent my entire life trying to be good, but that I didn't want to be good anymore. This statement would have not made sense to most people, but to her it made perfect sense. She understood me without hardly using any words.

I didn't feel like talking to anyone and even less to a therapist—to me a complete stranger who would possibly bring more pain out of me and make me feel vulnerable. All I wanted to do was run away to a place where I could be alone without worrying about hurting anyone. But the thought of leaving even for a week would have been detrimental to Mike and the boys. Against my wishes, I agreed to therapy! I felt like a wild horse being forced into her stall. I spent a couple of months visiting a therapist twice a week; again, doing the right thing. I didn't tell my mom or most of my friends because I thought this was weakness—that I had not found a way to overcome my crisis. As a matter of fact, I hardly shared details of my crisis with anyone. I constantly had to battle with what I tell and what I keep secret. I had always been good at putting on a smile and a great happy show because I love family and friends and I feared rejection. I now understand that it takes character and strength to share pain and to accept help when we need it. I am still a work in progress.

The therapist and I focused mostly on cognitive behavioral

therapy, and her advice on my approach to motherhood was helpful as I started to treat my boys like young men with their own agendas and dreams. By the time the therapist and I were to address my childhood wounds, I decided not to continue, since I felt maybe it would release darkness—stories of my father that I had pushed deep into the past and that I did not want to share aloud. Revealing to my therapist that I was hurt felt like giving power to my father. Right or wrong, I moved on to working with my mind on my own. Keeping my volcano silent, I continued with my life as it was.

Even though I quit my therapy sessions I used the techniques of Cognitive Behavior Therapy (CBT) that I'd learned. I became much more mindful of my Automatic Negative Thoughts (ANTs) and worked on replacing these with positive and more realistic thoughts or with no thoughts at all, while also practicing meditation on a more consistent basis. I had to remember that I could choose my own thoughts. That became my daily work. I also started the process of writing my childhood stories in digital format. Going into the past on my own allowed me to open my wounds in a safe environment—this was the real beginning of my healing process. During the evenings, I would read some of these pages to Mike. Through the act of writing and sharing them aloud, these stories gradually lost their grip on me, transforming into mere written words. They became stories meant for sharing and lessons to be learned from.

CHAPTER 24

Feisty 50s

"I am sensual and very physical. I'm very erotic. But my sexuality exists on a sort of a fantasy level." – Donna Summer

THE DAY BEFORE I TURNED 50, Mike and I drove to South Lake Tahoe to celebrate my birthday. I was feeling excited but nervous to arrive at the big day, when I could no longer say that I was in my 40s. I texted Bonnie and asked her to call me a few times that day to ask me about my age. And she did! We both laughed as I kept repeating how lucky I was to be in my 40s.

Tahoe, as always, was refreshing and beautiful, with still a little bit of snow in the high ski mountains. We had a nice meal at the hotel, and found a dance club, almost empty since it was still early in the evening. I had an interesting drink called *Wet Pussy* that the bartender said he would make for a special girl turning 50. I definitely appreciated the word *girl* more than ever before. Bartenders know what to say—naturally born to do the job. We had quite a conversation as I was explaining to the much younger man that I wanted to have fun, that I didn't usually drink or consume sugar, but that a drink would be helpful with the transition into my 50s. I had no intention of going to bed that night to wake up to a 50-year-old me. That night in Tahoe seemed endless, only because I kept counting the minutes. Mike and I danced for a couple of hours before ending our night with passion. Mike reminded me that night that, for many people, a more fulfilling, purposeful life starts in their 50s and even in their 60s. "Babe, we still have too many goals and objectives, trips and adventures to experience in our lives. We are young." He remarked with his positive outlook. I fell asleep with his words in my mind and his warm naked body entangled with mine.

The next morning, I felt quite all right. Nothing had really changed but somehow, I felt a weight lifted from my shoulders. I was 50, with a new outlook finding myself on the other side of a dark cave, and ready to explore whatever the Universe would bring next. Life quickly went on!

My midlife crisis was over, at least the worst of it—the negative sad emotions, the nostalgic thoughts, the anxiety, and the feelings of running to no land. The relationship between Mike and me had been put to the test, and it had endured. We had learned to feel and understand each other without needing to explain ourselves. He had shown remarkable resilience in love. While I might have appeared as the stronger one in the relationship, especially to my children, the truth is that we both possess our own strengths. There are times when I carry the weight, and other times when he holds us in one piece. I could now comfort in his strength, without ever feeling weak. To his *I love you*s I could find no weakness in expressing love back. *I fucking love you* or *I love to be loved by YOU*, became comfortable ways of expressing my love with words. Through endless conversation, we became more self-aware of our own patterns that would occasionally trigger his fear of losing me. During my late 40s, there was a possibility of him losing me as I was losing myself. But the situation had changed. Those years and emotions were part of the past; any remaining fragments that prevented us from feeling deeply connected needed to be swept away.

Mike understood that I needed my space to feel my own emotions without him questioning my love for him. I also learned to express myself so I could quickly remind him that my emotions did not signal doubts about the love I felt for him. I had to fight my tendency to be quiet, and he had to stop fixing my inner world because of his own fears. All I had left from my late 40s episode was a high level of energy and a strong desire to live with him a life with purpose, whatever that meant.

In my 50s, I was not willing to work as hard as I did in the last decades and was determined to bring fun and new adventures as much as I could into my life. Mike at times was wondering, scratching his head, whether his wife had turned 50 or 15. For the first time ever, speeding on non-congested freeways while driving alone became thrilling. Regardless of my new disposition for more fun and less work, turning 50 brought a new sense of self. A new version of me, more confident and much more able to enjoy the good in my life without ever feeling guilty. But most importantly, I could look at myself in the mirror, fully accepting myself with my faults and my virtues.

Seven months into my 50s, Mike, the boys, and I traveled to Fiji, New Zealand, and then Australia to visit my brother Memel, Sarah, and their kids, Ruben and Lola, for Christmas. The trip was exciting and a good break from my busy work and family life. My favorite spot was the week we enjoyed in Noosa at my brother's seaside house. We all hung out by the ocean, surrounded by *chiringuitos* that evoked memories of southern Spain. The mornings were incredible, with the hissing of snakes and bird sounds as I woke up and the jungle scenery from the balcony as I had my cup of coffee specially made by my brother.

As soon as we came back from our Christmas vacation, we left the boys with my mom, and headed to Nevis in the Caribbean to celebrate our 26th anniversary. We were attending Avaya's Circle of Excellence, an annual event honoring top sales reps. Mike was doing his job as a tremendous, dedicated husband, looking for opportunities to make our lives fun and passionate, while excelling in his sales quotas at his job at Avaya. In Nevis, I had the opportunity to dance every night, mingle with locals, enjoy time with Mike, and swim in the ocean. I found a deep connection with the island's people.

Right after my trips, I went back to teaching duties for the new spring semester. A few days later, Carmen gave birth to Hailey, a tiny, beautiful baby girl. Having spent 17 years together raising four boys, the arrival of a girl felt incredibly special. After a day of teaching, I drove as fast as I could, tears of joy blurring my sight. The doctor who delivered Hailey didn't allow me to be present during her birth. Carmen had been right next to me with Mike for the delivery of my three boys, and I had been there for Dani's birth until the last minute when the doctor took Carmen to an emergency C-section. My brain could not comprehend that this time it seemed to be different; I could not push for what I wanted.

I imagined the future, having to tell Hailey that I was not present the day she was born. I am not the father or the mother, but somehow, I was having a difficult time understanding, and it felt painful. I once believed that Carmen was born to be mine, and now her daughter seemed like another divine present for me. Before I met her, I already loved her as my own.

When I saw Hailey, I cried! I felt the same feeling that I'd once had when I held Carmen as a baby for the first time. Since then, my brain continues to go back and forth between Hailey and my memories of little Carmen. They are both so similar, from their big expressive eyes and goofy facial expressions to their smart, affectionate, strong characters. Hailey brought a lot of happiness, not just to me, but also to my mom. She gave her purpose at a time when she needed it the most. I believe Hailey has extended my mom's health and life.

CHAPTER 25

The Pandemic

"Wisdom means to choose now what will make sense later." – Tracee Ellis Ross

IN MARCH 2020, SIX WEEKS after the birth of Hailey, the COVID-19 pandemic hit California, and in a matter of weeks, we were all in lockdown.

I was 50 with high levels of energy, feeling strong and healthy again, keeping up with my daily Zumba routine and ready to have fun, but instead, I was locked down. I had to quickly figure out, as did the rest of the teaching faculty, how to bring my courses online, and how to keep my college students engaged.

During the first year of the pandemic, I held positions such as department chair and director of the graduate program. I was also involved in a data science research project with UC Berkeley. I spent most of my days in front of the computer, on a stationary bike, pedaling between lectures and meetings to stay active during the day, while engaging more than ever before with my boys' studies. My days seemed longer, work hours were never-ending, and motherhood became policing my boys about their schoolwork.

Once a week I would drive to my mom's house to drop food at her door, exchanging a few stories while keeping our distance outside the house. Then I would drive to Carmen's and see both Carmen and Hailey through the window glass. Carmen felt lonely and I felt heartbroken not being able to hold our new baby girl. The same crowded freeways that I had driven for decades were now empty. Suddenly nothing was the same. It felt like the end of the world!

My friends Bonnie, Trish, and I snuck into one another's backyards, each of us bringing our own food and drinks. Sitting far away from one another, we did our best to keep our friendship. We found a safe way to have plenty of conversations and fun during the cold nights of the pandemic winter. When summer came, one afternoon we wore our best dresses by the pool, listened to music, and took distant pictures of each other. We also kept a WhatsApp chat going, including Carmen, which was quite entertaining. We would text one another several times a day with silly conversations, but at times, they were full of meaning and support for one another. We kept one another in one piece!

Mike didn't blink twice when news of the pandemic hit. He started to work from home every day, no longer traveled or had long days out of the house, and no longer went to the gym after work. I loved having him at home *all* day long, and I was pleasantly surprised by his level of acceptance, especially considering I had never seen him skip going to the gym. He did the family's groceries every week, double masking and meticulously sanitizing all the items with alcohol. Mike and I were among those parents who took the threats of the virus very seriously, fearing that it could cripple or even kill one of us. Mike stayed focused on making the best of the situation, ensuring that no one inside the house broke down. We set up the garage as a gym with weights, put a big mirror on the wall with mats on the floor for dancing, and a speaker to play music. In the evening, the garage became our hang-out place. Mike would mostly lift weights while I enjoyed performing my Zumba routine. I even shared a few videos of my routine on YouTube. The boys also used the garage gym for their workouts during the day. It was our best outlet. We were all determined to keep in good shape.

My teenagers took interesting paths. Their schools went completely online for a year and a half. Dylan, in his last year of middle school, spent most of the class time falling asleep and staying up at night playing video games. Brandon, a high school freshman, was extremely committed to working out and often sneaked out during lockdown to meet his friends. He once broke his foot jumping from his second-floor bedroom window. His friends meant everything to him, and the virus meant nothing.

Michael at the beginning of the pandemic was in the last semester of his high school junior year. Before lockdown, I had burned most of my neurons trying to control his whereabouts. "I love you, Mom, you don't need to worry about me" was his favorite sentence, always stated with a smile and a hug. I googled and asked friends—*how can I control my teenager?* Every single answer made me laugh like a hysterical witch. Dylan was sure to tell me so. Either no one understood teenagers, or mine was truly a piece of work. Setting boundaries and enforcing consequences, as most experts' advice on books and social media, seemed impossible after years of trying. Deep within, I carried an immense amount of stress and concern. My thoughts were consumed by worry for him, both day and night. There are many aspects of those days that I yearn for, particularly my affection and devotion for that mischievous teenager. But it is his story to share and tell.

Mysteriously, however, after Mike and I announced lockdown to the boys, Michael, unlike his brother Brandon, embraced the situation. Every passing day, I expected him to dash out of the house to be with his friends, but he never did. He remained indoors for a full year and a month. In his senior year, he would wake up at five in the early morning to study the stock market. I saw him absorbed in books, actively learning, and meticulously taking notes about business, economics, and technology, ultimately losing interest in pursuing his high school education. He bought a large whiteboard and filled it with goals and concepts written in different colors. In a short time, he created an online business—an educational investment platform. With earnings from his subscribers, he began monthly investments in cryptocurrencies, making substantial profits. Eventually, he made the bold decision to drop out of high school and announced his relocation to the beautiful island of Puerto Rico, where he planned to manage his investments from a warm and cozy ocean.

Michael knew from an early age that he wasn't going to follow his mom's academic expectations. "I will not be a product of the system, Mom. I was doing school just for you; this is not my thing. I knew I wasn't going to finish high school," he said to me once. But for a long time, I was as blind as a donkey wearing blinders. He radically changed my understanding of teenagers, my role as a mother, and how we make life choices in general, often by allowing others or society to make these choices for us. He gave me daily speeches on why he didn't need a traditional education to be educated, and how the educational system was working against his goals, ambitions, and dreams. I found these conversations fascinating, against conventional thinking, but perfectly aligned with my rebellious entrance into my 50s.

The pandemic also brought drastic and unexpected changes to my professional life. Mills College was going through a merger, at the time with UC Berkeley, due to a financial crisis. There were many roles that I had to play as department chair and director of the graduate program that no longer aligned with my values. I was once passionate about recruiting; I believed in the powerful education and unique college experiences that we were providing to our students, but I could no longer appreciate an institution that was quickly becoming unstable. I was basically recruiting for programs that perhaps soon would not exist and that felt wrong.

The faculty, but mostly the department chairs, were being held accountable for the institutional crisis. If a merger didn't go through, Mills would not financially survive. I became one of many professors expected to work under hope toward intangible ideals that no longer aligned with reality and without being paid fair salaries. How could I empower our students and recruit new ones when I myself didn't believe that some of our programs would remain alive for much longer?

During the pandemic, the lack of in-person interaction with my students was devastating to me. Throughout my career as a professor, I had the opportunity to work with hundreds of college students. Some came to our programs with extreme confidence, but others came with broken souls, like the one I once had as a young woman. I could see in their eyes their untold stories, but I could also see their hidden powers and the potential to heal and create a better existence for themselves. Most of them did not trust my confidence in their potential and abilities, just like many years back I could not recognize those who strongly believed in me. Many of my students needed someone to tell them what they couldn't see in themselves. And that, together with my dedication to teaching cutting-edge computer science technologies and concepts, made me the educator I was. But now, after a year of Zoom, my motivation to continue working at that same intense pace had vanished. The days were long with a seemingly endless amount of work, and I could no longer rely on the energy of my students to push me forward.

I hit a steel wall of frustration, convinced that I could not continue doing a meaningful job and that my work-life balance had been an illusion, and even self-destructive.

Exactly one year after the lockdown, we gathered as a family around the kitchen table to discuss my early retirement from academia. Michael was convincing in his arguments, more than anyone he pushed me to slow down.

I started dreaming of having time for my family and my mom, but mostly myself. Time for my own projects, my own learning, and reading. The opportunity to write this book. I was over the moon thinking about the possibilities but scared to death of leaving what had been my life for 18 years. I would be walking away from being financially independent, at least temporarily.

Something I had worked on for my entire life. Mike had treated me all these years as his queen. In the back of my mind, I wondered if Mike's admiration and love had something to do with my accomplishments. But he had always been proud of me, even when I had nothing. Still this thought bothered me. Would he have felt differently if I had been completely financially dependent on him for the last 18 years? If I had decided to be a stay-at-home mom? For years he would massage my feet before going to bed while looking at me in awe, appreciating how much I was able to do in a day. He was in love with that dedicated hard-working woman. I was also in love with her. She walked her days with smiles for everyone.

It was a hard decision to make. But I so much wanted to walk away from all that—from any fears, doubts, or concerns. I trusted my feelings and the process of letting go! One more time in my life I had a burning desire to jump into the unknown. I needed NEW in my life. New episodes, new projects, new passions. For years I had done work that mattered. Guiding and mentoring students had been my true passion, providing a sense of fulfillment for almost two decades. But in this moment in my life, I realized the importance of letting go. The authenticity of love goes beyond titles and professions, as those who truly love me will love me forever. Embracing this understanding, the decision became much simpler for me.

I reflected on how difficult it can be to identify the things and people we need to put behind us because they no longer serve a purpose. As individuals, we often find ourselves unhappy in relationships and careers, yet we are not willing to move on.

Letting go of something that was once special, that perhaps required great effort, or for which we still hold hope can be incredibly difficult. The easiest path is hardly ever the one that will bring peace and joy. I reminded myself that life circumstances are just stories with an end—an end that must be embraced to make room for new opportunities.

Before making my final decision, I had a couple of conversations with my colleague, mentor, and great friend, Susan. On many occasions, she had been involved in guiding me to the next steps of my academic career. I have enjoyed working with her for 18 years, and I trusted her immensely. Those conversations were difficult. She had been my greatest support in my academic career, but this time I could not follow her logic or advice. I left Mills without a clear argument for leaving my position while simultaneously *lacking* the will to find one. My decision made no sense to those outside my family circle. And yet, I had the nagging desire to create the space to explore new projects and ideas.

The desire to live my life differently became an obsession, and I constantly imagined what it would be like if I had time to discover new passions. Michael was my inspiration—the driving force that completely transformed my thinking, challenging my beliefs and disrupting my way of life. He had done things differently. He had the courage to tell me with love and a smile that he had a different plan for himself. I embraced that courage when I told my peers, my provost, my students, my friends, and my family that I would not continue my academic path, not for now, not this way!

Without further analysis or a set plan for the future of my

professional career, I quit my full-time tenured position as a computer science professor at Mills College. The provost recommended to the board of trustees that I hold the title of Emerita status, and it was approved, allowing me to still be able to teach courses without the commitment of a full-time position.

A month after quitting my job, in April 2021, Michael left for Puerto Rico. The day Michael left home was a painful one. I cried the entire day and could not think of anything but how much I was going to miss his mischievous laugh. He didn't see me cry—no one did—but my heart was broken. I was not ready to let go of my son yet. But *life doesn't knock* on your door; it just happens. During the car ride, he spoke the whole way with his dad about cryptos, but he stopped once and said: "Mom, I will find the nicest beach spot, and I will send you pictures," and he did. That was his way of saying, *Don't worry, Mom, I will be connected to you.* He took with him the book that I mostly read to him: *Only One You* by Linda Kranz. I believe that he followed every single piece of wisdom in this little book, especially, "*Find your own way. You don't have to follow the crowd.*"

Michael was not the only one making abrupt decisions. To everyone's surprise, Dani, a sharp high school student, decided to pursue a career as a United States Marine instead of going to college as planned and expected. He had excellent grades and had even taken advanced placement courses. But, in August, our Dani departed for boot camp in San Diego, leaving Carmen devastated and me overwhelmed by sadness. Our minds were filled with a torrent of apprehension, contemplating the many possibilities that could unfold in the life of a Marine. At the same time, we were proud of him for choosing the hardest path to follow, exactly what he wanted to do. How could I not express support for his unexpected decision when he seemed so happy and determined? I thought about my car rides with him on Fridays on our way to our house and how much I enjoyed his selection of music— mostly old songs with meaning behind each word—our conversations, and his unique teenage way of making me happy. This was all coming to an end.

Mike and I said goodbye to Dani with two special trips: one to Puerto Rico to see Michael, and the second to our favorite place in the mountains: Graeagle, the place where Dani and the other boys had pushed themselves beyond their strength and abilities since they were very little. In those mountains, the boys had hiked for hours over the years, jumped into cold lakes, and explored the wilderness. On our last hike with Dani in Graeagle, preparing himself for bootcamp, Dani guided us through the most challenging paths. I felt a few times completely out of my safety zone having to push myself beyond my physical and mental abilities. To keep up with my boys, stepping up to a higher level of toughness was not uncommon. I enjoyed every second of Dani on those last two trips. I knew how special they were since traveling with him in the future would not be as easy anymore. Eighteen years had not been enough for me; I selfishly wished those boys would stay with me for a little bit longer.

CHAPTER 26

Life Purpose

"The meaning of life is to find your gift. The purpose of life is to give it away." – Picasso

BY THE END OF THE PANDEMIC, I hardly recognized my life. During my midlife crisis, I lost all sense of direction, believing that my efforts were not producing the results I had envisioned. I had never before questioned my life purpose, maybe I never had the luxury to do so. My goals were pragmatic; they were my focus. With resilience, as most of us do, I endured challenging times. But I was holding an external identity that was growing apart from my true self. I was driven to keep an eye on the prize, and once achieved, my eyes fluttered on to the next. But now I felt free without any rush or financial pressures to choose my next steps.

I reflected on whether achieving goals translated to fulfillment and a feeling of purpose—but they don't always. Purpose is more meaningful and aligns with our authentic values. Goals are measurable; purpose is the way we feel about ourselves in our daily lives. Goals may suffocate us while purpose gives us life. My goals are backed by reason. For example, when I received tenure, I also got job security and an increase in salary. But at the end of the day, it didn't change my level of life satisfaction or my quality of life. I was still hungry and in a rush for my next career move or life goal, while blind to whether I was also pursuing my most basic core values.

I was driven by self-fabricated needs to follow a system that does not always correlate to human nature. People are not meant to live to work in pursuit of materialistic goals or recognition; this only makes sense when the goals and the daily job align with our beliefs. How often do we pause to ask ourselves the reasons behind our actions or choices?

Now in my 50s, newly retired from my full-time academic career, it seemed critical that I define personal and specific desires that could drive the next decades of my life. But first I needed to go deeper into understanding the meaning of purpose. I started by exploring how others view purpose by collecting family and friends' responses to the question in the form of a text, "*What is the purpose of life?*" Each response provided insight into my own journey to find purpose. The most interesting replies were:

- *(My sister Ana) Honest answer? I have no idea. Maybe we are farm food for aliens.*
- (My mom) *There is no meaning. Our brains don't have that ability.*
- *(My sister-in-law Lina) To use and share the talents/skills that we have, build upon them, and pay forward by sharing them with others to inspire them to do the same thing.*
- *(My brother Memel) The meaning takes place as the journey happens.*

- *(My friend Bonnie) At this moment in my life, I think it's raising my kids.*
- *(My sister-in-law Sarah) What a serious question. How interesting. I think my life has been about meeting lots of people from different parts of the world and making connections.*
- *(Mike) Take care of my wife, and my kids.*
- *(My son Michael) To do things differently.*
- *(My friend Sonia) What we do for ourselves dies with us. What we do for others and the world is immortal.*

I connected with their responses and identified with most of them. Some seemed like practical goals, while others felt like distant dreams. A few sounded like philosophical statements, and many were rooted in wishful thinking. After some contemplation, I first concluded that I had been lost at times, too preoccupied with pursuing goals to be conscious of my purpose. There were moments when I believed my purpose was defined by clear, progressive, linear steps, guided by good intentions but leaving little room for reflection. I've come to realize that my definition of life's purpose is ever-changing, depending on my circumstances, age, experiences, the cultures around me, and my capacity for self-reflection.

It wasn't until I stopped stressing about what the purpose of life was and took a break from setting goals and working hard that my mind was given time to reflect. I eventually understood the reason why this question became so important to me. A bigger lesson was to identify goals that were shaping my identity before I could uncover and define my own answers. I remember during my teaching career telling my students to walk away from debugging their computer programs whenever they felt stuck. Moving away from the intensity of wanting to solve a problem can do wonders. And that is exactly what I did.

I had to stop doing, achieving, and obsessing over improving my resume, professional website, and LinkedIn profile. My constant chasing of predefined steps during my academic years was killing my soul. It was one of the greatest challenges to leave my academic career and my tenured status, to get up every day and not sit in front of the computer for hours non-stop. I still struggle with this. Not talking to students, giving lectures, preparing new curricula, or attending meetings felt wrong. *If I was not a computer science professor, who was I?* I found the courage to let go so I could explore my real self, relish the possibility of new experiences, challenge myself in different and uncomfortable ways, and find new sources of life purpose.

As I continued my meditation practices, I became aware of my thoughts as I woke up in the morning. I had a sense of uncomfortable freedom of choice. I didn't want to use the word *goals* any longer, so I asked myself to clarify the intention for the day. As I tried to find just one, I found myself wanting internal peace. I introduced the habit of doing yoga in the morning to break the habit of sitting in front of the computer first thing in the morning. During yoga practice, the words *transformation* and *connections* would often go through my head. I thought about their meaning several times during the day. I even wrote about it.

To me, transformation meant that I had to help transform and create change in positive ways, mostly myself, and sometimes those around me—a need to make something better. It could be having an encouraging conversation with one of my former students, a simple laugh with a friend, or giving a hug to one of my boys. Or feeling peace under struggles. My purpose began to be clearer.

I realized that I had been transforming and connecting, in a way fulfilling my purpose, all along without thinking much about it. I thought and wrote about situations in my life where I felt a strong sense of deep accomplishment accompanied by joy and happiness. Moments that were so intensely meaningful that they didn't need to be shared to feel the excitement. These moments were not associated with titles, awards, or external achievements but with silent contributions to better the world around me. My purpose was not the same as my goals, but many of these goals allowed me to experience a sense of purpose.

I wrote in my journal about the time a student was about to drop out of the computer science undergraduate program because she was having a difficult time keeping up with her coursework. I stayed with her in my office until late that evening telling her stories of my struggles as a young immigrant woman in the US. I did not let her go until I felt her confidence coming back, making sure she was ready to fight for her potential again. Not only did she graduate from our program years later, but she pursued a master's degree in cybersecurity. I felt joy and pride beyond any external recognition. My life struggles had made me a compassionate mentor all along.

At home my connections to my boys gave me purpose once I realized that purpose in this case had to be detached from wanting to control the outcome. My purpose was not to create their destinies, but to be a mom in its simplest form.

There have been many occasions when embracing spontaneity and showing care has brought immense personal fulfillment. I find myself wondering if my purpose in life is simply to stay true to myself as authentically as I can. In a society that often prioritizes external motivations driven by recognition and rewards, practices like self-exploration and meditation become crucial in the pursuit of self-discovery and finding meaning. Purpose can be found in every aspect of our lives and is in everything we do. It lies in the unspoken moments and untold stories, which cannot be captured in words or displayed alongside degrees, titles, or social media posts. When my mind yearns for grand gestures, I remind myself to appreciate the small things. When the urge to shout to the world arises, I understand that it is during those moments that silence becomes my greatest ally. I may not always succeed, but at the very least, I am aware of this journey.

Today, I give myself the freedom to define purpose in many ways. It is my purpose to learn from my mistakes no matter how small they may be. To recognize them and to let them go. A negative thought is a mistake, I say to myself, toward me or others. I work to be self-aware of my intentions. Failures don't have to be significant to give us the opportunity to learn and grow. I experience daily failures because I am human, and I take myself at times out of my comfort zone. It is my purpose to be truthful to myself, to be me, even if it requires discomfort and moving backward. At times to move forward we first have to backtrack and feel some pain. To grow means to slow down and take steps that don't feel productive. It is my purpose to share my successes. It is my purpose to walk away from accomplishments that may only feed my ego.

I remind myself of the concept I have taught for 18 years to my software engineer students: "I am because we are," the team concept of *Ubuntu.* If you were in my class, this lecture would be the most important because, without the concept of a team, no software product can ever succeed. *Ubuntu* is an ancient African word that reminds us to come together as humans, and that we cannot succeed in isolation. Asking for help is not a weakness but a sign of strength. When I ask for help, I am saying, *I am not better than you, I am vulnerable and incomplete, with the courage to ask.* It is only when we are ONE that we can feel complete and satisfy our purpose, whatever it may be. I have for so long misunderstood the meaning of weakness. I now see weakness as my own perception of my determination to endure, to push my limits and to pursue happiness.

It is my dream to be present in all my endeavors, to continue building connections with the world around me, to search for opportunities to inspire, to help but also learn from others, and to accept my constantly changing reality. It was my 14-year-old Dylan, my thinker, who told me once, "Mom there is nothing that you can do about it. Accept it! You can't control everything." And maybe he's right, but deep inside, I believe that there is always something I can do. *That is my truth—that is my purpose.*

CHAPTER 27

A Note to My Father

*"I could easily forgive his pride if he had
not mortified mine."* – Jane Austen

NIGHTMARES HAD COME to haunt me in my sleep as I
relived traumatic moments that existed in the shape of you, my
father. I loved you once, but only briefly. I hated you for the rest
of your existence. Dreams have dragged me back to that house
where I lived without meaning, without hope, suffocating under
your merciless dictatorship. You stole my mom's happiness and
health and my sense of self-worth. In my dreams, I was a teenager
again, and I had lost it all: Mike, my boys, and my new life. The
only thing that I could feel was your strong presence.

But one day, my dream changed. I went back to the house, and
I found my mom. She was smiling. She told me that things were
different now, that we would be happy in that house, and that I
had to trust her. I told her I could not stay, but she insisted. I took
a stick and hit the walls looking for the disgusting cockroaches
that used to terrify me as a teenager. But none came out. I told
Mom that I could now afford to remodel the house and that I
wanted to change the entire bathroom. You were there too, Papa,

but you had no power. I couldn't see you. I knew you were there, but it meant nothing to me. The cockroaches were my only concern because you did not matter. The next day I woke up, and in the afternoon, you passed away. I had no tears, and I still don't. The only sadness I felt was the sadness of not feeling your death. I didn't need to grieve because I had no love for you. You died at the age of 81 in the Philippines, with none of your six children next to you. In our last phone conversation seven years before your death, after enduring your insults, you asked me an interesting question: You needed to know why I hated you so much. Not much thinking was needed to share my feelings. I let you know that I had tried to forget how you treated me as your daughter, yet I reminded you of the husband you were to my mom. You had no words, but I know you were listening. With no compassion left to give, I let you go forever.

I wished for decades that I would forget the years that I had to surrender to your authority. I wished for your own good that you could have asked for forgiveness from all of us—your own mom, your kids, your ex-wives, and all the people that you have hurt along the way. But you didn't! Instead, you gave a twisted account of our stories from a place of denial and superiority.

Since your death, I have twice dreamt of being lost in a parking lot, unable to find my car with a cell phone that doesn't work properly. In both dreams, your voice comes out of my phone, and you tell me not to worry, that you would come to help me, to protect me. It makes me happy. In these dreams, you might have been the person you were born to be, and not the one that lived. I am not angry, nor do I feel hate anymore when I think of you.

Does this mean that I can forgive you? Forgive how you treated my mom? I don't think I can. I would be living a fraudulent life if I forgot or forgave how you hurt my mom. Through her, you almost killed my spirit. My past is part of my reality. I am who I was. I never believed in ignoring or putting a bandage on my wounds, but in healing them and moving on. For me, healing means neither pain nor anger, nor hatred, nor forgiveness. Negative experiences live in our subconscious, affecting every aspect of our lives unless we resurface them and put them emotionally behind us.

I was hoping that you would read my book. Maybe then you would understand my pain. The pain that I so long carried from the suffering of my mom. But you would have not been interested in either reading my book or hearing my thoughts. Your pride and mental sickness blinded your truth.

You are a reminder that the dark side in our physical world is real, a place to avoid; a reason to trust, love, and work hard to lean toward the light. To keep our spirit alive means to be determined, to walk away from victimization, and to believe that we can live better lives. Our strength comes from our suffering and moments of despair. It is a source of growth.

CHAPTER 28

Now and Forever

"You asked me if I ever stood up for anything. Yeah, I stood up for my life." – Tina Turner

MY SENSE OF JOY TODAY is connected to people from all walks of life, past and present. From the older lady in Heathrow airport who helped me find my hotel in London to all my professors, my mentors, my brothers, and sisters, my mom, my sons, other family members, my friends, and my soulmate, Mike. All these people contributed to who I am today, my accomplishments, my happiness, and my suffering. Some of them have spent their lives by my side, but others made an impact in only a fraction of a second. Their compassion at times gave me hope, their words and actions guided me in the direction of growth, and their love built my strength. Every connection I have made has allowed me to learn, share, give, explore my biases, practice empathy, and view life through different lenses. I have not always been good to everyone, and everyone has not always been good to me, but these moments, too, were necessary for personal growth as well as self-preservation. I look back, telling myself that no one ever intentionally tried to hurt me, but that I was in their path of distress. I have to trust at times without the ability to understand the situation or take a moment to react to protect myself, but I am now aware of who is holding my hand, suspicious when I have to be, but comfortable enough to hold the hands of the ones I love. I cannot imagine a life without real love, without Mike, without holding his hand as I fall asleep every night feeling that whatever happens to us, we together will find a way to persist.

As I reflect on the friends I've lost and the ones who have suffered, I now see that it was through them that I could disconnect from the external world and ultimately from the ego that seems to grow over the years. With each loss, I came closer to understanding and truly accepting myself. It is only through my real self that I can reach out to them. The absence of their presence allowed me to genuinely value their friendship, and in a strange way, the longing for them continues to deepen our connection.

Through my relationships, I've ultimately been able to work toward consciousness and self-awareness. I feel conscious when my intentions are clear, my thoughts are in everyone's best interest, and my actions have meaning. It is only then that I can be aware of my own perceptions and views of reality. Human connections provide us with opportunities to bridge differences, practice empathy and foster authentic friendship. We must remember that we are not alone. We may be tempted to feel that way during the dark hours of the night—I certainly do. In reality, we live for others and others live for us. We are much more connected than we are able to understand, but our minds play bad tricks on us. Once we understand the games of the mind, we can be the masters of our existence.

I have come to understand that without darkness, there can't be light, and without connections, I couldn't have moved forward toward growth. Walking through moments of uncertainty and pain used to be terrifying and lonely at times, but now I understand that I was never truly alone. My life connections and I were moving together. Each person holds a special place, for we are all part of someone else's path through darkness. Even if we don't realize it, we serve as pillars and teachers to one another.

My four sons have been my greatest teachers. Because of my unconditional love and devotion to them, I had no choice but to persist. Adopting their perspectives, I continue to experience unknown worlds as they push my thinking and expectations in extreme directions. As soon as they became teenagers, they taught me very quickly to let them walk their own paths, no matter how small or insignificant or unconventional their goals seemed to be. I still found ways to show them that I cared, maybe not with as much physical affection anymore, but by expressing my commitment to stand by them and—try to—understand their choices.

I have learned to withhold initial judgments, certain opinions, and sometimes my tears. Having boys has been like constantly living on the edge. They can bring intense mixed emotions in a matter of minutes. A storm can quickly follow a moment of joy and vice versa. I have been constantly tested both physically and mentally. I tried to breathe during times of chaos, with the hope to co-regulate, somehow influencing their untamed, fearless spirits. As they grow older, seeing my boys turn into men, a piece of my heart hurts but another one brightens with pride. *I have nothing to fear; a mom is forever,* I tell myself at night as I fall asleep. I am excited about their future while looking for windows of opportunity to fully enjoy their presence in my life.

People and relationships are at the center of my growth, but external obstacles and internal conflicts continue to make me resilient. Reflecting on my flaws, my internal crises, and my times of suffering has forced me to learn tough life lessons. I have learned that the easiest way out of suffering is not usually the immediate path toward growth, but a downward spiral into darkness, self-destruction, and even cruelty. By allowing myself the sensations of suffering and discomfort, I become more capable of enduring adversity, understanding that obstacles and conflicts will always come my way in different forms and shapes.

Life has unique ways of awakening us, granting us opportunities at different ages and stages through hardship. It is through this process that we can truly relish the simplicity of life and treasure its special little moments. Now and forever, I will remain humble, for I am no stranger to encountering darkness as life progresses. Yet, I am now conscious that these moments will persistently ebb and flow, and even in the worst times, there is still much to live for.

Embracing a fresh outlook on reality, I have relinquished the urge to gravitate toward unhealthy paths. I have come to terms with the inevitability of aging and change, recognizing that my authentic essence remains unaffected. I no longer wish to cling to the youth I once possessed, as doing so obscures my present existence and impedes my capacity to wholeheartedly embrace new experiences.

The different roles I have taken on and my few significant transitions have taught me a few things. I am quick to free myself of belief and personal perspectives, or even the way I feel about myself, because I am forever transforming. My opinions tonight could be dated by sunrise. This realization is important to cultivate relationships but also for self-compassion. Every instant is a new beginning full of possibilities. When I make a mistake, say something inappropriate, or do something hurtful, I let go of any judging thoughts and start again with a new me. I never quit trying because this is my only life. I will forever forgive myself. I have learned that maybe I have followed my intuition too many times without a plan, that I have doubted myself millions of times when I really didn't have to, and that I have been too quick to jump to new opportunities.

My long-lasting traits are that I deeply care about people; I torment myself with the suffering of others; I need human connection; I need the ocean in my life; I am a victim of love; I constantly doubt myself but persevere anyway. I believe in smiles and kindness; music and dance are my energy source; I have an intrinsic motivation to achieve dreams, and I have a natural *growth mindset*[2]. I recognize that some days I will feel like a failure, others like a superwoman ready to conquer new heights, and that the days in between are the times of joy.

Through my experiences, I have realized that the reach of our human potential and abilities are beyond our comprehension. That our own opinion of ourselves is false and limited, as we are capable of so much more. Desire accomplishes dreams. I have separated myself from my thoughts; rumination has been my worst enemy.

Dreaming of the unknown, without judging myself or holding expectations, I look forward to the next episodes of life, smiling toward the future. Many of my dreams in the past became real because I desired to experience an extraordinary life, to see the world from different perspectives, to indulge my passion for learning, and the excitement of starting new adventures with curiosity and excitement. Now, my new passion for writing reminds me of how I fell in love with Mike decades ago—*It doesn't make sense, but it feels right.*

Acknowledgements

I extend my grateful thanks to the people who have traveled with me through my life stories. While there are too many to name, each one holds a special place in my heart.

Mike, with his astonishing determination, has taught me to love without a shield. Through him, I experience passion, trust, and true love. To my son Michael, I am grateful for teaching me to live differently than expected, to confront my fears, and to conquer without limitations. To Dani, I owe a million precious moments. He is a teacher of compassion, empathy and strength. Brandon, my middle son, despite his mischievous moments and undefeatable arguments, lives with integrity, mastering right from wrong, even when right means hard. Dylan, my young thinker, has a unique ability to see through me. He sits next to me without words but love, during unbearable times. Through the influence of these young men, I have come to appreciate that there is no other life I would rather live than my own life.

My mom and grandma, both named Clotilde Solsona, gave

me the courage to persevere through life's hardships. Ana continues to show me the meaning of super resilience, continually pushing boundaries and breaking stereotypes. Carmen, my life companion, is a fountain of love, wisdom, precision, creativity, and laughter; we are ONE. Hailey is an extension of the love I have for Carmen, my opportunity to experience a daughter. Chino, with his restless optimism and tenacity, has been a role model to me, teaching practicality and confidence. Memel, who is strong and handsome, shares my enthusiasm for new dietary discoveries. His loving heart and incredible determination have made him my hero.

My young brother Jefferson, brilliant and self-assured, follows in the footsteps of all his older siblings, redefining perseverance and success. With Jessica, my friend and my father's ex-wife, I've navigated through challenging moments while battling my father's negative presence in her life.

My forever sister-in-law Lina, for being part of my American life from the very beginning and for her valuable feedback after reading several versions of this book. Sarah, for the fun times and shared experiences of motherhood. With her, I always have a smile. Kirk, my brother-in-law, brings vast knowledge and caring into our family. My nephews Justin and Ruben, and nieces Lola, Lucy and Olivia, have always filled my heart with love and hope for the future.

Gina, my free-spirited woman, has let me be part of her entire life, giving me the privilege of learning from her experiences and reflecting on my own. She was the first person to encourage me to write a book. Arlene has guided me toward inner love.

My uncles, aunts, and cousins are my strongest connection with Spain, especially Aruca, who will always make sure to stay connected with me, preventing time and distance from affecting our friendship.

Countless Mills College students have reminded me of the uniqueness of each individual. They have pushed me to be a better teacher, to embrace sharing stories, and to be more compassionate. I see a piece of myself in all of them, as I remain deeply connected to their efforts, abilities, and dreams.

To all my friends from different countries, cultures and backgrounds, thank you for being an integral part of my life and making a difference in both the good and challenging moments.

I extend my thanks to beautiful Shaina, a teenager from Reunion Island, for allowing me to be part of her life despite the distance. She is a constant reminder of the societal battles we face in a world riddled with inequalities. I believe in her inner strength, as one day she will surprise us all.

I am also deeply grateful to my horse Keziaa, who shook my adventurous spirit to new heights. Her intelligence, immense power and beauty are unmatched in the human world.

On a professional level, I would like to express my deepest gratitude to my consultant, Tristine Rainer. Her guidance, extensive experience, honest feedback, and words of wisdom have brought my writing journey to new heights and inspired me to contemplate publishing my work. I admire her mind as much as her writing.

Seta Salkhi, the young daughter of my dear friend Bonnie, deserves special mention for dedicating her summer to editing and providing invaluable feedback on parts of my stories, encouraging me to delve deeper. To Claire Strombeck, who proofread my final version, and to David Prendergast, my amazing *creative* book cover and book format designer, I extend my appreciation. I also want to express my heartfelt gratitude to Sheila, Gina and Sofia for their enthusiasm in reading an earlier version of the book and for providing feedback. I am thankful for the support and advice of colleagues like Carlota, Kirsten, Pamela, Diane, and Susan. I deeply appreciate the encouragement from Arlene's Book Club—The San Francisco Girls Club. Their encouragement during the manuscript review process were the sources of courage I needed to take the final step in sharing my story with the world. Special thanks to my friends Bonnie, Wendy, Trish, sister Carmen, Nikki and Gunilla for reading my manuscript and for their patience in hearing about my book for the last four years.

Finally, I would also like to dedicate my work to Cristina, who represents the generations that follow, offering them a story so they may believe in their future and the power of their convictions.

To all my readers, I want to express my sincere appreciation for taking the time to read my story. Thank you!